D1453821

The Flirt's Tragedy

THE

Flirt's

TRAGEDY

Desire without End
in Victorian and Edwardian Fiction

RICHARD A. KAYE

University Press of Virginia
Charlottesville and London

The University Press of Virginia
© 2002 by the Rector and Visitors of the University of Virginia
All rights reserved
Printed in the United States of America on acid-free paper
First published 2002

1   3   5   7   9   8   6   4   2

Library of Congress Cataloging-in-Publication Data

Kaye, Richard A., 1960–
  The flirt's tragedy : desire without end in Victorian and Edwardian fiction /
Richard A. Kaye.
      p.   cm.
Includes bibliographical references and index.
  ISBN 0-8139-2100-7 (acid-free paper)
  1. English fiction—19th century—History and criticism.   2. Courtship
in literature.   3. English fiction—20th century—History and criticism.
4. Darwin, Charles, 1809–1882—Influence.   5. American fiction—History
and criticism.   6. Man-woman relationships in literature.   7. Mate selection in
literature.   8. Seduction in literature.   9. Desire in literature.   10. Women
in literature.   11. Sex in literature.   I. Title.

  PR878.C69 K39   2002
  823'.809355—dc21   2001005899

Contents

Acknowledgments

Many individuals helped with the writing of this book. I would like to thank U. C. Knoepflmacher for his patient, expert, and always spirited attention, Talmudic in its intensity, to the details and substance of my writing. To Elaine Showalter, whose good humor, erudition, and warm encouragement have been everywhere in evidence, my fondest gratitude.

Special thanks to Deborah Epstein Nord, whose enthusiasm and learning about all matters Victorian greatly helped me in formulating my ideas. Jane Eldridge Miller read the entire manuscript and provided much helpful advice. Suzanne Churchill again and again proved herself a tremendous friend and a cogent critic.

Others who offered their insights or suggestions at various stages in my writing include Eric Anderson, Rachel Asher, Nina Auerbach, Jeanne-Marie Baron, Robert Caserio, Doreen Cooper, Nick Cull, Joshua David, Richard Dellamora, Maria DiBattista, Caryl Emerson, Laura Engelstein, Casey Finch, Billy Finnegan, Carter Foster, George Ganat, Michelle Gittelman, Ken Halpern, Beth Harrison, Anthony Heilbut, Stephen Hirsh, Elizabeth Hollander, Anne Humpheries, Claudia Johnson, Jennie Kassanoff, Carole Kaye, Kevin Kopelson, Joshua Landy, George Levine, Vittorio Lingiardi, A. Walton Litz, Mary Long, James Longenbach, Chris-Ann Matteo, Michael McKeon, Mark Melchior, Lee Clark Mitchell, Nick Moschkovakis, Adrienne Munich, James Najarian, Thomas Pavel, Arnold Rampersad, Bruce Redford, Katie Roiphe, Charles Rosen, Marcia Rosh, Talia Schaffer, Todd Shepard, Kathy Silberger, Jonathan Smith, Katherine Stern, Lisa Sternlieb, Katherine Stevens, Maja Thomas, Mark Turner, Marilyn Walden, Susan Wolfson, and Phoebe Zerwick.

At Eugene Lang College and the Parsons School of Design, Bea Banu, Caroline Payson, and Arnold Klein offered invigorating conversation. At Davidson College, Jonathan Berkey, Vivien Dietz, Ramón Figueroa, Ann Fox, Gail Gibson, Cynthia Lewis, Maggie McCarthy, Shelley Rigger, and

Mary Thornberry offered advice and friendship, while David Boraks, Michael Oldani, Deidre Prosen, and Chris Wooten supplied much-needed distractions. At Hunter College, Richard Barickman, Nico Israel, Margaret Laurino, Harriet Luria, Kate Parry, Thom Taylor, and Sylvia Tomasch have offered a lively academic environment. I know that for many of my friends and colleagues, as with so many of the coquettes and flirts I deal with in these pages, the anticipation has been maddening—and exquisite.

Over the years, many of my students have galvanized my thinking on the history of the novel and Victorian fiction, and I have space here to thank only Merritt Abney, Alexis Boehmler, Vic Brand, Jamey Heit, Robert Hester, Rhonda Hinds, Sam Kuykendall, Erin Smith, and Jim Stuntz.

To Jill R. Hughes, Carolyn Sherayko, and the anonymous readers at the University Press of Virginia, I am grateful for astute suggestions. To Cathie Brettschneider, who expressed interest in my manuscript at a very early stage in its conception, I offer my salute to an ideal editor.

Finally, my family has been a constant source of encouragement throughout my work on this project. This book is dedicated to the memory of my father, Walter Kaye.

The Flirt's Tragedy

Introduction
Fiction and the Poetics of Flirtation

[S]he had not, then, eloped in order to be married to Mr. Stephen Guest—at all events, Mr. Stephen Guest had not married her—which came to the same thing, so far as her culpability was concerned. We judge others according to results; how else?—not knowing the processes by which results are arrived at.
—George Eliot, *The Mill on the Floss* (1860)

Was it love, she wondered, or a mere fortuitous combination of happy thoughts and sensations?
—Edith Wharton, *The House of Mirth* (1905)

TAXONOMIES, ARCHETYPES, MYTHS

"All the great European love stories take place in an extra-coital setting," observes the narrator of Milan Kundera's novel *Immortality* (1991), noting the stories of Madame de Lafayette's *Princess of Clèves,* Bernardin de Saint-Pierre's *Paul and Virginia,* Eugène Fromentin's *Dominique,* Goethe's *The Sorrows of Young Werther,* Knut Hamsun's *Victoria,* Romain Rolland's *Peter and Luce,* and Nastassia Fillipovna's unrequited love for Prince Myshkin in Fyodor Dostoevsky's *The Idiot.* Concludes Kundera's speaker: "The love of Anna Karenina and Vronski ended with their first sexual encounter, after which it became nothing but a story of its own disintegration."[1] As *Immortality* implies, it was not the rebellious nature of Anna and Vronski's love that dooms this couple but the notion that the consummation of their desires might placate their anguish. This is why, for Kundera's mournful speaker, immortality does not adhere to romantic passion per se but rather to passion's calculated postponement.

What Kundera's novel in part addresses is one of the great, often noted paradoxes of realist fiction, which is that its task has been simultaneously to encourage and expose the illusion that desire is attainable. To the extent that desire feeds on illusions, it is isomorphic with the enterprise of fiction itself, in which the satisfaction of characters must be deferred, as their fantasies of love are sustained, in order for narrativity to occur. The most articulate exponent of this view is Peter Brooks, who explains that this seemingly irreconcilable "double logic" is the "peculiar work of understanding that narrative is required to perform." For Brooks, it is the modern detective story, in which the plot of the inquest of a crime is made necessary by the crime itself, that most overtly displays this special logic.[2] Writing of the novel of realism, Leo Bersani has defined desire in analogous terms as a "hallucinated satisfaction in the absence of the source of satisfaction," a definition that strikes at the heart of the necessarily delusional nature of erotic desire as well as the experience of reading a work of fiction.[3]

There are, nonetheless, as many forms of desire as there are novels to narrate them, and it is fair to ask what happens when desire is not "repressed" or "hallucinated" but deliberately deferred (although not denied) as it is self-consciously and playfully managed. What occurs when desire refuses to follow the libidinal model, which is to say, a paradigm stressing the hydraulics of repression and liberation? What happens when eros is neither completely submerged nor fully expressed but suspended in a series of deferrals? The activity that most successfully fosters this dynamic is what I have chosen to term *flirtation*. An acknowledgment of the dangers of romantic ardor, flirtatious eros is a recognition that untrammeled and hallucinatory, desire frustrates reason and creates havoc.

Desire, particularly as opposed to romantic love, has been the subject of intense, widespread critical scrutiny in the last twenty years in the works of postmodern Continental theorists and those writing in an Anglo-American context. Roland Barthes's strict distinction between desire as opposed to romantic love has been extremely influential. Thus Robert Polhemus, implicitly expanding on Barthes's distinction, has used the term "erotic faith" to describe romantic love, noting that throughout European culture narratives of love have served to imagine "forms of faith that would augment or substitute for orthodox religious visions."[4] Critics addressing the strictly formal dimensions of literary texts, as well as theorists seeking a more politically pronounced emphasis on how fiction operates in a matrix of cultural determinants, have turned to desire as a crucial locus of meaning. René Girard's exploration of "triangular desire"; Barthes's intensely personal endorsement of "bliss" and "pleasure"; the hymeneal "dissemination" evoked by Jacques Derrida; Julia Kristeva's semiotic, signifying stress on process; Leo Bersani's focus on the fluid, fragmented staging of desublimated carnality; Judith Butler's elaboration of sexuality as sheer "performance"; Tim Dean's Lacanian exploration of desire as fundamentally impersonal—have all accentuated an eroticism that is mutable and unstable, in which functional desire emerges as a historical aberration. For many postmodern critics, that aberration is a scandalously successful nineteenth-century literary invention that has come to legitimize patriarchally and heterosexually structured social scenarios.

Still, while library shelves creak beneath the weight of critical volumes devoted to the exploration in eighteenth- and nineteenth-century fiction of desire as it exfoliates into various definable plots—seduction, courtship, and marriage—sportive, unconsummated sexuality for the most part remains uncharted critical terrain. This omission seems curious, for as Kundera suggests, flirtation's place in the history of the novel is undoubtedly paramount. Beyond the works cited by the narrator of *Immortality*, flirtatious desire is a preeminent thematic issue in such major works of fiction as *Vanity Fair* (1847–48), *The Mill on the Floss* (1860), *Sentimental Education* (1869), *Far from the Madding Crowd* (1874), *Daisy Miller* (1878), *The Ambassadors* (1903), *The House of Mirth* (1904), *The Age of Innocence* (1921), to name only canonical texts of European and American literature. In terms of individual authors, flirtation is an integral feature of all of the works of Jane Austen, much of the fiction of George Meredith and Anthony Trollope, and the greater part of E. M. Forster's novels. Indeed, the novel as a genre in many ways is as deeply preoccupied with flirtatious desire as it is with what is conventionally considered romantic eros. When Mikhail Bakhtin attempted to isolate the generic uniqueness of novelistic discourse, he discussed the novel as a "force" that "novelizes" other genres by "inserting into these other genres an indeterminacy, a certain semantic open-endednesss."[5] Bakhtin's definition points to one of the reasons that novelistic discourse has proven especially accommodating to a thematics of flirtation: the novel's formal attributes mimic the procedures of flirting, which require an analogous "open-endedness." Most importantly, unconsummated carnality expressed as flirtation emerges as an activity as complex and as constitutive of the self as any other theme explored by Victorian and Edwardian novelists.

In this study of coquettish females and flirty males, of artfully managed attractions and deliberately deferred desires, I consider flirtatious eros as a largely unexcavated, distinct realm of experience in nineteenth- and early-twentieth-century fiction. Flirtatious desire undermines the still-influential libidinal model of sexuality by its reiterated suggestion that the aim of desire is not necessarily the realization of desire but rather deferral itself. Seductive behavior without seduction, attention without intention, flirtation in the Victorian and the Edwardian novel seems playful, even pointless, yet nonetheless carries powerful emotional associations and unleashes perilous consequences. Containing its own distinct rules and attributes, relying on elusive and multifarious plots, flirtation has its flowering in Victorian fiction for reasons that I shall explore in depth throughout the following chapters.

In an era that placed an exceptionally high value on the accelerated production and consumption of goods, as well as on linking individual worth to rapidly disseminated effects, flirting—the libidinal form of loitering without intent—fostered insurrectionary energies. In a male-dominated order, in which marriage was prized as a satisfying resolution, flirting represents a reckless adventurism that violates—and sometimes succeeds in undermining—the smooth functioning of middle-class interests and aspirations. Within the context of nineteenth-century fiction, that violation often emerges as a subtly intimated, dissident gesture at the center of a larger, apparently well-settled narrative of connubial bliss. An exemplary text in this regard is Austen's *Pride and Prejudice* (1813), where it is Lydia, and not, notably, Elizabeth Bennet, who wins the hand of George Wickham. In *The Mill on the Floss,* the plot of flirtation that briefly ensnares Maggie Tulliver and Stephen Guest strongly confirms the illegitimacy of the (stalled) romance between Maggie and Philip Wakem. Philip, alarmed by the intense *amitié amoureuse* flaring up between his adored Maggie and her new acquaintance Stephen, strives to resolve the long-standing familial feud that he imagines has obstructed his fitful pursuit of Maggie. Yet with the introduction of Stephen into the last third of her narrative, Eliot suggests possibilities for the representation of erotic desire that seem outside of her power as a novelist; indeed, flirtation occurs exactly because Eliot is able to take this proto-Lawrentian interlude no further. Maggie's near-romance with Stephen brings *The Mill on the Floss* and the Victorian novel itself into a new register of feeling, paving the way for Eliot's unlikely but unmistakable position as a precursor, along with Emily Brontë, of D. H. Lawrence (whose Ursula Brangwen of the 1915 *The Rainbow* echoes Maggie in her renunciation of her would-be romantic savior, the initially intoxicating but ultimately feckless Anton Skrebensky). As I suggest in my discussion of *The Mill on the Floss* in chapter 3, Maggie's "flirtational" rapport with Stephen has too often been downplayed by critics of Eliot's novel. Yet this section of *The Mill on the Floss* is pivotal to its success, for had Maggie never gone on her boating trip with Stephen, she indeed would have been the drearily self-renouncing Victorian heroine, trapped in a life of dingy pieties, that many readers have accused her of resembling.

For the nineteenth-century novelist, who labored in a literary market-place where protracted plots were financially profitable, flirtation as the-matic material had obvious advantages. At its most basic, flirtation es-chews an exclusive, familiar trajectory, instead favoring plots that in retrospect seem to have metastasized into a further stage in courtship when, in fact, such plots were not necessarily directed toward anything so coherent. This is especially true of Thackeray's productions, which were composed in a breakneck, improvisational spirit demanded by their ap-pearance in monthly installments. Having earned 1,200 pounds for twenty monthly installments of *Vanity Fair,* Thackeray capitalized on that novel's success by contracting 2,000 pounds for the same number of installments for his subsequent work of fiction, the sweeping bildungsroman *The History of Pendennis* (1848–50). Midway through the publication of *Pendennis,* however, the novel was expanded to what Thackeray called a "Homeric" twenty-four numbers, with a proportionate increase in payment for its author. The last-minute resolutions of these works—in their market-driven formlessness, truly the "loose baggy monsters" that Henry James criticized as all too typical of nineteenth-century fiction—depend on the fortunes of inveterate coquettes, Becky Sharp and Blanche Amory. Becky, after evidently poisoning Jos Sedley, ends up a prosperous woman, while Blanche is rejected by Pendennis for Blanche's worthier, more pa-tient rival, Laura Bell. Whatever their ultimate resolution, plots of flirta-tion continually raise the question of which paths most satisfyingly reflect the deepest impulses of characters. As Eliot demonstrated in *The Mill on the Floss,* it is not through "results" that one gains an expanded sense of Maggie Tulliver but rather through the hidden "processes" whereby Eliot's heroine confusedly struggles for a sense of identity after her elopement with a man she can call neither lover nor fiancé.

In such a way do novelists take flirtation, which embodies the indeter-minacies of erotic impulses and relations, as their formal inspiration. The flirtatiousness of Rosamond Vincy, Becky Sharp, and Daisy Miller is a generative metafictional motif. Recent theories of fiction are dense with in-sights about the necessary shifts in narrative discourse that occur between the start and finish of a novel, but my focus here is primarily on the long course of the "middle," before closure is in sight, and during that extended moment when the form of desire radically challenges all trajectories and repetition impedes steady advance. As decisive as such technical issues are, flirtation had more than a formal impact, as indicated by the alarmist reaction of the Victorian critics of Darwin's theory of sexual selection. My concentration on flirtatious desire aims to recast some of the continuing critical controversies that have surrounded the question of sexuality in the Victorian novel and in the Victorian era generally—arguments concerning, most recently, whether one should regard Victorian culture as steeped in illicit eroticism or as an integrated cultural system that adhered to a shared, sensibly conceived code of the senses.[6] An emphasis on the centrality of flirtation in nineteenth-century British fiction helps to undermine the still-influential libidinal model of sexuality as dependent on a mechanistic system of repression and cathexis. As John Kucich argues in a discussion of the fiction of Charles Dickens, George Eliot, and Charlotte Brontë, the purpose of desire in Victorian fiction is not necessarily the realization of erotic need but the maintenance of deferral. Along with Kucich, I regard the ceaseless emotional convolutions of Victorian protagonists as the aim, rather than the problem, of nineteenth-century subjectivity.

Why have critics failed to register such a powerfully constitutive component of the novel? Why, in a period in which feminist criticism of Victorian fiction has come to accentuate the "transgressive" possibilities of various dissident female figures, would the coquette escape extended treatment? How, when the recent insights of queer theory have so powerfully redefined the ways in which we read texts, allowing us access to forms of desire that refuse to fall into a pinched (and, as Michel Foucault has demonstrated, relatively recent) binary of heterosexual and homosexual, would the erotics of flirtation fall off the radar screen in examinations of fiction? One possibility is that flirtation would seem to resist the "deep" decoding afforded by other forms of erotic desire, suggesting as it sometimes does a kind of empty intimacy—playfulness without import, a parody of the earnest love plots that continue to draw readers to Victorian fiction. A more likely answer, I suspect, is a methodological one—namely, the dominance in recent discussions of Victorian fiction of paradigms adapted from the work of Foucault. For the Foucauldian understanding of Victorian fictional practice stresses, among other issues, the ways in which novels replicate the prevalent discourse of surveillance, in which the "gaze" becomes a dominant means of understanding relations between characters in fiction. My own debt to aspects of Foucault's thinking is considerable. One of the central claims informing *The Flirt's Tragedy,* that sexuality is shaped as it is articulated and by its resonances in the public sphere, is Foucauldian at its core. Nonetheless, what cannot be explored in a discussion where "carceral" Foucauldian prototypes obtain is the ever-changing give-and-take, the fast-shifting, elusive, fluid dynamic of personal relations (which are ocular but not only ocular) on which flirtation thrives.

The most influential critic of the "Foucauldian school" of criticism of Victorian fiction is D. A. Miller, not only in *The Novel and the Police* (1988), but in the less explicitly Foucauldian, earlier study *The Novel and Its Discontents* (1987). That narrative closure is an insufficient gauge of totalizing meaning is one of Miller's more persuasive arguments, as when he notes that the marital "narrative of happiness" is inevitably frustrated by the fact that only "insufficiencies, defaults, deferrals" can be successfully narrated. Yet even as he accentuates the limits of a focus on erotic closure, Miller's discussion comes to reconfirm the dead end provided by deferred desire. Thus Miller tends to stress clammy insufficiencies and defaults where one might just as easily locate exquisite enhancements and delirious raptures. In some ways this is an anticipation of Miller's exploration of Victorian fiction as functioning "panoptically" in *The Novel and the Police.* In the more recent study (one of the most cited critical texts on the Victorian novel of the last twenty years), Miller emphasizes the restrictive energies of Victorian fiction, critiquing, in an analysis of *Bleak House* (1853), *Barchester Towers* (1857), *The Woman in White* (1859–60), and *David Copperfield* (1849–50), the Victorian novel's claim to transform the inward, the individualistic, and the domestic into a sheltered sphere that functions as an oppositional "outside" to established power.[7] In a work preoccupied with the exposure of the Victorian novel's most punitive tautologies, every relation is reducible to a relation of power—indeed, for Miller, "power . . . encompasses everything in the world of the novel."[8] Moreover, all expressions of rebellion, all depictions of fantasy, are merely further evidence of the novel's scrutinizing, interrogative devices. Miller's approach has been especially far-reaching in influencing readings of the Victorian novel within the critical framework provided by queer theory, most conspicuously in the work of Eve Kosofsky Sedgwick, for whom the "closet" trumps the "panopticon" as a ruling metaphor for the practices of the Victorian novel insofar as it deals in homoerotic desire.[9]

One problem with Miller's Foucauldian perspective is its implicit analogy between scientific and juridical models of human behavior and Victorian fictional character. Miller contends that nineteenth-century fictionalists shaped their characters so that, one and all, they typified a dynamic of surveillance. Yet it is a highly individuated kind of fictional character that one finds in Victorian fiction—indeed, individuated character arguably is the Victorian novel's most basic constitutive feature. If Miller were correct in perceiving uniform discursive practices across nineteenth-century fiction, one would surely expect far more commonalities than differences between particular characters in the fiction of the period. Yet, as I argue, novelists such as Austen, Charlotte Brontë, George Eliot, and Hardy reactively sought to detonate types (especially theatrical types) so that their characters nurtured an unending opacity. "We cannot say that we like or understand Bathsheba," complained Henry James in his 1874 review of Hardy's *Far from the Madding Crowd,* but it was the flirty Bathsheba's resistance to ultimate discernment, James should have realized, that kept her from collapsing into other characters.[10] *The Novel and the Police* sees a single species as inhabiting the era's fiction, available to scrutiny and coercion because he or she must surrender to a discourse of knowledge. We are asked to accept this delineation of Victorian fictional character at the precise moment in the history of the novel when protagonists in fiction were becoming not only more nuanced, more unfathomable, and more closed to systematizing processes, but also more distinct from one another than characters in fiction had ever been before.

Despite the subtlety and power of Miller's analysis, his stress on the supervisory function of an external regime of power as it monitors and infiltrates an "internal" realm reinscribes a rigid, unchanging binary in which an external force invades and comes to assume a self-policing internal power. At the erotic level, however, an activity such as flirtation involves a constant, continuous usurpation of the boundaries of the internal and external. The problem stems, too, from the limitations of the panopticon as a metaphorical tool for nineteenth-century fiction, given its near-absolute emphasis on the visual. In the multivocally structured nineteenth-century novel, however, flirtatious scenarios are not only visual but involve the entire body. Moreover, Miller's description of nineteenth-century realism, in its oft-repeated insistence on the Victorian novel's policing strategies and complicity in the curtailment of opportunities for freedom, tends to minimize the variety of "realisms" available throughout the Victorian era, flattening all texts into a single paranoid narrative, so that a "policing function" gives a forced coherence to such disparate literary subgenres as sensation novels, detective stories, and autobiographical fiction.[11] Latent, too, in Miller's Foucauldian understanding of Victorian fiction lies not only a skepticism toward modernity, particularly as regards the city as a site for swiftly moving change, but a refusal to see the ways in which urban locales produce a range of new social arrangements commensurate with the anarchic energies of city life. The particular form of erotic relations focused on in this study, flirtation, intensifies the *unknowability* of the self as it changes with each interaction, generating not only paranoia in individuals but also a heightened, imaginative capacity for the pleasures that only the metropolis can provide.

One alternative to Miller's Foucauldian comprehension of the Victorian novel lies in the work of the German social thinker Georg Simmel. Simmel offers, I would suggest, a more complex theory of modernity, especially in its newly urbanized forms, and one that provides a more suggestive means of exploring erotic relations in the nineteenth-century novel. Simmel directly examined the subject of flirting in a 1909 and 1923 pair of essays on flirtation ("die Koketterie"), where Simmel, largely celebrated today for his meditation on the contradictory benefits and drawbacks of the "money economy" in *The Philosophy of Money* (1900), examined flirtation as a significant yet overlooked area of social experience. Just as the medium of money became the mechanism of an increasingly objective, distanced existence in cities, so too did flirtation emerge as the inevitable mode of relations for the metropolis, according to Simmel. Although Simmel's attitude toward urban life was in some ways an ambivalent one, he shares with Walter Benjamin a sense that the metropolis creates its own unique social forms. Whereas Foucault sees an accretion of power in the new urban regimes of knowledge, Simmel locates a social realm of intensified, dizzying, protean fluidity in which power is one of many components of the metropolitan landscape. It remains a curious aspect of Foucault's intellectual achievement that although one of the most influential postmodern theorists of modernity, his work devotes little sustained analysis to the city as a distinct arena of experience. In the final pages of *Discipline and Punish,* where he does provide a coherent view of the metropolis, Foucault offers a stark image of the "carceral city" as the culmination of those ever more canny punitive procedures that Foucault sees the Enlightenment as having generated. Urban life, for Foucault, is an unending gothic scenario, so nightmarish as to defy description, its seeming "freedoms" the very apotheosis of modern disciplinary regimes: "The notions of institutions of repression, rejection, exclusion, marginalization, are not adequate to describe, at the very centre of the carceral city, the formation of the insidious leniencies, unavowable petty cruelties, small acts of cunning, calculated methods, techniques, 'sciences,' that permit the fabrication of the disciplinary individual." [12]

For Simmel, however, the city is a site of multiple freedoms that have little to do with eluding detection or punitive scrutiny, while the pervasive impersonality of urban life, its excess of "external and internal stimulation," demands a new, "nonjudgmental" perspective. Foucault perceives a univocal discourse permeating social institutions in and outside of the city, in which power is forever deployed and sustained, whereas Simmel sees the key to the analysis of modernity as lying not so much in seemingly all-determining social systems or institutions but in the "invisible threads" of social reality in diverse "momentary images" or "snapshots" ("*Moment-bilder*"). The multiplicity of everyday stimuli engendered by city life is precisely what lends urban existence its quality of excitement, danger, and risk (a perspective on urban existence that links Simmel not only to Walter Benjamin, with his focus on the urban flâneur, but to Mikhail Bakhtin, who in his elaboration of "speech acts" accentuated daily interaction, in which the individual actively creates the society in which his or her discourse occurs).

As Jürgen Habermas notes, Simmel had a "sensitive awareness of the attractions typical of his times; of aesthetic innovations; of spiritual shifts of disposition and changes of orientation in the metropolitan attitudes to life; and of subpolitical transformations of inclination and barely tangible, diffuse, but treacherous phenomena of the everyday." [13] The idea that modern everyday life held danger stemmed from Simmel's observation that faced with a colliding array of impressions, the individual might seek to create psychological and emotional distance between himself and his social environment, the pathological deformation of which is so-called agoraphobia. [14] Simmel's thinking was governed less by a concern over the pathologies produced by random encounters with strangers, however, than by an appreciation of the experimental excitement of encountering others en masse. By implicitly linking the new social relations of urban environments to Darwinian sexual selection, Simmel went far in naturalizing the flirt, just as Baudelaire had done with the flâneur in describing his domain of the crowd as what the "air is to the bird or the sea to the fish." (Benjamin, similarly, romanticized Parisian flâneurs, quoting Hugo von Hofmannsthal to the effect that they had transformed Paris into "a landscape made of living people." [15])

"Flirtation" for Simmel emerges as a uniquely potent activity for city dwellers as an antidote, one may assume, to urban indifference and anomie. As we shall see, his theory of flirtation understood flirting as increasing in modern times owing to an expansion in the number of individuals drawing one's attention. It is the novel, with its absorption in daily life in all its detail as well as in the individual's attempt at negotiating the chaotic flux of a modernity, that most energetically embodies Simmel's stress on the power of momentary encounters. The significance of the new, intensified role of flirting in modern life is such that flirtation becomes thematically crucial not just in those novels of urban, bohemian ambition such as George Henry Lewes's *Ranthorpe* (1847), William Makepeace Thackeray's *The History of Pendennis,* and Gustave Flaubert's *Sentimental Education* (in which unconsummated relations symbolize all the unachievable desires of the grappling artist living in the city.) Flirtation dominates even those works, such as *Middlemarch* (1871–72) and *Under the Greenwood Tree* (1872), that are set in rural, "primitive," or rustic locales, where life in small towns, far from madding crowds, reveals designs supposedly inherent in human nature and outside of those accelerated historical processes associated with metropolitan experience.

Whether it is Bathsheba Everdene shifting between three suitors in her isolated farm community, or Daisy Miller flirting before the social potentates of the American exile colony in Rome, urban life has altered the value of flirtation, augmenting its potential to enhance the self. That augmentation takes place through an erotics of the everyday as opposed to the momentous, and it is the everyday, as Laurie Langbauer has demonstrated, that is the foundation for realism. Langbauer brilliantly establishes that with the rise of serial fiction later Victorian and early modern novelists demonstrate a preoccupation with commonplace events as a means of conveying the tedium along with the mystery of cosmopolitan life, the daily deconstruction of illusions, and the unendingness of life in urban lo-

cales. (Such a preoccupation on the part of writers such as Oliphant, Trollope, Galsworthy, and Woolf was, as Langbauer shows, one reason the
novel was frequently derided as a genre of mundane, "feminine" concerns.) For the coquette, the city signifies an enticing series of new, impersonal opportunities, just as Baudelaire saw the flâneur as entering into
"the crowd as into an immense reservoir of electricity." [16] Zuleika Dobson,
the coquette-heroine of Max Beerbohm's 1911 satirical novel, fantasizes
about expanding crowds once she has vanquished a would-be suitor: "And
now not on him alone need she ponder. Now he was but the center of a
group—a group that might grow and grow—a group that might with a
little encouragement be a multitude. . . . With such hopes dimly whirling
in the recesses of her soul, her beautiful red lips babbled." [17]

An enhanced exploration of flirtation in the novel does not so much
unravel questions concerning Victorian sexuality as intensify and complicate them. Because of the changing direction of character in the nineteenth-
century novel, scenes of flirting in the fiction of Jane Austen, Charlotte
Brontë, William Makepeace Thackeray, George Eliot, and Thomas Hardy
contribute to a sense of desire itself as paradoxical, unknowable, and beyond the author's (or reader's) purview. This problem in the understanding of the sexual self (one might call it a crisis in an erotic "epistemology")
often forces a resolution in the narrative that has little relation to the dynamics of the erotic relationship proper. Frequently it is as if the energies
released by flirtation cannot be assimilated fully by available sanctioned
plots. Scenes such as the murkily depicted, apparent death that ambigu-
ously concludes *Villette* (1853) and the equally implausible flood at the end
of *The Mill on the Floss* are conclusions that suggest authorial ambivalence
before a marriage plot that has been assiduously avoided throughout the
course of the novel. Scenarios of flirtatious desire occur at the crux of
plots and at the heart of the thematic concerns animating such plots. The
consequences of Becky Sharp's equivocally sketched encounter with Lord
Steyne, to take a prime example from Victorian fiction, is rendered by
Thackeray as a battle as pivotal as Waterloo in determining the fate of the
heroine of *Vanity Fair*. For Thackeray, history as exemplified by a European military conflagration is simply an uncontrollable juggernaut, lay-
ing waste to thousands. That Waterloo kills off Amelia's husband George
and renders her a young widow is a tragedy, yet *Vanity Fair* gives pride of
place not to historical debacles but to its heroine's endless coquetries. The

exposure by Becky's husband of his wife's seeming infidelity is, for Becky, a metaphorical Waterloo in the form of abandonment and (temporary) financial ruin. Her ambiguous encounter with Steyne, moreover, stresses the unknowable, continuing enigma of the relations between two people.

Scenes of flirtation in Victorian fiction are not always in the service of comic revelations and outlandish twists of plot, however, as the title of this book should indicate. My inclusion of such "earnest" Victorian texts as *Middlemarch* and *Daniel Deronda* (1876) will undoubtedly strike some readers as misguidedly stretching the activity of flirtation, so seemingly droll a theme, to the brink of its suggestiveness as an interpretive tool. The significance of flirtation for the Victorian novelist lay precisely in the risks involved, in flirtation's potential to deal the flirt a tragic fate, although in having no legal consequences such risks cannot be discussed in the terms of the state's apparatus of laws and surveillance explored by Miller. Whatever comic power coquetry obtains in a novel such as *Vanity Fair,* what made flirting so richly evocative a subject for nineteenth-century writers was the possibilities the topic offered for suggesting implied-but-never-satisfied inclinations. Flirtation represented a useful paradox not only because it was tragically and comically resonant but also because it reflected the self at its most intensely sociable and most frustratingly secret.

Far more than Thackeray, Hardy and George Eliot reveal an intensely unresolved attitude toward flirtatious behavior. Hardy's literary career is bifurcated by the contradictions presented by erotic play with ancillary romantic interests during courtship and before and after marriage. While he mined coquetry in *Under the Greenwood Tree* in order to create a rural comedy of manners in which a female held all-commanding power in *affaires de coeur,* it was the horrifying vicissitudes of indecisive feminine mischief that came to preoccupy the novelist in such works as *Far from the Madding Crowd* (1874) and *Jude the Obscure* (1896). Hardy remained fairly obsessed by the ways in which the serious play that is flirtation turns deadly serious. When he turned exclusively to poetry after the succès de scandale of *Jude the Obscure,* that preoccupation remained. He made flirting the focus of one of his most memorable dramatic monologues, "The Flirt's Tragedy" (1911) (from which I have adopted my title), in which a male speaker bitterly recalls in old age how he contracted a "needy Adonis" to woo and then abandon his too-flirtatious beloved. But the jealous lover's curiosity backfires, and confronted with the tale of his woman's "betrayal," he murders the young man in a showdown in Venice ("And there in the gloom of the *calle* / My steel ran him through.") Returning to his lover in England, he marries her as a way of redeeming himself. When the woman gives birth to a son, the boy suspects that his "false father" has murdered his "true" papa. The child flees, leading his mother to drown herself. Flirtation unleashes the murderous, competitive beast in man, engendering anxieties over romantic faithfulness that congeal into a cross-generational curse.

For George Eliot, often dependent on the creakiest trappings of nineteenth-century fiction yet continually frustrated by the limitations such devices placed on her imaginative powers, coquetry was also far more than an opportunity for the staging of playful amorous mischief. It was valuable as a means of bringing to the surface latent love plots, testing the seriousness of her heroines' romantic inclinations, and ascertaining the depth of emotions. Just as in *Villette* Charlotte Brontë understood that the naughty coquette Ginevra Fanshawe allowed Lucy Snowe to recognize flirting as a means of asserting female interests, in *Middlemarch* George Eliot grasped that sanctioned plots of desire thrive on illicit ones. Although Eliot needed to contain flirtation's dangerous energies (punishing such flirts as Rosamond Vincy for their reckless wooing of other men after marriage), she often intimates that the plot of flirtation does not function as a hindrance but as an inspiration to connubial schemes. Dorothea's accidental discovery of Ladislaw with Rosamond indirectly secures her happiness when she forces herself to reach a final estimation of her young suitor. Such scenes abruptly and crucially alter the course of events in Eliot's fiction. In a replay of this scene of Rosamond and Ladislaw's exposure, *Daniel Deronda*'s Grandcourt discovers his wife privately receiving Deronda at home and immediately decides that she must be removed from England. Only on a private yacht in the Caribbean can he be assured that she will not turn parlor-room tête-à-têtes into galling spectacles of moral salvation with his "rival."

In Eliot, as in Hardy, the process of Darwinian sexual selection, whereby males compete for female approval, continues even after marriage vows have been sealed. (The exposure of Gwendolen's indiscretion seals both her fate and that of Grandcourt when she, in a negative act of "choice" that perversely abides by the logic of Darwinian sexual selection, passively elects to watch her husband drown.) Climaxes in which flirtations are dramatically exposed, suddenly and unexpectedly transforming the novel's action, echo with the breathless *coups de théâtre* of the eighteenth-century stage, where, I argue, coquetry finds much of its literary ancestry. Ultimately, however, such scenes serve to advertise the realist novel's generic superiority to the theater, since ambiguous encounters between illicit suitors in Victorian fiction are sufficiently opaque as to require a novelist's infinite demurrals, speculations in the absence of "hard evidence," and nuanced elaborations.

When novelists depicted characters who suspend rather than indulge their carnal impulses, they also indicated that the novel, although its chief subject might be desire, could not be confused with what, according to recent historians such as Robert Darnton, constituted the single most powerful rival for the attention of readers throughout the eighteenth- and nineteenth-centuries: pornography.[18] Regardless of class, sex, or age, the heroes and heroines of pornographic literature are eager to respond with swift, athletic alacrity to the first sexual overtures. Although many Victorian pornographic texts do enlist postponement as a narrative technique (allowing heroines, for instance, to be glimpsed, teased, and pursued in successive, protracted episodes), an erotic "endism" invariably prevails in such works. Existing in an eternal present tense of instant gratification and release, pornographic narratives generally differ from their counterparts in both "high" and popular Victorian fiction, in which time functions in a forever-postponed conditional tense and in which consummation is not always a certainty, as it usually is in pornographic works.[19] The coquette, in particular, locates her very identity in the manipulation of time. A popular send-up of coquettish females entitled *The Natural History of the Flirt* (1851) noted that during a ball the coquette is "skilled in saying with great coolness," when the slower of her admirers asks if it is not now the dance for which he will be her partner, " 'No, I think it was the next'." [20]

As I suggested, with serialized fictions such as Thackeray's *Vanity Fair,* Eliot's *Middlemarch,* and Hardy's *Far from the Madding Crowd,* flirtation held the obvious advantage of allowing novelists to protract desire over the course of several months and sometimes even years. Less apparent, however, are the ways in which flirtatious scenarios have allowed nineteenth-century fictionalists the opportunity to explore seemingly dissident forms of eros supposedly "repressed" by Victorian society or the expectations of Victorian readers. In Austen's (pre-Victorian) epistolary novel *Lady Susan* (1805), Charlotte Brontë's *Villette,* Charles Dickens's *David Copperfield,* and Eliot's *The Mill on the Floss,* characters flirt across authorized boundaries and with forms of desire often deemed outside the scope of the nineteenth-century British novel. In all of these works "rebel" erotic impulses are depicted and then withdrawn, fleetingly proffered but then tucked back under more pronounced narratives of courtship and marriage. Such scenarios—situations momentarily staged in lieu of fixed erotic "identities"—do not exist merely in opposition to more conventional dynamics of romantic desire. Rather, flirtation binds the dissident libidinal impulse to the erotically "authorized," as heroines and heroes learn from coquettes and flirty males how to assume sociable selves in order to engineer their own plots of erotic happiness. The erotic "tutoring" fostered by these female and male coquettes lends the Victorian novel a built-in dialectic; Lucy Snowe requires her Ginevra and Catherine Morland her Isabella Thorpe, for no angelic heroine can function without a demonic coquette-sister in close proximity. Similarly, Hardy's Gabriel Oak of *Far from the Madding Crowd,* loyal and stalwart, gains in the eyes of Bathsheba Everdene as he is contrasted to the preening Frank Troy. This dynamic functions in tandem with other potent dialectical pressures informing the novel in this period: British earnestness versus French erotic fluidity, Puritan as opposed to Cavalier literary traditions, bourgeois versus aristocratic ethics of social behavior, and nineteenth-century as contrasted with eighteenth-century conceptions of femininity.

At the same time, flirtatious desire becomes more than a formal strategy and a keen thematic preoccupation as it emerges as a recurring metaphor for both the challenges and limits of literary representation. It is through flirtation that novelists link problems in the depiction of desire to ambiguous sexuality. When Austen's Lady Susan toys with her daughter's fiancé, is it the mere exercising of a merry widow's impish impulses, or the callous betrayal of a child? When Becky Sharp saps Lord Steyne of funds in a series of flirtatious encounters enacted in the drawing rooms of London, is Thackeray's antiheroine committing a kind of adultery, or aiming to increase her family's fortunes in a financially unstable period? When a half-dressed Steerforth gazes at his new friend David Copperfield before retiring for the evening and asks, yawning, "You haven't got a sister, have you?" (because, Steerforth assures David, he is certain a Miss Copperfield would have been a "pretty, timid, bright-eyed sort of girl"), is Steerforth declaring an (unconscious) attraction to David, or to an imaginary young lady?[21] Lady Susan is socially shunned, Becky Sharp becomes a respectable society matron (an ironic fate for a bad girl), and Steerforth is killed off in the narrative, but such questions remain unresolved.

These characters make their exits, leaving behind them large doubts as to what may be represented in fiction, but they do more than raise doubts. By elevating flirtation to a superdeterminant position in the narrative, a novelist such as Thackeray insists on the superiority of *Vanity Fair* not only to earlier fictional enterprises but to other literary genres as well. Only the novel of realism, insists Thackeray's eagle-eyed puppeteer-narrator, can isolate the now-apparent, now-veiled dynamic whereby flirtatious desires are enacted. In an analogous deployment of flirtation for a shift in the novel relation to realist representation, the bewildering shallowness of James's Daisy Miller marks a move toward the Symbolist style that James would embrace in such late works as *The Golden Bowl* (1904). Daisy's very "emptiness" (that is, her character's beguiling yet maddening openness to multiple interpretation) makes her an ideal literary "symbol," since symbols, in being open-endedly suggestive, provide the terms for a modernist representation of opaque signification.

This crucial relation of flirtation to the ever-changing aesthetics of realism helps to explain the upheaval evoked by the actions of fictional characters who flirt too recklessly: the horror provoked by Susan Vernon in Austen's novel, the destruction of Becky's marriage signaled by the climactic disclosure of her near or actual affair with Lord Steyne, the emotional havoc generated by Steerforth, and the challenge to social mores and male comprehension of Daisy Miller's self-immolating fickleness. At such moments in narratives, the attentive reader should grasp that nineteenth-century fiction pivots around coquettish figures and flirtatious scenarios that indirectly evoke adulterous, incestuous, same-sex, and bisexual erotic impulses. Such intrusions into the plot of the novel frequently jump-start sanctioned connubial resolutions. It is only after the coy Steerforth perishes that David marries the feather-brained Dora (although, in temporal terms, these two events occur simultaneously). A counterdynamic that dissolves marital union also abides in the wake of flirtation: in *Daniel Deronda,* it is only after Grandcourt discovers his wife Gwendolen at home with Daniel Deronda, where the two are engaged in a suspicious tête-à-tête, that he whisks her out of England for a Mediterranean cruise, in a move that brings their woeful marriage to its deadly denouement.

Through unresolved scenarios such as that between Maggie and

Stephen, Countess Olenska and Newland Archer, Gabriel Nash and Nick Dormer, the nineteenth- and early-twentieth-century "love plot" comes to exist in tensile, symbiotic relation to narratives of a well-managed erotic carnivalesque. And as the example from *David Copperfield* might suggest, homoerotic propensities may emerge in the absence of socially possible homosexual identities. Before the appearance of the "homosexual" as a well-defined category, the nineteenth-century novel accommodated what we would today recognize as homoerotically coded impulses—but only insofar as those inclinations appear entangled with more sanctioned narratives. However, with the emergence of the self-consciously designed "homosexual novel of manners" exemplified by *The Picture of Dorian Gray* and *The Tragic Muse* (both of which first appeared serially in 1890), male coquettes such as Lord Henry and Gabriel Nash permanently sidetrack the Victorian marriage plot, drawing the young heroes of these novels out of the arms of eligible females and into either gothic self-annihilation (*Dorian Gray*) or a life devoted to art (*The Tragic Muse*).

With a variety of techniques, Victorian novelists continually remind their readers that flirtation is not simply another form of eros—amorous dallying—but an activity that speaks to the impermanent, shifting vocabulary of erotic desire, a language, as I argue, that the novel fosters above all other literary genres. A private language enacted in public, flirtatious desire in Victorian fiction is also, far more than romantic love, one that must be forever aware of itself, as participants remain conscious of their physical deportment and the social ramifications of their behavior. As I suggest by linking Darwin's theory of sexual selection and Victorian fiction in chapter 3, the evolutionist complicates the idea of flirtation as conscious game-playing through an argument (partly forced on him by those critics who rejected Darwin's notion of animals as aesthetic "choosers") that coquetry might be unconsciously driven. Darwin's conception of unconscious flirtation paves the way for James's Daisy Miller, whose coquetries are defended by her friend Winterbourne as "innocent," harmless and characteristically American, until Daisy dies of Roman fever. It is as if Daisy's body (rather than her conscience) registers her moral trespasses as well as the truth of Darwinian law.

Simultaneously anticipating, enhancing, and revising the precepts of sexual selection, both Eliot and Hardy represent flirtation as accruing intensity when it is enacted in the presence of others, not only before rivals (although this too is typical in their work) but also in the presence of family members, friends, and acquaintances. Eliot and Hardy depict flirtation as inherently social, distinct from an eros that exists in a wholly personal realm. In all of his major fiction, Hardy remains fascinated by women whose allure grows—and, indeed, whose very characters are formed—through an increase in the number of men vying for their approval, as in *Jude the Obscure* or *Far from the Madding Crowd.* Bathsheba Everdene's sexual charisma is magnified in direct proportion to her restlessly changing mind, which enacts its uncertainties regarding a proper suitor as an entire farming community looks on, overhears, and judges. At another level, Hardy remains intensely preoccupied with the various ways in which any given fate may obscure the possibility of other destinies. Flirtation for Hardy becomes an ideal metaphor for hidden patterns, undisclosed impulses, and alternate but never-taken paths embedded in nature, the consciousness of which generally weighs heavily on his male protagonists but that offers his heroines a clandestine sense of power. In an uncharacteristically mirthful Wessex novel, *Under the Greenwood Tree,* published one year after Darwin's first extended articulation of his theory of sexual selection, Hardy supplies a final image of his smug heroine Fancy Day, affianced to Dick Dewy, cherishing her secret knowledge that she had earlier accepted—and then abruptly rejected—another man's proposal of marriage.

To write about flirtation in the novel is to risk the accusation that one is exploring an activity that is at best trivial, at worst shallow, and that in any case is far too amorphous to have historically specific, identifiable characteristics, let alone a distinct literary genealogy. Critics of my focus on Victorian and Edwardian fiction might argue that unfulfilled eroticism as literary material may be traced back to Petrarch and Chaucer, or note that the language of Troubadour poetry is celebrated for giving voice to the vicissitudes of unrequited eros. Pushkin's *Eugene Onegin* (1830), with its story of Tatyana's long-sustained unrequited love for the foppish Onegin, is yet another case of a work of poetry that would seem to militate against an argument stressing the novel's unique generic accommodation of flirtation. At the same time, Pushkin's poem (so novelistic that it is sometimes called a "novel in verse") looks backward, as many formalist critics have pointed out, to such fictions as Laurence Sterne's *Tristram Shandy* (1759–67), and if it points at all forward, toward the nineteenth-century Russian novel. Some might argue too that the coquette is a transhistorical literary figure: Shakespeare's Cleopatra (and to a lesser extent, Dryden's and

Shaw's) is perhaps the archetypal "flirt," no more so than when, after Antony's death, she tries to flirt with Octavius and, only after realizing that this rigid patriarch won't play, commits suicide. (A comparably "mythic" coquette in the Victorian period is Tennyson's Vivien of the poet's 1859 *Idylls of the King,* a woman who elicits and then mocks male desires and whose unalleviated malevolence has repelled generations of readers.) Confirming a sense that flirtation functions transhistorically, a recent account of the "history" of flirting by the French journalist Fabienne Casta-Rosaz begins in 1870 and culminates in the years 1950–65, just before an era of uninhibited sexuality, which Casta-Rosaz views as a watershed for flirtatious behavior.

To the charge that flirting is either too murky or too widespread to be calibrated in a study of the novel, I would respond that while flirtation never ceases to animate the preoccupations of pre-Victorian poets and writers, there are historical moments when the subject of coquetry takes on special intensity for fiction makers. Despite its ubiquity as a theme in literature, erotic indecisiveness expressed as flirtation has a distinct history and definable parameters within the history of the novel. The protracted novel of seduction exemplified by Samuel Richardson's *Clarissa* or *Pamela,* so closely related to the pornographic, functions differently than the Victorian and Edwardian fictions of modesty and immodesty I explore here. Learning to flirt in an increasingly crowded universe, in which flirtation hints at hidden, nebulous depths of the self, is central to the very enterprise of nineteenth-century fiction. To be sure, flirtation became a focus of conduct books, courtship guides, religiously inspired manifestos on women's role in society, and treatises on ladylike deportment through the Victorian epoch. Yet the prickly problems of form confronting the authors of such works were by no means identical to those encountered by writers of fiction. Although recent critical attempts at blurring the once-sacrosanct distinctions between fictional and nonfictional texts on themes of desire have identified many affinities across discursive modes that once seemed foreign to one another, the authors of conduct books did not so much concern themselves with an elaborate depiction of flirtation as with its condemnation *tout court.*[22] Far more than those moralizing on the limits of female behavior, Victorian novelists were obliged to address the paradoxical nature of flirtation. The very qualities that are engendered by coquetry and which lend it a dialectical force—an impenetrable, complicated inner life; secrecy in protracted, intimate relation with a much-scrutinized public self; a vital hesitancy permitting the contemplation of alternative choices; artful erotic dissembling in defiance of sincerity; ever more intricate plot-hatching—represented an embarrassment of riches for the Victorian novelist. The tonal monotony and emotional flatness of most conduct books tellingly contrasts with the continually perplexing Rubik's Cube of a work of overt fictionalizing such as *Villette* (where the restless heroine semisecretly flirts and denounces flirting in equal parts). The aesthetic advantage of Victorian fiction, moreover, stems from the unresolved nature of flirtatious desire throughout the nineteenth century.

NAMING FLIRTATION

"Can you think of anybody besides Lady Rosina?"

"I suppose you will wish to have Mrs. Finn?"

"What an arrangement! Lady Rosina for you to flirt with, and Mrs. Finn for me to grumble to."

"That is an odious word," said the Prime Minister.

"What; flirting? I don't see anything bad about the word. The thing is dangerous."

—Anthony Trollope, *The Prime Minister* (1876)

While I have sought a comfortably capacious definition of flirtation, I also have tried to discuss flirting in fairly restrictive terms since it is one of my basic contentions that flirtation is a distinct, overlooked category encompassing its own rules and dynamics. At the same time, my terminology favors a certain degree of linguistic multiplicity. In my first chapter, which discusses the forced march of the eighteenth-century coquette into nineteenth-century narrative, "coquette" and "coquetry" are favored terms. Employing words with Gallic associations is appropriate for a section that focuses on the sense in a number of British texts of flirting as a distinctly French (and aristocratic) invasion. Interestingly, in a reciprocal act of linguistic invasion, the English word "flirtation" came into common usage in French in 1817, causing consternation among purists of the French language, subsequently getting cut to "flirt" (again, meaning "flirtation") in 1866, a term that endures as *the* word for flirtation until today.[23] In England, the word "flirtation" was still fairly newfangled in the eighteenth century, when Samuel Johnson, who customarily refused to insert into his 1755 dictionary terms that previously had not appeared in print, balked at Lord Chesterfield's suggestion that he include "flirtation" in his dictionary (a word that Chesterfield promoted because, he claimed, it belonged to a lady of fashion who had "the most beautiful mouth in the world.") For Johnson, who wished his dictionary "to shew that the end of learning is piety," the problem with coquetry lay precisely in its suggestions of excessive verbal license on the part of women. When "flirtation" did show up in the lexicographer's dictionary, it was defined without erotic suggestions as "A quick sprightly motion. A cant word among women." For a verb to describe the activity discussed by Chesterfield's lady, Johnson chose "To coquet," which he defined as "To entertain with compliments and amorous tattle; to treat with an appearance of amorous tenderness"— significantly, given the term's associations of feminine wiles, a word indicating a game that Johnson defined as one that both sexes could play.[24]

If coquettes and flirts were invariably women, the activity of flirtation transcended such categories, denoting behavior generally initiated by women and reluctantly engaged in by men. In countless eighteenth- and nineteenth-century conduct books and popular novels (whose heroines mightily strove to adhere to pieties defining the rules of female modesty), writers in Britain warned of the perils anyone entailed in employing verbal cues and nonverbal gestures in acts of flirting. The authors of these cautionary texts exhorted their readers that coquetry was becoming an increasingly rampant problem, an art of socializing with origins in a discredited aristocratic class that was dividing the sexes. Males who assumed the roles of coquettes risked charges of effeminacy. David Garrick's confessedly timely farce "The Male Coquette: Or Seventeen Hundred Fifty-Seven" (1757) concerned a young man named Daffodil who boasts that "I give 'em all Hopes, without going a step further." Confronted by the women with whom he has trifled, he is scolded in the play's last lines by a male rival, who addresses the male coquette's female victims: "In you Coquetry is Loss of Fame / But in Our Sex, 'tis that Detested Name, / Tha marks the Want of Manhood, Virtue / Sense, and Shame."[25] "You are a strange young man," a society matron accuses young Mortimer in Amelia Opie's popular novel *Dangers of Coquetry* (1790). "Your sex, in this age, seems to idolize coquetry, for when were they more attentive to ours? Search throughout the beau monde, and you will scarcely see a woman that is not versed in every art of it." In seeking to defend his sex, Mortimer likens coquettes to rakes: "A coquette in your sex is, in my opinion, as detestable as a libertine in ours, and certainly has less excuse for her fault than the latter can boast."[26] Although his analogy is flawed, it calls attention to the fact that the activity of "coquetting" was increasingly understood as a socializing game involving both sexes.

A remark offered by Austen's Lady Susan intimates that men might be flirts—but only when they are fooled or charmed into engaging in spirited repartee with a coquette. "He is lively and seems clever," she observes of Reginald de Courcy, "and when I have inspired him with greater respect for me than his sister's kind offices have implanted, he may be an agreeable flirt."[27] By 1814, Austen could write in *Mansfield Park* of a male character "Becoming soon too busy with his play to have time for more than one flirtation."[28] The linguistic distinction between "flirts" and "coquettes" was kept alive well into the nineteenth century, although in the twentieth the latter increasingly suggests the social *environs* of a vanished upper class.[29]

In the absence of a secure definition of what constitutes flirtatious behavior, authors of moral treatises and conduct books repeatedly pointed to specific acts of female coquetry as meriting concern. With considerable frequency, "glances" generated special alarm in that they expressed erotic interest at the same time that they called attention to the "glancer." Far more economical, timewise, than verbal prowess, glancing eyes might take in two men or twenty in less time than it could take to utter a fetching sentence. The chief advantage of glances, however, was that they left no solid traces and thus no incriminating "evidence." The proverbial Victorian good girl could be a bad girl and then a good girl again, while the social universe itself could be evoked, as in any number of teeming scenes in Thackeray, with a series of swift, panoramic movements. Stendhal (Marie-Henri Beyle), whose tonic taxonomy of desire in *De l'amour* (1822) was as mordant a send-up of romantic ardor as that provided by Thackeray in *Vanity Fair,* displayed a fondness for military analogies when he called glances "the big guns of the virtuous coquette." Noted Stendhal: "Everything can be conveyed in a look, and yet that look can always be denied, because it cannot be quoted word for word."[30] As Stendhal intimates, if flirtation is a language, it is often an adamantly nonverbal one that lacks lasting, evidentiary power.

At the same time, flirtatious acts of communication are far too nuanced to be considered merely a primitive form of communication between interested members of the opposite sex. In a chapter on "Friendship and Flirtation" in *The Daughters of England: Their Position in Society and*

Character and Responsibilities (1842), Sarah Ellis declared that "all women plead not guilty to the charge of flirtation in themselves" and "yet, all are ready to detect and despise it in their friends," and then offered a "catalogue of folly" that itemized, along with a beautiful young woman's glances, nearly every artful social activity in which a young woman might engage:

> when the bland and beaming smile is put on for the occasion; when expressive looks are interchanged; when glittering curls are studiously displayed; when songs are impressively sung; when flowers which have been presented, are preserved and worn; when unnecessary attentions are artfully called forth . . . when conversation is so ingeniously turned as to induce, and compel some personal allusion, in which a compliment must almost unavoidably be couched. And in all this system of absurdity, containing items of folly too numerous for tongue or pen to tell, from the glance of a beautiful eye, to the expression of a mutual sentiment; from the gathering of a favourite flower, to the awakening of a dormant passion; from the pastime of an idle moment, to the occupation of years; in all this, it is deeply to be regretted, that the influence of man is such, as to excite, rather than to repress—to encourage this worse than folly, rather than to warn and to correct. . . . Time was, when warriors and heroes deemed it not incompatible with glory or renown, to make the cause of helpless woman theirs.[31]

That a "compliment" could not be directly proffered but must be surreptitiously "couched" within a "personal allusion" suggests the thin line dividing social propriety from social peril. A daughter of England scarcely could be blamed for not wishing to leave the bedroom, let alone the home. Daughters of France were no less vulnerable, and the statesman Talleyrand may only have been half joking when he observed of a certain woman that "Because she did not want to be considered a flirt, she allowed herself to be easily seduced."[32]

The distinctions between coquetry and flirtation would seem to have become arbitrary by the end of the century, although some observers sought to claim flirting as a relatively innocuous sport, in contrast to the time-honored craft of the professional coquette. Thus the popular novelist Paul Bourget (a friend of Edith Wharton and Henry James) insisted on the flirt's relative innocence in contrast to the coquette. In a philosophical "meditation" entitled "Du flirt et des coquettes" in *Physiologie de l'amour moderne* (1890), purportedly the posthumous fragments of a work by Bourget's alter ego, Claude Larher, Bourget noted that the "woman who flirts is often confounded with the coquette" but asserted that an "abyss, however, separates them. The first likes the upheaval that she inspires in men. She wants to desire and savor the honor that this desire gives to her charm, to take part in it, to amuse herself, and then it's finished. The second wants to be loved without loving, to provoke those passions which she doesn't share. . . . The coquette is always a cruel woman."[33] Novelists in France were far more likely to portray the phenomenon of flirting in socially positive terms. In a droll *nouvelle* entitled "Flirting Club" and first published in a collection dedicated to Henry James, Bourget himself strongly hinted that unfulfilled desire constituted the very distillation of love. "Flirting Club" tells of a lively English organization in which men are not allowed to become the lovers of the women with whom they flirt, a program that proves of particular benefit to a young woman who, as the wife of a paralyzed husband, finds herself enjoying heightened emotional relations with several men at once.[34] As if to drive home the point that flirting had replaced adultery as the favored game of the *haute bourgeoisie*, the popular French novelist Paul Hervieu composed a comic novel that may be translated as *Flirtation: A Novel of Parisian Life* (1889).[35]

Recent disputes over appropriate conduct in the work environment, sexual harassment, and most recently, whether children can be considered as indulging in "natural" activity or legally actionable behavior when they make overtures to their classmates, have rendered flirting an ever more vexing type of behavior, with men and women frequently holding very different views of what comprises a winking expression of affection versus a lecherous play for power. In some ways, flirtation held as much peril in the 1990s—and continues to do so in a new century—as it did for Victorians, perhaps even more so, given that the separate-sphere culture of Victorian life precluded women appearing in the workplace, the site of so much wrangling over sexual signals over the last few years.

As with the Victorians, an accusation of flirting today poses the greatest danger to those upholding an unyielding set of social values. Several years ago, a newspaper article reported that then–Secretary of Housing and Urban Development Jack Kemp discovered that an open microphone at the G.O.P. Convention had captured his "honeyed compliments, some of them whispered," to a television reporter, and noted that "In the Republican Party of rigid family values, even the harmless flirtation that was once the best part of politicians' lives is fraught with peril."[36] Throughout the early 1990s, the perpetual presidential noncandidate Mario Cuomo, famous for his verbal eloquence, symbolized the risks of playing the coquette in the hardened realm of American politics; one observer expressed despair in "watching Cuomo flirting with the Presidency and teasing the press with his mystifying soliloquies."[37] Given that it thrives on public versus private conduct, secret as opposed to open sentiments, flirtation was a special temptation for those occupying the political arena. Flirtation has always thrived where behavior is monitored, so that the term never quite sheds its implications of risk. As psychotherapist Adam Phillips observes, the enduring seriousness of flirtation as an enterprise is suggested by the way in which today one generally is said to flirt with trouble and danger, say, but not, for instance, with pleasure or happiness. Choosing to stress flirting's positive value, Phillips has employed flirtation as a broadly applicable metaphor for the "non-contingent" nature of stories relayed within the framework of psychoanalysis.[38]

For Austen, Eliot, Hardy, James, and Wharton (all of whom were drawn to the depiction of love problems within the context of tightly woven, self-regarding communities), the more thoroughly regulated realm of Washington politics would have been the ideal setting for a depiction of flirting. (Indeed, when James revised *Daisy Miller* (1878) in his more purely comic story "Pandora" (1884), the setting shifted from the American exiled community of Rome to the European emigré cenacles of Washington, D.C.) All of these novelists understood coquetry as increasing in frequency and gravity in direct proportion to the monitored calibration of personal relations, in a social environment in which even momentary "commitments" may have grave consequences. Flirtation increasingly raised epistemological problems for fictional characters as well as for attentive readers. How can one ever be certain if characters in a particular scenario harbor a playful interest in one another, given the necessarily secretive—and also sometimes nonverbal—nature of this erotic game? Flirtation at once engendered and confounded the aims of realist fiction in forcing the social sphere to surrender to documentary representation, as readers were induced to strive for the extraordinary position of Austen's Isabella Thorpe, who is said to be able to "discover a flirtation between any gentleman and lady who only smiled at each other."[39]

SURVIVING DESIRE: GEORG SIMMEL AND THE ART OF FLIRTATION

As a subject of serious theoretical discussion at the turn of the twentieth century, flirtation arose as a question of considerable topical interest, stemming from the period's extensive debates on relations between the sexes. At the very moment when flirtation already had witnessed its hey-day as richly coded subject matter in nineteenth-century narrative, Simmel focused on flirting as a quintessentially metropolitan activity, open to all city dwellers, and no longer the telltale marker of specific class allegiances. Simmel insists on three basic categories of flirtatious activity: flirtation as flattery ("although you might indeed be able to conquer me, I won't allow myself to be conquered"); flirtation as abject contempt ("although I would actually allow myself to be conquered, you aren't able to do it"); and flirtation as provocation ("perhaps you can conquer me, perhaps not—try it!").[40] After offering a rather too-schematic delineation of the various forms coquetry takes in social life, Simmel attempted to formulate a theory of flirtation. For Simmel, flirtation is neither a trivial social activity nor a mere stage in romantic courtship. Citing an anonymous French philosopher who argues that flirtation may be attributable to an "advance in culture," Simmel suggests that a "large increase in the number of provocative phenomena" has generated "an erotic repression in men."

According to Simmel, that increase arises from life in the new urban locales. Beginning in the 1830s in Europe and America, for the first time most people found themselves living in cities. Since it is simply impossible to possess all the attractive women or men one meets in the more mobile world of modern times, Simmel claims, flirtation emerged as a kind of remedy for this condition. "By this means, a woman could give herself— potentially, symbolically, or by approximation—to a large number of men, and in the same sense, the individual man could possess a large number of women." Simmel's essay further argues that although men engage in flirtation, "refusing and conceding are what women, and only women, can do in consummate fashion." Coquetry—and here Simmel clearly is borrowing a leaf from Darwin's formulations concerning sexual selection—is the culmination of the female's role throughout the animal kingdom, which is to be the "chooser." In a later discussion of coquetry published in 1917, Simmel emphasized that flirtation was in essence a two-way street: "In order for coquetry to grow on the soil of sociability, as we know from experience it does, it must meet with a specific behavior on the part of the male." According to this new elaboration, as long as the male is the "mere victim" who "without any will of his own is dragged along by its vacillations between a half 'yes' and a half 'no,' coquetry has not yet assumed for him the form that is commensurate with sociability."[41]

Simmel's understanding of flirtation stems from his general conception of urban living as outlined in his essay on "The Metropolis and Mental Life" (1903), where he insists that the "psychological foundation of the metropolitan personality type" is an "increase in nervous life, which emerges out of the rapid and unbroken change in external and internal stimuli." [42] The experience of living in cities allowed for the cultivation of such values as "caprice, self-distanciation, of fastidiousness"—values that led to an intensification of the impulse toward coquetry, since the "metropolis exacts from man as a discriminating creature a different amount of consciousness than does rural life." The city dweller, even as he appears in a "thousand individual variants," develops a psychic organ that protects him against the "threatening currents and discrepancies of his external environment which would uproot him. He reacts with his head instead of his heart." [43] Negatively, this organ emerges as a "protective antipathy" arising from the need to particularize oneself even as one is conscious of the self-protecting insulation of others. Alternatively, coquetry takes on added value as an erotic adjustment to the new social arrangements engendered by modernity, to what Baudelaire identified as the "ephemeral, the contingent, and the fugitive," and what Benjamin saw as the quintessential experience of the urban flâneur, who turns ocular restlessness into a social role. Like the Benjaminian flâneur, the individual favoring games of coquetry is aimless, emotionally detached, given over to the "spectacle of the moment," a self-conscious spectator rather than an unthinking participant. Both Benjamin and Simmel understood that the citizen of the metropolis, confronted with a surfeit of urban stimuli, becomes more detached. (Simmel writes of the "blasé" attitude as a characteristic urban trait.) However, unlike many Frankfurt School theorists who stressed the anomie generated by urban living, the bewilderingly anarchic quality of city life, and the temptations toward totalitarianism of crowds, Simmel saw the intensified urban landscape as potentially harboring positive social implications. By linking the rise of flirtation to what he views as the fleeting, provisional, fragmentary nature of modern life, Simmel also gave the nebulous phenomenon of coquetry—in some ways, a transhistorical experience—its own distinct history, and one whose pace parallels and interacts with the history of the novel as a changing genre. [44]

Simmel's "Flirtation" was itself part of an extensive twentieth-century discussion with roots in the late-Victorian period that sought to deal with the dramatically changing positions of women and men in society, a debate centering on the increasing social power of the "New Woman" and a concomitant crisis in masculinity. To be sure, Simmel's argument concerning coquetry is fraught with generalizing assumptions concerning woman's "true nature" that might strike contemporary theorists as ahistorical at best, laughably essentialist at worst. (As Habermas remarks, Simmel "is nowadays in a peculiar way both near to and far away from, us."[45]) Still, Simmel's analysis of flirtation explains why the activity of flirting came to signify a domain of power for so many female protagonists in Victorian fiction. Because the swiftly changing nature of cosmopolitan life required the stress of non-emotional encounters, it encouraged the suspension of desire, the individual's "survival" of conventional romantic bonds in favor of more distanced, noncommittal relations. Like Homer's Penelope, with her never-finished, perpetually worked-over tapestry, Simmel's temporizing female (who is viewed by Simmel as inwardly resolved even before flirtation has been inaugurated) is a figure who suspends male hopes—a suspension that ends with the act of choosing. "Once she has decided, in either direction," Simmel writes, "her power is ended." But flirtation, maintains Simmel, keeps "in play" values such as joy, relief, liveliness, and above all, the freedom to experiment and to eroticize without the fear of the usual consequences that arise from consummated sexuality. It is in its "freedom from all gravity of immutable contents and permanent realities" that coquetry comes to have the character of "suspension, distance, ideality," according to Simmel, and allows him to think of the "art" of flirtation and not only of its "artifices." According to "Flirtation," Kant's celebrated claim concerning the nature of art—that it is "purposiveness without purpose"—holds true for the playfulness of flirtation.[46]

As I have been suggesting, there are significant feminist implications at the heart of Simmel's theory, although they are masked by Simmel's repeated tendency to see flirting as an inherently "female" art. Surviving the ordeal of desire becomes, for many Victorian female protagonists, a form of social freedom as well as a shrewd gambit in self-preservation. If flirtation's social value lies in what Simmel, in a memorable phrase, calls the "simultaneity of consent and refusal," then it allows women as much as men a relatively equal social position to possess yet not to possess simultaneously. Although Simmel clearly considers coquetry as related to romantic love, he nevertheless insists that flirtation must also be disconnected from the process of love and lovemaking. What Plato understood as the very essence of desire—that is, an intermediate state of having and not having, the interpenetration of the two—is for Simmel less the nature of desire than of flirtation. Simmel also suggests (but does not develop completely) a notion of flirtation as sometimes harboring within itself a tragic dimension in which love is not simply deferred but impossible.

For all his attention to flirtation as an "art," however, Simmel restricts the phenomenon of flirting to its social manifestations. And despite the richness of its understanding of his subject, as a theoretical tool for appreciating the nineteenth- and early twentieth-century novel, Simmel's understanding of the socially beneficial aspects of flirting has its limitations. As much as George Eliot or Hardy, Simmel must be considered in historical context. In 1909, he may hail coquetry's liberating possibilities, but most Victorian novelists were struggling either to reassert some version of the rigidly enforced sociosexual conventions that flirtation allows characters to evade or to expose the hypocrisy of those conventions. Simmel's positive view of coquetry ran counter, as well, to prevailing nineteenth- and twentieth-century scientific discourse, which viewed flirtation as an abnormality, including it among the symptoms of male hysteria, for example, as an excessive concern with self-preening behavior. The physician Emile Batault observed in 1885 that "hysterical men" were "coquettish and eccentric," preferring "ribbons and scarves to hard manual labor." [47] In his widely translated sexological study *Sex and Character* (1906), Otto Weininger subsumed a brief discussion of coquetry under an exploration of the prostitute, whose "readiness to coquet with every man," according to Weininger, is "an expression of her nature." (According to *Sex and Character,* the purpose of coquetry "is to picture to the man the conquest of the woman before it has occurred." [48])

Other writers saw flirtation as a flight from the claims of a mature erotics. Writing in 1915, shortly after the outbreak of the First World War, Freud insisted on a sharp distinction between an American activity and Continental practices—much as Henry James had done in *Daisy Miller.* Flirtation (or at least American-style flirting) became for Freud a convenient metaphor for modern man's refusal to see that living involves real risk. Two years before he introduced his concept of a death instinct in *Beyond the Pleasure Principle* (1920), Freud hazarded that "Life is impoverished, it loses in interest, when the highest stake in the game of living, life itself, may not be risked. It becomes as shallow and empty as, let us say, an American flirtation, in which it is understood from the first that nothing is to happen, as contrasted with a continental-love affair in which both partners must constantly bear its serious consequences in mind."[49] For Freud, an "American flirtation" is a refusal to accept the weightier entanglements of romantic love, with its deeper access to the sources of psychic hurt, betrayal, and fantasy. War, in tearing away civilization's consoling illusions, forced individuals to see that death was a constant actuality. "American" flirting—a refusal to engage in love—emerges here as the analogue for the denials fostered by modern social arrangements. In an assent to Simmel's formulations, Freud grasped that flirtation is less a subspecies of romantic desire than an utterly separate—and, for Freud, even diametrically opposite—experience.

Throughout Victorian fiction, the "liberating" effects of flirtation often operate just a hairbreadth away from disenchantment, danger, and tragedy. A sense of flirting as riskily close to the wrong side of the law occurs at the end of Anthony Trollope's *The Last Chronicle of Barset* (1867) when Madalina Demolines, with whom John Eames has been conducting a lengthy flirtation (he is engaged to another woman), suddenly insists that she assumes they are betrothed. After summoning her mother, she threatens to bolt the door to keep Eames from leaving. (As if in fevered sympathy with his trapped hero, Trollope abruptly begins to refer to Madame and Miss Demolines through the remainder of the chapter as the "dragon" and the "tigress.") An alarmed Eames cries out for a policeman from an open window and, once out of the house, must offer him a bribe in order to avoid trouble. The unexpected turn in tone in Trollope's novel (from light comic satire to lurid gothic) drives home the point that flirting in a nineteenth-century context was as "liberating" as Thomas De Quincey's opium—and as hazardous.

In George Meredith's *The Egoist* (1879), the hero Sir Willoughby Patterne pursues Clara Middleton, but her mercurial nature leads him to secretly propose marriage to another woman, Laetitia Dale—an act that, once disclosed, leads Clara to reject him forever by marrying another man. Meredith's tone is droll, but this is not the comic resolution of Congreve or Austen, in which appropriate lovers are ultimately and happily affianced. Meredith's hero is trounced, as his treachery backfires, while his final betrothal to Laetitia occurs in an atmosphere of total disillusionment since Laetitia, confronted with unbridled male ego, accepts her suitor out of mere "egotism." Similarly, twentieth-century writers such as James, Wharton, and Forster remained preoccupied with the depiction of the *perils* accruing to flirtatious behavior. These novelists not only registered new avenues for the expression of amorous impulses but also gave imaginative form to retreats from the possibilities opened up by such paths. Daisy Miller's reckless walking with Giovanelli dooms her to a death by Roman fever, just as the appearance of an affair—the basis of which lies in a rumor—condemns Lily Bart to pariahdom and evident suicide. In *A Passage to India* (1924), the fiasco in the Marabar caves that began as a congenial cross-cultural outing jump-starts a cataclysmic international incident.

As a discrete sphere of human relations with rules and dynamics of its own, flirtation offers the literary critic an especially valuable means of discussing at once the thematics and stylistic strategies of a number of major texts seldom connected to each other. If the dynamic of erotic deferral, playful capering, and friskily parried indecision may be said to constitute a plot in the novel, then such a narrative trajectory frequently takes the form of what I have chosen to call the "plot of flirtation," one that sometimes functions so that it is not apparent to the participants themselves. The flirtation plot stands alongside the more conspicuous central narrative, intersecting rather than paralleling the courtship plot. If Peter Brooks is correct in suggesting that the motive for plots in literature lies in a "universal need" on the part of authors and readers to impose a coherent order on reality, then the plot of flirtation might be understood as stemming from a concurrent and competing impulse to escape a socially determined scheme.[50] In place of what Brooks has termed, in a discussion of a Freudian "masterplot," the reader's "fear of endlessness" or an "improper end," I would suggest that there is also a fear of closure, one that is satisfied in the unfinalized plot of coquetry.[51] The inassimilable nature of Maggie and Stephen's eroticized friendship is underlined by the way in which Victorian readers of Eliot's novel were far more disturbed by Maggie's attraction to Stephen than by the grisly natural accident that kills off the heroine and her brother.

The anxiety that scenes of flirting created in the novel is related to the acute oppositional tension between deferred desire and the demand for satisfying endings required by plots of marriage, seduction, and adultery. For it is precisely out of such moments of erotic uncertainty and doubt—especially, when they are calculated—that flirtation is formed. Yet it is out of that very tension, too, that nineteenth-century novelists enhanced their characters' erotic desirability—for other characters and for readers. In the opening pages of *Madame Bovary* (1856), Emma offers a cordial to Charles

Bovary, to whom she has just been introduced, and, in what may be one of the more overt displays of erotic interest in nineteenth-century literature, finishes her own drink by dredging up the last bit of liquor with her tongue. Whatever Emma's intentions in this scene, the chief result is that the young medical student returns to his home thinking to himself that he must marry the beautiful young woman. Emma's daring gesture, although it may represent an unconscious indulgence in a sensual pleasure, becomes not so much an expression of sexual desire as a declaration of the young woman's erotic worth. The "risk" of Emma's act is that unlike a ladylike declaration of interest in Charles, it could very well repel him, foreclosing marriage. In its carnal assertiveness, Emma's gesture hints at a future adulterousness—and is impossible to imagine in a work of nineteenth-century British or American fiction of the same period.

In Victorian fiction, flirtation as thematic material had been ideally suited to those serially published novels in which authors could defy the reader's desire for resolution. There is little doubt that without Thackeray's pressing interest in securing devoted readers (who he dreamed of training so that they might buy each installment of his fiction with unhalting regularity), our whole conception of the nineteenth-century coquette would be fundamentally different. These material factors surely underpin what Bakhtin has termed the essential "unfinalizability" of the novel's dialogical structure. Such a structure is connected to what the Russian critic has characterized as the novel's multivocal, conversational formal architecture, in which, as Caryl Emerson and Gary Saul Morson have noted, "identity is always postponed and about to be postponed."[52] Perhaps more than any other Victorian novelist, Thackeray embodies the Bakhtinian ideal of the author devoted to a "multivocal," open-ended structure in his fiction (a tendency only partly undermined by Thackeray's fondness for seeing himself as all-controlling "puppeteer").

At the same time, as I try to suggest in my exploration of Wharton, James, Wilde, and Forster, flirtation becomes not simply a postponement of erotic play but a means of keeping one's sexual identity open-ended and deliberately unstable, especially at those moments in the history of social relations when masculine and feminine roles are undergoing radical transformations and in which same-sex sexuality is an option if still taboo. Forster, whose *A Passage to India* is the last novel I consider, is also one of the first novelists to publish his works in single, "modern" editions, as distinct from the Victorian triple-decker. *A Passage to India* (which I read as

a self-consciously antimodernist text as well as a partial revision of Lawrence's 1921 *Women in Love*) aims to preserve the vestiges of sexual difference on which flirtation depends but within the context of same-sex carnal relations.

Since flirtatious communication so often relies on an intensified appreciation of the arbitrary and ambiguous nature of language itself, such a
mode of sending signals would seem to substantiate more recent conceptions of language as insecure, unreliable, utterly open-ended in its ability to generate a seemingly infinite number of interpretations. It is likely,
for example, that coquettish language, either of words or of gestures,
throws into high relief Ferdinand de Saussure's insight that most of us have
grasped the codes of everyday language so thoroughly that we do not even
realize we are applying them. Those indulging in flirtatious language,
however, are likely to be far more conscious of the coded nature of language. Aware of the special signs and signals they are employing, two
people engaged in a flirtation are closer to players involved in an explicitly
coded game, such as chess, than ordinary users of language. Unlike a game
of chess, however, the game of flirtation is based on rules that are liable to
change at any moment and that may never have been clear in the first
place. For flirtation gets its primary charge from what Philip Wheelright
has termed "plurisignation" (what might be termed "both/and" possibilities) or what William Empson would call "ambiguity" ("either/or" options). Empson maintains that ambiguity itself can indicate an indecision
as to what is meant, an intention to mean several things, a likelihood that
one or the other or both of two things are meant and the possibility that a
statement has multiple meanings. (A narrower definition, and one that
would exclude Simmel's notion of "simultaneous rejection and refusal," is
suggested by Monroe Beardsley, who confines ambiguity to linguistic expressions that are doubtful in meaning. He argues that such expressions
could have either but not both of two possible meanings and provide no
ground for a decision between them.)

While flirtation is often structured like a metalanguage, a hypercon-
sciously adopted linguistic system, the activity of flirting frequently functions so as to frustrate language. This is partly because flirtation as a social
activity is inextricably connected to bodies, adopted as a strategy because
exalted romantic love is held in suspicion. Flirtation replaces the conventions of courtship even as marriage is embraced as a mercenary option. In
the autumnal world of *Persuasion* (1818), for example, flirtation again and

again emerges as an obstacle to true feeling, happiness, and marital resolution. Whereas the wrong pairings that flirtatious eros encourages may
cause comic delay in *Pride and Prejudice,* in *Persuasion* there is the nagging
threat that time is running out, that a right pairing will never occur, and
that only solitude beckons. Captain Wentworth's aimless fooling with
Louisa Musgrove even causes the young woman to suffer a near-death fall,
although in this case, too, flirtation is functional; Wentworth, chastened
by the accident resulting from his dallying with Louisa, takes advantage of
the incident in order to spend more time in Anne's company).

Simmel's idealized view of coquetry minimizes not only the perils of
flirting but also the anger it frequently provokes. Flirtation, much as romantic passion breeds disillusioned casualties, also creates "victims,"
those who misread flirting as a serious seduction or actual romance.
Isabella Linton of *Wuthering Heights* (1847) is a paradigmatic case here.
Heathcliff, desiring only Catherine and unable to have his passion acknowledged in socially approved terms, flirts cruelly with Isabella and
goes so far as to marry her so as to remain in close proximity to his beloved. Flirting is part of the worldly learning that the once untutored or-
phan (as a boy too "primitive" for sociability) adopts while educating
himself in self-exile; by turning Isabella into the target of flirtatious ve-
nality, he effectively destroys her. In a similar spirit of flirtatious cold-
bloodedness, Vladimir Nabokov's Humbert Humbert coquets with and
then marries Charlotte so as to attach himself to her daughter, Lolita. With
a vindictiveness worthy of Brontë's malevolent antihero, he declares: "To
break Charlotte's will I would have to break her heart." For Nabokov, as
for Brontë, flirtation is not simply an order of experience distinct from
love but an antithetical shadow game that mocks true romantic ardor. In
his *Physiologie de l'amour moderne,* Bourget taxonomized, with appropriate culinary metaphors, two stages in the process of being flirted with: the
first allows one the "piquant taste of an innocent infidelity" in which you
"realize how happy you feel being a sweet, an *hors d'oeuvres.*" The second
stage results in rage, however, when one "realizes there is an actual dinner
and you are not on the menu." [53]

"You commit the inexcusable triviality . . . of turning this evening into
a *flirtation!*" the hero of Christopher Isherwood's *A Single Man* (1964) tells
a young man he cannot seduce. "You don't like that word, do you? But it's
the word. It's the enormous tragedy of everything nowadays, flirtation instead of fucking, if you'll pardon my coarseness." [54] Still, those whom flirts

would make the target of their heartless toying exact their own poetic justice. On realizing that the narrator has been flirting with her in order to take possession of the precious papers of Jeffrey Aspern, Miss Tina in James's *The Aspern Papers* (1888) burns the letters with exquisite, protracted sadism that mimics his toying with her ("last night . . . one by one"). Stage and screen adaptations of James's *Washington Square* (1880) allowed Catherine Sloper a poetically just retribution denied her by the Master himself. In the very last scene of William Wyler's 1949 film *The Heiress*, Catherine, whom James had insisted had "not a grain of coquetry," coquets with—and then jilts—Morris Townsend when he returns to her drawing room years after he first abandoned her.[55]

On the other hand, flirtation does not necessarily compete with those plots of marriage and seduction so familiar from eighteenth-century and nineteenth-century narrative. In *Vanity Fair,* Thackeray diagrams how basic the operations of flirtation are for the eventual triumph of romantic happiness. In the last pages of the novel, Dobbin, remembering Becky's "desperate flirtation" with Osborne on the morning of Waterloo, recalls that "he was too much hurt or ashamed to fathom that disgraceful mystery."[56] Dobbin emerges as Amelia's true match, however, only because that "desperate flirtation" helped uncover Osborne's adulterous leanings—a fact that frees Amelia from her devotion to an undeserving dead husband. Whether or not Becky Sharp ever wished to betray her friend Amelia increasingly becomes a moot point in *Vanity Fair* (Becky's flirting so often renders irrelevant *all* issues of intentionality). There is little question that her actions have worked on behalf of Amelia's liberation from her morbid attachment to her dead husband. Still, Becky's determined toying with Lord Steyne, a pivotal event that at last destroys her marriage, has as one of its rationales the financial buttressing of her household. In a context in which flirtation operates beyond or above libidinal desire, Becky's outraged cry on being discovered—"I am innocent!"—is more than technically true. More than any other novelist of the Victorian period, Thackeray has as his most characteristic narrative style a technique that thrives on flirtation's radical unknowabilities. The scene in which Becky is discovered with Steyne, for example, immediately splinters into a series of ponderously entertained imponderables: "What had happened? Was she guilty or not? She said not; but who could tell what was truth," and so forth, in an unending sequence of never-quite-answered rhetorical questions and evasive minicommentaries that guaranteed the popularity of *Vanity Fair* as serial fiction.[57]

Flirtation differs from "desire" as it has been defined by recent theorists in that when both parties are in accord, it remains a controlled indulgence in the erotic—"managed desire" would be the most accurate way of describing it—whereby individuals remain conscious of their interests, aims, and actions. That a Becky Sharp finds a comfortable place in the last pages of *Vanity Fair* suggests not so much a complete transformation in her character as a continuation of her earlier role of a woman who sins. Despite its associations of dissembling calculation and thoughtless cruelty, flirtation has the potential to be chivalrous. In Eugene Fromentin's 1862 *Dominique* (forgotten today but extravagantly admired in its own time by Flaubert and George Sand), there is a scene involving two characters who have never touched each other although they have adored each other for years: the cultivated, levelheaded heroine Madeleine and her friend Dominique. The would-be paramours go horseback riding, and Madeleine suddenly breaks into a mad gallop, an apparently impulsive act. (In fact, her seemingly reckless action is calculated to insure that Dominique, who has continued to follow her by horse although he is a poor rider, will not be injured in trying to keep pace with the woman he loves.[58])

It is one of the salient paradoxes of flirtation that it simultaneously signals wholly inconsequential activity as well as a mature, adult consciousness of the risks of desire. If Daisy Miller conveys an image of total triviality (rendered significant only by the gravity of her death), the heroine of Trollope's *Miss MacKenzie* (1865), a middle-aged "spinster" with several "lovers," reveals Austenian reserves of modesty, dignity, and shrewdness in what Trollope admitted was initially an attempt "to prove that a novel may be produced without any love."[59] In its most idealized, "Simmelian" sense, flirtatious desire, as a different order of erotic feeling, may also function without the consciousness of risk that occurs with blatant acts of adultery. In Stendhal's *Le chartreuse de Parme* (1839), Count Mosca returns to his home to find Fabrice engaged in an intensely amorous conversation with his wife. As he strolls around the drawing room in a state of jealous anxiety, Mosca's distress increases as he imagines that the pair talking before him is brazenly betraying him. "He was going quite mad; it seemed to him, that as they leant towards each other they were kissing, there before his eyes." Yet clearly it is only an optical illusion born of an agitated psychological state. In actuality, Fabrice and Countess Mosca are not engaged in physical contact at all, but are flirting so comfortably, so "safely," that they are completely oblivious to Mosca's presence in the room. (As Mosca departs with ridiculously awkward formality, the flirting duo gives no indication of having observed either his entrance or his departure.)[60] Here, flirtation has the outward appearance of lovemaking. The potential "openness" of flirting—after all, no one engaging in it, strictly speaking, is betraying anyone else—serves as a protection against coarse accusations of adultery.

FLIRTATION AND THEORIES OF THE NOVEL

In charting flirtation as a separate emotional and erotic terrain, I am aiming to complicate, rather polemically at certain points, several influential studies of the novel that have appeared over the last twenty years, works that have sought to describe the relation between desire and the novel as a genre. Coquetry is linked to the performative and the theatrical, both subjects that recently have been the subject of much critical discussion in the work of Judith Butler and Eve Kosofsky Sedgwick. As a highly performative figure, the flirt has her sources in the cultural energies explored by Terry Castle in her study of eighteenth-century masquerade. Castle contends that the demonic, mysterious nature of theatricality is characterized as female by definition. If performance represents potentially infinite repudiations of those ontological fixities that codify culture, as recent theorists such as Judith Butler have argued, then the flirt, with her refusal to be "sincere" and her juggling of self-contradictory masks, is a carnivalesque subversion of such fixities. This is surely why characters who assume roles as actresses in so many Victorian texts—Becky Sharp, Laure in *Middlemarch*, Gwendolen Harleth—are so frequently identified with flirtation. These highly conflicted representations of the flirt, seeing her as dazzling manipulator, draw much of their force from what Jonas Barish has identified as a persistent nineteenth-century psychomachia, the "antitheatrical prejudice." More generally, the flirt is of particular importance for a discussion of literary narrative in that, like the author, she is a powerful generator of plots.

My emphasis on flirtation as it serves as a vehicle for the expression of "dissident" sexualities in the novel differs from that of literary critics who regard it as a mere stage within the development of courtship or seduction. The two great theorists of desire as it determines the novel, René Girard and Roland Barthes, seldom make a distinction between an erotics of self-willed delay and the postponement that they believe inevitably must arise from desire. In *A Lover's Discourse* (1977), Barthes does supply a few aphoristic thoughts on flirtation as a "paradisiac realm of subtle and clandestine signs: a kind of festival not of the senses but of meaning."[61] Such luminous *aperçus* do not, however, emerge into a unified theory of flirtation with regard to fiction. Nor does Girard, in his influential study *Deceit, Desire and the Novel* (1961), discriminate between the managed eroticism that is flirting and the delusion that is erotic love. But the romantic "lie" that Girard sees as concealed and enabled by the European narrative tradition (and that is "disclosed" to the reader and sometimes to the characters themselves) is immediately exposed with the deployment of flirtatious desire. The delusion we may share with Leo Tolstoy's Anna Karenina is surely different in kind from what we share with Hardy's Bathsheba Everdene, which is akin to something like bemused horror at her confused but deliberate toying with three male suitors.

The Flirt's Tragedy implicitly expands on, and seeks to challenge, some of the premises underlying several more recent, influential studies of the novel, those by Nancy Armstrong, Joseph Allen Boone, John Kucich, and Ruth Bernard Yeazell. In *Desire and Domestic Fiction: A Political History of the Novel* (1987), Armstrong underscores how heroines are recuperated to the domestic sphere under male protection, in a reinscription of male and female power that Armstrong sees as the cultural project of courtship fictions from the late eighteenth century until the Victorian period. Viewing "ordinary" and "popular" reading materials as providing the foundation for this enterprise, Armstrong posits a causal theory of the production of desire that, she argues, was energetically sustained, not by high-minded "serious" novelists, but by hack writers, booksellers, and publishers.[62] Armstrong is especially persuasive in articulating how the writing process was transformed by historical and cultural pressures throughout the eighteenth century. My argument stresses the way in which the Victorian novel thrived not on myths of courtship but by flirtatious energies that were inassimilable to plots of marriage.

Writing of the Anglo-American tradition of the novel, Boone's *Tradition Counter Tradition* (1988) gives some attention to a strain of same-sex eroticism first noted by Leslie Fiedler in his study of the masculinist romances of Herman Melville and Jack London. Boone maintains that the formal design of the nineteenth-century novel embodies either traditional or countertraditional paradigms. *Tradition Counter Tradition* offers an extended critique of a long-standing stance that considered nineteenth-century fiction as inextricably bound with closure in the form of marital union, articulated most energetically in Forster's *Aspects of the Novel* (1927) and D. H. Lawrence's "A Propos of *Lady Chatterley's Lover*" (1929). Utilizing feminist insights into the relation between sexual politics and social organization and recent sociolinguistic theories of the means by which narrative structures encode ideologies as well as generate erotic pleasure, Boone's highly schematic study posits a "tradition" and a "countertradition." The first of these affirms a paradigm in which "the very dynamic of narrative, the structure of desire in traditional fiction, has been coerced into upholding a restrictive sexual-marital ideology," while the second subverts that paradigm through such means as making drama out of the divided identity and shattered relations resulting from an insistence on a heterosexual order.[63] According to Boone, the ideal of marriage is asserted most efficiently in the courtship narratives of *Pamela* (1740) and *Pride and Prejudice,* the seduction plots of *Clarissa* (1747–48) and *Tess of the D'Urbervilles* (1891), and the domestic dramas of *Amelia* (1751) and *A Modern Instance* (1881). Boone claims, however, that endings that stress, for instance, death (Heathcliff's, for example) or unhappiness (say, Gwendolen Harleth's) act as a counterweight that keeps desire open. This concomitant "countertradition," emphasizing irresolution and open-endedness, works at undermining what are for Boone the necessarily patriarchal myths of difference and stability that he views as promoted by the courtship plot. Disregarding the long "middle" section of the novels he analyzes, Boone overemphasizes novelistic closure as the all-determining criterion for locating a given fictional work's ideological "weight."[64]

Among other critical studies of fiction of the last few years, Ruth Bernard Yeazell's *Fictions of Modesty: Women and Courtship in the English Novel* (1994) shares many of the interests of my own study. With a stress on the complexities of modesty that intersects with my treatment of flirtatious desire, Yeazell considers conduct books, eighteenth-century and Victorian novels, as well as scientific texts—specifically, works by Havelock Ellis and Charles Darwin. Locating discursive forbears for Ellis's and Darwin's notions concerning feminine modesty—in which the female's "seeming reluctance" was intended less to inhibit sexual activity than to increase it—Yeazell examines how the figure of the modest woman has dominated English fiction since the late seventeenth century. According to Yeazell, Ellis and Darwin overturned prevailing Victorian claims that construed feminine modesty as a sign of female erotic anesthesia. Instead, both theorists followed the logic of many of the era's courtship novels in suggesting that the modest woman was secretly the most sexually loving. As I indicate in my chapter on Darwin's theory of sexual selection, Yeazell's account subtly elucidates Darwin's reliance on previous plots of sexual selection that were pervasive in nineteenth-century fiction. Where I part from Yeazell is in her account of such plots, which she reads as single-minded retellings of erotic narratives that involve a deferring female and an aggressively pursuing male. (In this, Yeazell shares much in common with Gillian Beer, whose 1983 *Darwin's Plots* also understands the evolutionist's principles of sexual selection as substantiating conventional Victorian belief.) One of the more intriguing aspects of *The Descent of Man* (1871) is that in failing to conceive of a strong female libido in nature, Darwin seemed to leave open the possibility of "unnatural" plot lines in which heterosexual relations might be deferred or sidetracked. Not all of Darwin's narratives, moreover, ended "happily" or even conclusively.

Beyond my disagreement with its understanding of Darwinian sexual selection, Yeazell's *Fictions of Modesty* presents several problems that *The Flirt's Tragedy* seeks to redress. Not only does a concentration on female modesty inevitably minimize the male's role in scenarios of heterosexual courtship, but modesty lacks those dynamic qualities—that crucial dialectical momentum—that renders flirtatious desire so integral to the success of fictional characters and, indeed, particular novels. Thus, Yeazell's emphasis on modest deportment as a the locus of those socializing restraints that command women to inhibit their erotic impulses tends to downplay the way in which the novels of Austen or Eliot actually represent modesty as existing in tension with desire. Yeazell's one-sided accent on feminine restraint in courtship stems in part from her tendency to see the novel as simply replicating attitudes toward female behavior pervasive in contemporary conduct books and scientific treatises. *Fictions of Modesty* never considers that there may be specific forms of eros that the novel *as a genre* is especially adept at representing. Yeazell's study is too little interested in how a conduct book differs from a work of fiction in representing the socially available, but impossible to pin down, rumblings of flirtation. When Maggie's brother Tom accuses her of behaving "as no modest girl would" in undertaking what he calls a "clandestine relation with Stephen Guest," he yet again reveals himself as dim-witted for relying on an inadequate vocabulary for what *The Mill on the Floss* has just demonstrated is something deeper and more perplexing than romantic betrayal.[65]

Yeazell's notion of the novel as simply another discursive site for a (fun-

damentally conservative) comprehension of female behavior places her in
the mainstream of literary critics over the last fifteen years, who largely
have moved from a consideration of the "novel" to a stress on "narrative"
proper. Beyond simply thwarting the "traditional" plot of marital happiness, plots of flirtation frequently comprise, as well, a liberating design, as
constitutive of novelistic form as the plot of matrimony. Unlike Boone,
moreover, I would suggest that such plots do not encompass a "tradition"
but lie at the heart of the most paradigmatic nineteenth-century texts. Not
only does a text such as *The Mill on the Floss* confound categories such as
"traditional" and "countertraditional," but in its depiction of Maggie's relations with Stephen Guest, also insists on the necessity of female decision-
making as a foundation for self-enlightenment. No doubt because *The
Mill on the Floss* hints at erotic possibilities that will not find full expression in the English novel for some fifty years, Maggie and Stephen's relationship was considered alarming by Eliot's Victorian readers. They were
for the most part shocked that Maggie might be attracted to such an oddly
self-fabricated figure as Stephen, introduced to the reader as he fusses over
Maggie's curls. Leslie Stephen, who famously derided Guest as a "mere
hair-dresser's block," undoubtedly had grasped that Eliot was importing
to the Victorian novel a (dormant) strain of eighteenth-century foppery.
(Austen, in inserting the swank, self-preening Frank Churchill into the
staid community of Highbury in her 1886 *Emma,* was adding a similar ingredient to her work.)

Eliot's linking of flirtatious delay and masculine artifice continues to
trouble readers of *The Mill on the Floss.* Recent critics have questioned why
Eliot would choose to tempt her heroine with such a flashy interloper as
Stephen. My reading of *The Mill on the Floss* not only accentuates the centrality of Maggie and Stephen's encounter but the way in which Eliot saw
in Stephen a means of working out her conflicted views of the figure of
aesthete-dandy. A decade before Darwin's *Descent of Man,* Eliot highlighted the links between aestheticism and sexual selection in a novel in
which female choice is a burning thematic issue. And just as Hardy suggested that the most crucial exfoliations occurred outside of "results," re-
siding, rather, in a half-secret pattern in nature, Eliot implies that half-
hidden "processes" were the greatest subject for the Victorian novelist.
Indeed, in *The Mill on the Floss,* she goes far in implying that the novelist
must depict emotional and erotic links that continually border on lying

beyond narration. It is the power of flirtatious eros to undermine secure conceptions of character—what Lawrence once denigrated as the "old, stable ego" fostered by nineteenth-century fiction—that adds a complicating wrinkle to a process in which Victorian fictional character is being formed through increasingly complex calibrations of the self. Through the Maggie "affair," Eliot intimated that the meaning ascribed to fictional character is more than the sum of a narrative's concluding pages. With the now-you-feel-it-now-you-don't nature of flirtatious desire, one witnesses not only an alternative story line composed of mischievous social games but, more powerfully, a compelling reassessment of the concept of a coherent identity.

In *Repression in Victorian Fiction: Charlotte Brontë, George Eliot, and Charles Dickens* (1987), John Kucich offers a powerful, revisionist advance in discussions of the Victorian novel. Eschewing both a standard view of repression as an enemy of the self and the Foucauldian view, as expressed by critics such as Miller, that repression is a displacement of sexuality into a discourse about the self, Kucich defines an extremely cooperative relationship between a dynamics of repression and libidinal impulses. Kucich conceives of repression as eroticizing inwardness at the same time that it submerges such conventional Victorian ideals of duty, self-sacrifice, and service within the domain of secret passion. Inward-turning eroticism is intensified by repression, just as, for Kucich, private passion exalts inner conflict. As Kucich comments, "'Power' for Foucault is a kind of mystified, ontological absolute though it masquerades as the end of ontology."[66] For Jane Eyre, Dorothea Brook, and David Copperfield (to mention several of the figures Kucich investigates in depth), the sublimation of desire evinced by convoluted denials and interminable evasions is actually the eroticization of self-negation. "By marking an inward instability, an eccentricity of the self to itself," Kucich contends, "passionate expression actually defeats any knowledge of its nature by others."[67]

In addition to rethinking frequently unquestioned Freudian conceptions of the self, Kucich critiques Foucault's tendency to collapse repression, desire, discourse, and subjectivity into an all-encompassing notion of "Power."[68] My study also rejects the "repressive" hypothesis whereby desire is invariably understood as operating so as to overcome repression. However, I view the dynamic of flirtation as a more viable means of discussing what Kucich calls repression, a term that despite Kucich's skillful

rehabilitation of the concept as self-consciously and sometimes pleasura-
bly deployed, cannot escape its suggestions of retreat, negation, and (as
Freud continually recognized) morbidity.

   To be sure, flirtation becomes a source of apprehension in such works
as Ivan Turgenev's *First Love* (1860) and fin-de-siècle texts such as Bram
Stoker's *Dracula* (1897), where flirtatious desire is increasingly depicted as
an aberrant, artificial path of pursuit, engaged in by sexually loose women,
a route unsanctioned by either society or nature. Just how vexing a preoccupation flirtation became for the Victorian novelist is suggested by the
fact that when flirtatious eros is spoofed in explicit terms, it is not in a
novel but in a Savoy operetta—"popular culture" for the Victorians—
Gilbert and Sullivan's *The Mikado* (1884), one of the most successful works
of popular entertainment of the Victorian era.[69] It is not until Max Beerbohm's *Zuleika Dobson* (1911) that one finds a work of fiction that offers a
similar send-up of flirtation as death-dealing activity; its final image—
Zuleika, having already generated mass suicide at Oxford, calmly studying
a train schedule to Cambridge—foretells the obliteration of an entire
male ruling class. Beerbohm's comedy of manners has a camp afterlife in
Gore Vidal's *Myra Breckinridge* (1968), whose heroine gives off the glint of
a hypertalkative Zuleika Dobson gone Hollywood. The novel's opening
line—"I am Myra Breckinridge whom no man will ever possess"—
echoes Zuleika's fundamental appeal as a personality wholly given over to
the denial of the heterosexual male libido.[70]

   At the risk of positing a theory of the novel that is overly synoptic, my
exploration of flirtation stresses literary cross-fertilization, as it encompasses a variety of European and American texts. Just as Wharton is critiquing the European tradition of the novel in *The Age of Innocence,* James
took cues from Turgenev's portrait of the doomed coquette Zinaida in
First Love when he created an "innocent American flirt" in Daisy Miller.
Zinaida's fondness for "knocking people against each other" pits a young
man against his father in a doleful homosocial rivalry. Turgenev's absorption in eroticisms played with and then abandoned informs his most celebrated work of fiction, *Fathers and Sons* (1862), in which a duel arises
from a misunderstood flirtation, in a fight that kills off—because it results
in an uncauterized wound—the paradigmatic nihilist Bazarov. In Turgenev's novel, flirtation is inextricably bound up with the novel's more
pronounced political concerns—what Irving Howe has termed its "politics of hesitation"—so that it becomes impossible to consider flirting as
frivolous behavior.[71] Rather, coquetry for Turgenev parallels the crisis of

political will depicted in the novel. Princess Odinstov's cat-and-mouse game with Bazarov and Bazarov's failure to seize the Princess's hand are the erotic parallel for the novel's taxonomizing of Russia's political predicament. Both matters reflect on the difficulties, and finally the impossibility, of commitment and resolution. When Princess Odinstov fails to respond to Bazarov's overtures, withdrawing from an initial expression of interest, she condemns him to a total "negation," one that mocks his own self-professed nihilism. Bazarov's subsequent duel with Pavel Petrovich after the older man imagines he is courting Fenichka arises from a mistake. (In fact, Bazarov has kissed Fenichka after the princess has rejected him; his flirtation with her arises from profound self-disgust.) Ironically, the duel between Bazarov and Pavel is a fight of two opponents in political ideology who have both met very much the same romantic fate. Like the hero of Balzac's "La Duchesse de Langeais," both have been destroyed by aristocratic coquettes. In Turgenev's novel, coquetry reaches its apotheosis in a cul-de-sac that links amorous and political crises. In a shattering denouement, the "nothing" of Bazarov's ideological nihilism mirrors the erotic "nothing" offered him by Princess Odinstov. Through the figure of the glittering, useless coquette, the ancien régime trumps both fathers and sons.

Like James, Wharton was powerfully influenced by European novelists—far more, in fact, than most critics of her writing until now have suggested.[72] (In her single critical work devoted to fiction, an overview of the novel entitled *The Writing of Fiction* (1924), she focused almost entirely on British and Continental authors yet gave scarce attention to American writers other than several comments on the work of her friend Henry James.) In my chapter on Wharton, I focus on *The House of Mirth* (1905) as well as what I take to be the novelist's rewriting of Flaubert's *Sentimental Education* in *The Age of Innocence*.

In my final chapter, I explore what I call the "homosexual novel of manners," chiefly Wilde's *The Picture of Dorian Gray* and James's *The Tragic Muse* (1890). These works have an entwined history in that, as many critics have observed, the figure of James's Gabriel Nash is clearly modeled on Wilde. Both texts include opening scenes in which men flirt seductively with one another as aesthetics, in a coy metafictional conceit, is the ostensible subject of their discussions. The foremost concern of this last chapter, however, is the competing notion of homoerotic relations in the fiction of Forster and Lawrence, novelists who, like Wilde and James, forged their fiction out of a rancorous personal relationship with each other. Given the implications of carnal danger adhering to flirting, it should be no surprise that the first appearance of a homosexual "couple" in European fiction involves a little-noted but remarkable scene of male coquettishness in nineteenth-century fiction. In Tolstoy's *Anna Karenina* (1877), Vronski arrives at his officer's club and is approached by the an older officer and his younger friend, known as the "inseparables" (a standard colloquialism for a homosexual pair in Tsarist Russia), who teasingly inquire about whether Vronski has gained weight. (Although he is clearly disgusted by them, Vronski thereafter informs a fellow officer that he has no appetite.) In late-nineteenth-century fiction in Britain and America, homosexual characters were required to be more coy. Wilde and James offer scenarios in which flirtation, because it is homoerotically conveyed, remains doubly coded. Such scenes strongly suggest that homoerotic desire was allowed a sustained, if limited, field of expression in the turn-of-the-century novel.

In making this point, I seek to destabilize the model of "homosexual panic" so prevalent in recent estimations of same-sex desire as played out in fin-de-siècle fiction. It is time, I think, for new, more expansive theoretical models in which to grasp the depiction of late-Victorian homoerotic relations. For just as the clunky device of the "panopticon" cannot serve as a useful metaphor for the Victorian novel, neither can the "closet" characterize the range of devices whereby authors represented same-sex eroticism before the "homosexual" was conjured up as a distinct category. As with the male aestheticism encouraged by Darwin's theory of sexual selection, Wilde's and James's works highlight the relation between Kantian aesthetics and flirtatious desire to which Simmel only summarily alludes.

The post-Edwardian *A Passage to India,* meanwhile, brings to the forefront the political dimensions of flirtation as debased upper-class activity that are discussed in detail in my first chapter. Whereas coquetry once served as metaphor for a feminized, useless aristocratic class, in Forster's novel flirtation represents the relations girding the entire Imperial enterprise, through which Englishmen and women are permitted to encounter—but never connect with—their Indian subjects. Providing an occasion for a fragile, momentary paradise of personal communion between Mrs. Moore and Dr. Aziz, flirting produces a trap of damaging ambiguities for Aziz and Miss Quested. There are contradictions in Forster's novel, as well, that are related to the writer's relation to literary modernism. On the one hand, flirtation diminishes with the rise of modernist representation, particularly in the fictions of a novelist such as Lawrence, for whom flirtation is always something to be surmounted (yet for that very reason is an obstacle that needs to be depicted). At the same time, however, by deliberately revising the scene in the Marabar caves so that it is difficult to ascertain what happened therein, Forster lends his novel the classic Jamesian note of heightened subjectivity, in which the attack on Adela Quested, like the incident in "The Turn of the Screw," is so beyond a wholly explanatory narration as to accrue a metaphysical supernatural meaning. (Such moments are not, sui generis, modernist; in *Vanity Fair,* Thackeray also favored scenes of flirtation in which Becky Sharp gets off the hook because she seems to have eluded even the all-seeing puppeteer of *Vanity Fair.*)

My focus on the homosexual novel of manners relates to a larger claim underpinning my discussion of the novel as a genre. Given the nature of flirtation—its mutable qualities, its inherently contradictory nature, its dialectics of acceptance and negation, its irreducibly ambiguous character—reaches its apotheosis in the novel as a genre. The Renaissance scholar Bruce R. Smith has made the case for literary works as the most efficient avenues for the depiction of sexual desire, particularly homosexual eros. Given the relevance of Smith's points to my own argument, I quote him at length:

> The mode of discourse that gives us most intimate access to these scripts of sexual desire is not moral, legal or medical, but literary. There are two reasons why. First, literary discourse, unlike moral, legal, or medical discourse, does not have to be logical or consistent. Fiction is able, in Wolfgang Iser's phrase, to show the "simultaneity of the mutually exclusive." In fiction, as in dreams, logically separate experiences can be "bracketed together" for the space and time of the fiction in a way they cannot be in everyday life—or in the logically rigorous confines of moral, legal, and medical discourse. Fiction is uniquely fitted to address the contradictions that must be covered up to make ordinary life possible. Second, literary discourse involves a power relationship between speaker and listener that is far more complicated than in other modes of putting sex into discourse. In legal discourse, as in moral discourse and medical discourse, the writer speaks from a position of complete authority. The reader's role is assumed to be one of passive acquiescence. In fictional discourse, "authority" is not so absolute: in creating a hypothetical imaginary world author and reader are, in a sense, *collaborators.* Between them power is constantly being renegotiated as the writer keeps offering new details of the hypothetical world he is constructing, as the reader draws on his own experience to amplify those details and gives or withholds his imaginative assent.

For Smith, the special qualities adhering to literary texts allow such works to serve as an ideal vehicle for the expression of illegitimate forms of sexuality. "Moral, legal, and medical discourse are concerned with sexual *acts*," notes Smith, "only poetic discourse can address homosexual *desire*."[73]

Given that flirtation is less a series of isolated acts than a relational activity, works of fiction are the best venues for its depiction. (With the late-Victorian representation of homoerotic flirtation in James and Wilde, such a process is obviously intensified.) The loosening of the restrictions on the literary representation of sexuality inevitably renders flirtation less crucial as well as less insurgent. The moment Ronald Firbank's debauched Cardinal Pirelli chases choirboys around the table of his church, the necessity of coding homoerotic desire via subtle evasions becomes an empty literary mannerism. Similarly, when Lawrence's Constance Chatterley moves down the social scale for a taste of "blood consciousness" with her gamekeeper Mellors, flirtation as "aristocratic" courtship ritual has been given a severe blow.

Since my analysis of flirtation and fiction stops with Lawrence and Forster, I do not examine the fate of flirting in post–World War II and postmodernist fiction, though I would venture to say that it is not until Nabokov that flirting is retrieved in the novel as viable material. A work by Nabokov that successfully explores the thematics of flirtation—and one that is often taken to be the writer's greatest short story—is "Spring in Fialta" (1938), which details an "affair" that endures decades and over several continents but never comes to a head. With playful self-consciousness, Nabokov explores how uncompleted desire inflects a given narrative. "Again and again she hurriedly appeared in the margins of my life," the narrator writes, "without influencing in the least its basic text. . . . Occasionally, in the middle of a conversation her name would be mentioned, and she would run down the steps of a chance sentence, without turning her head."[74] Today, flirtational narratives are powerfully amplified by telephonic and Internet venues (memorably captured in Nicholson Baker's best-selling 1992 novel about phone sex, *Vox*), in which flirting has the potential to become a thoroughly disembodied adventure in which participants need never meet.[75]

"[A]ll this rubbish about love, love in a church, love in a cave, as if there is the least difference," sighs an exhausted Mrs. Moore in *A Passage to India*, a novel of flirtations, cultural and personal, turned calamitous.[76] Mrs. Moore mournfully signals the demise of those distinctions that make coquetry so decisive to the rendering of Victorian personal relations. It is no accident, then, that Forster's novel begins with a discussion of Queen Victoria's death, given that Forster's novel at least partly reflects his interest in exporting Austenian fictional conventions to India now that literary modernists such as Lawrence have made such impulses difficult to sustain in England itself. Lawrence foregrounds issues of homoerotic friendship in *Women in Love,* a work we know Forster had in mind during his composition of *A Passage to India.* In his greatest, most geographically expansive novel Forster struggled to keep homosexual relations from going the way of the globally resonant Whitmanesque "adhesiveness" that Lawrence so admired. I explore the conclusion of *A Passage to India,* in which Fielding and Aziz jointly recognize the failure of their attempt at camaraderie, as a meditation on the bisexual credo announced by Rupert Birkin in the finale of *Women in Love.*

It is, however, Mrs. Moore who represents the voice of intractable historical and literary change in Forster's novel. Like Mrs. Wilcox, who dies before the conclusion of *Howards End* (1910) but endures as that novel's abiding spirit, Mrs. Moore is the touchstone of meaning in *A Passage to India*, an eagle-eyed, all-understanding observer who sounds the death knell for the cultural assuredness whereby possessing but not possessing, embracing India but not succumbing to its beguilements, once was thought possible. Her barefoot, moonlit rendezvous with Dr. Aziz in the opening pages of *A Passage to India*—itself reminiscent of the "Moony" chapter of *Women in Love*—momentarily restores Mrs. Moore's youthful romantic ardor. It would be overly simplistic, however, to understand the relationship between Mrs. Moore and Aziz as speaking of suppressed possibilities for love in a British India. Forster was interested in representing a couple who can find no place in any preexisting romantic story line, who discover an eroticized idyll that lacks any "pre-text." The excitement these two marital veterans experience is glimpsed by Miss Quested, who catastrophically does not know how to assimilate it, as they do, into an exalted, enduring mysticism. It is Mrs. Moore who represents the passing of flirtation as an all-determining theme in the novel, the historical phase-out of what Nanki-Poo in Gilbert and Sullivan's *The Mikado* calls "modified rapture"—desires suspended but no less rapturous in being so.

❧ 1 ❧

Dialectical Desires

The Eighteenth-Century Coquette and the Invention of Nineteenth-Century Fictional Character

> He was to be a plaything for her whims; he was to surmount one obstacle after another while making no advance, like an insect which, teased by a child, hops from one finger to the next in the belief that he is getting away while its malicious tormentor keeps it stationary.
> —Honoré de Balzac, *"La Duchesse de Langeais"* (1834)

BALZAC AND THE PERILS OF THE COQUETTE-ARISTOCRAT

Despite her ubiquity in eighteenth- and nineteenth-century French and British literary narrative, the figure of the coquette has eluded a sustained critical consideration in discussions of the novel. Although both men and women may play at flirtatious games, it is largely the coquette who in the novel of realism becomes the living symbol of a dangerous form of eros, as well as an enduring exemplum of a French aristocratic class so given over to glittering effects that it has lost its purpose. As we shall see, by importing the eighteenth-century coquette to nineteenth-century fiction, Victorian novelists come to highlight problems of female sociability as well as seemingly "unnarratable," dissident desires. Additionally, the artful, "aimless" carnality of Congreve's Millamant (the prototypical eighteenth-century coquette explored in this chapter) offers a paradox in literary narrative. For as integral to realist fiction as the coquette's strategies become, coquetry always threatens to stall a plot that strives to move toward a resolution in marriage. At the same time, coquettish desire signifies an unmentionable female eroticism precisely because it would seem to defy narration.

The *grande cocotte* who Balzac makes the subject of his novella "La Duchesse de Langeais" (1834) has her origins in French salon culture in which female conversational prowess found a place. Recent historians of eighteenth-century French literary culture such as Erica Harth, Joan De-Jean, and Mary Vidal have examined the place of salon-based conversation in French high society of the ancien régime—a central aspect of culture in France before the Revolution—and have explored its paramount role in the development of the modern French novel. Harth, for example, argues that the eighteenth-century "art of conversation" was a uniquely accommodating sphere for female interests, one that functioned in keen opposition to the period's all-male academies.[1] Through her social inroads into salon life and her transformation of this once exclusively male preserve into an arena of feminine power, the salon's grande dame exemplifies the potential for greater female agency. That power is acquired not through the privileges of birth but through conversational talent. The site of female cultural achievement, the salon also signaled an independent aesthetic system in its own right, one that relied on literary nuance, intellectual badinage, and playfully orchestrated scenes of social performance. With the rise of a more constraining post-Napoleonic social ethos, however, the high mandarins of official French culture increasingly regarded "la parole," or salon-based "speech," not as an unassailable realm of achievement for women but as a site of feminine uselessness—and peril.[2]

Throughout the eighteenth century, French and British writers continually linked female coquetry to a once-exalted aristocratic ethos that had disintegrated into wicked, erotic gamesmanship. Thus, in Pierre Choderlos de Laclos's epistolary novel *Les liaisons dangereuses* (1782), the amoral aristocrats the Vicomte de Valmont and the Marquise de Merteuil take professional pride in toying with a young woman and forcing her to acknowledge their power over her. In explaining why he delays lovemaking with the ingenue Cécile Volanges, the vicomte tells his sometime-lover and fellow gamester the marquise, "My plan . . . is to make her perfectly aware of the value and extent of each one of the sacrifices she makes me; not to proceed so fast with her that remorse is unable to catch up." The point of his cruel enterprise, notes the marquise, "is to show her virtue breathing its last in long-protracted agonies; to keep that sombre spectacle ceaselessly before her eyes; and not to grant her the happiness of taking me in her arms until I have obliged her to drop all pretence of being unwilling to do so. After all, I am not worth much if I am not worth the trouble of asking for."[3]

Aware of the passing authority of his class and the devaluation of his own precarious "worth," the marquise's letter suggests a large dose of sexual sadism. Society itself, meanwhile, has adopted aristocratic games of coquetry as an everyday ritual: indeed, it is a fundamental prerequisite for a social identity. "Mother Perpetué was right, I think," Cécile glumly confides to a friend. "One turns coquette directly one enters society."[4] Feminist intellectuals of the period depicted coquetry as a largely male invention designed to diminish female power and autonomy. In *The Vindication of the Rights of Woman* (1792), the pioneering advocate of women's rights Mary Wollstonecraft reprimanded Jean-Jacques Rousseau for insisting that a "woman should be governed by fear to exercise her *natural* cunning, and made a coquettish slave in order to render her a more alluring object of desire, a sweeter companion to man, whenever he chose to relax himself."[5] For Wollstonecraft, coquetry was an unnatural distortion of the female's innate powers of mind. In rebuking the author of *The Social Contract* and *Emile,* Wollstonecraft affirmed that the tensions surrounding flirtation occurred at the cultural borders separating France and England. Indeed, the contributions to realist fiction of novelists such as Charlotte Brontë and George Eliot involved the intensification of a process whereby, in the era following the French Revolution, British fictional character was formed in marked opposition to French culture. Thus a reprimand of French conceptions of femininity provided the basis of Brontë's *Villette,* whose heroine Lucy Snowe demonstrates her probity by obsessively castigating Ginevra Fanshawe, an English-born coquette who nonetheless flamboyantly continues to declare her Gallic lineage.

In popular fiction and conduct literature of the nineteenth century, the female flirt denoted less female sexual misbehavior per se than the *potential* for misconduct in woman, a distinction that stymied ethical and legal categories even as it formed the foundation of energetic inquiry on the part of novelists. "I do not say that she is actually guilty," observes Lord Bertie of the irresolute Louisa Conolly in Opie's *Dangers of Coquetry,* "but the woman who is not startled at indulging the adultery of the mind, is not far removed from yielding to that of the body; and the former, I am sure, she is not far from."[6] With the deployment of such distinctions, the public realm became a dangerous place for a young woman setting out into the world. An increasing number of writers seized on elaborate, Thackerayan military metaphors for what they considered a continual war between the sexes. "Renée was downcast," observes the narrator of George Meredith's *Beauchamp's Career* (1876). "Had she not coquetted? The dear young Englishman had reduced her to defend herself, which fair ladies, like besieged garrisons, cannot always do successfully without an attack at times, which, when the pursuer is ardent, is followed by a retreat, which is a provocation; and these things are coquettry. Her still fresh convent-conscience accused her pitilessly." [7] In Lady Charlotte (Campbell) Bury's popular 1841 novel *The History of a Flirt (As Told by Herself)*, the contrite narrator traces her coquettish behavior to her mischievous girlhood:

> I remember, at eight years of age I was a flirt in every sense of the word. My brother's playfellows were my earnest quarry: and I coquetted with undefined but strong feelings of pleasure, if I only drew their attention from kites and balls. To win any notice which might have been directed towards my sisters was triumph to the uttermost; yet I loved them in my heart, and would not willingly have given them pain under any circumstances; but the demon of coquetry was strong within me, and provided that passion was gratified, all was well. But sometimes it was not gratified; it would happen that my happiest efforts failed, when Charlotte with her gentle *insouciance* won the heart I only wished to act and trifle with; and then anger and revenge urged me to do and say a thousand things I bitterly regret now. Oh! the diary of a flirt is a heartless, hopeless catalogue of vanity and injustice.[8]

The drama of this emotionally fraught family romance is not, significantly, simply one of sororal competition for a coveted male; rather, two distinct kinds of desires come into marked conflict: Charlotte's sincere attraction to a young man, and the narrator's "heartless" impulse both to beguile and deny the opposite sex, an impulse that begins in childhood games.

The fundamentally literary challenge confronting novelists such as Jane Austen, Charlotte Brontë, and George Eliot was that despite their interest in creating improved, morally deep-grained models of female behavior, the feminine art of coquetry was an ideal means of enhancing those aspects of their literary craft that distinguished them from the authors of conduct literature and popular fiction. Flirtatious activity fostered the multidimensionality of character so crucial to the makeup of Victorian heroines, and multidimensionality of character was precisely what remained absent in the works of conduct book writers. Indeed, Austen, Brontë, and Eliot had turned to the novel at the precise historical moment when fictional character was becoming more nuanced, more nebulously elliptical, and more difficult to evoke in a few thumbnail descriptive calibrations. Wollstonecraft, although she had no rivals in her hostility to the idea of coquettishness as an essentially female attribute, found herself acknowledging the enchantments of flirtation when, in the midst of an otherwise ferocious critique of Rousseau's idealized, coy "Sophia," she noted that the Frenchman's depiction of his heroine was "undoubtedly a captivating one."[9] Still, neither the notion of character fostered by Rousseau's image of a coyly doting female nor that engendered by Wollstonecraft with her idealized, clear-eyed daughter of the Enlightenment would suffice, given the increased demands placed on the art of the novel. However shocking the moral outrages of the heartless coquette, the nineteenth-century novel heralded by Austen, Brontë, Thackeray, and Eliot *needed* its Lady Susans, Ginevra Fanshawes, Becky Sharps, and Rosamond Vincys. The new aesthetic of the realist novel demanded them.

Coquetry serves a dialectical purpose in the realist novel, for it is an activity that strikes at the tensions between a wanton female sexuality fostered throughout eighteenth-century culture and a more restrained Victorian ethos. In a sense, the coquette functions "dialogically" in the terms established by Mikhail Bakhtin, but she does so through a dialogism of competing desires. For Bakhtin, dialogic tensions arise not only from opposing ideologies animating fiction but also from the generic clashes that the novel at its most "novelistic" epitomizes. Lady Susan, Isabella Thorpe, Becky, Ginevra, and Rosamond, in their clashes with idealized heroines, at once enact a generic and ideological battle that is ostentatiously dialogic in nature. Furthermore, in terms of the changes in the way Austen, Brontë, and Thackeray render character in fiction, coquetry had distinct advantages as thematic material. Most significantly, flirtation enhanced the dialectical tensions of a private identity functioning in marked conflict with a public persona, an inner self continually checked by external societal pressures. Coquettish behavior exists in an ever-changing matrix, one that fosters a highly mutable erotics arising from simultaneous affirmation and refusal. In generating unnatural narratives, coquetry hints too at unsanctioned impulses that otherwise seem resistant to representation in nineteenth-century fiction.[10] Even when she is frustrated, the eighteenth-century coquette as she reappears in the Victorian novel reveals the residual, inadequately repressed traces of an older, dominant class, an ancien régime that refuses to disappear.[11]

Thus, Becky Sharp's success at conquering London in Thackeray's *Vanity Fair,* in a series of triumphs that reach their apotheosis when she meets the Prince Regent, indicates more than an aristocratic culture open to

permutation by an increasingly assertive "populace." That a Becky Sharp
becomes so decisive to the disruption of the central plot in *Vanity Fair*
suggests, at a much deeper level, the intractable endurance of both an aristocratic presence and a Restoration archetype in nineteenth-century fiction after the novel has been "democratized" as a genre. Indeed, Becky's
triumphs make it difficult to conceive of Victorian fiction as a series of
"evolutionary" advances on the eighteenth-century novel. Like the deluded insect of Balzac's analogy, the novel of courtship only appears to
push forward the novel as a genre. In actuality, the machinations of the coquette keep the novel stalled, its phylogenesis retarded by a series of deferrals. In a paradox, given her centrality in Restoration theater, the coquette is crucial to nineteenth-century fictional form. Thwarting the
systematic epistemological enterprise that the novel historically aspires to
promote, she nonetheless helps to give that project a purpose and a focus.
In a configuration that animates the large part of *Vanity Fair,* female coquetry as a social activity threatens the conventions of mimesis, suggesting a hidden world of personal relations that resist literary representation.

Imported to the nineteenth-century novel to be routed, the coquette
often helps to jump-start the marriage plot, although, to be sure, this is
not her only or even her most significant function. In the much-noted
process of "democratization," explored by Ian Watt in his classic 1957
study *The Rise of the Novel* (and more recently critiqued by Michael
McKeon in *The Origins of the English Novel*), in which the novel emerges
as the vehicle of middle-class interests, writers such as Austen, Charlotte
Brontë, and Thackeray discipline the coquette on behalf of emergent class
aspirations and a new, concomitant conception of the feminine. Mischie-
vously maneuvering on the perimeters of Victorian narrative, the coquette
is arguably as pervasive as the archetypal Madwoman in the Attic, the
culturally resonant "Demonic Woman," or the proverbial Angel in the
House. At once the focus of intense erotic desire yet also herself obdurately
immune to eros's power to disrupt the certainties comprising the stable
self, the coquette is the flip side of MacKenzie's Man of Feeling, the sentimental novel's representative figure, whose tears are empirical evidence of
unknown depths of feeling. Thus Lady Susan undermines the evidentiary
value of the emotions. "I have subdued him entirely by sentiment and serious conversation," she confides to Mrs. Johnson.[12] With increasing intensity, the coquette undermines concerted attempts at eliciting verifiable
evidence of sincerity.

The coquette suffers a contradictory fate in nineteenth-century fiction: she is introduced into fictional narrative so as to be extirpated. She receives this reprimand not only because of a more conservative social ethos but also because of a radically altered conception of fictional character. In the eighteenth century, both *The Way of the World* and the *Tatler* conclude with their coquettish females in positions of considerable power. But in nineteenth-century fiction, the coquettish woman becomes, most importantly, a fallen female signifying that which cannot be evoked explicitly. Austen's Lady Susan and Isabella Thorpe, Charlotte Brontë's Ginevra, and Thackeray's Becky Sharp all represent the perversely unnarratable, women of dangerously theatrical qualities. This paradox—that she is alluded to obliquely but cannot be rendered directly—haunts the coquette's appearances in the nineteenth-century novel. As Leo Bersani notes in an essay on "Realism and the Fear of Desire," realist fiction typically "admits heroes of desire in order to submit them to ceremonies of expulsion. This literary form depends, for its very existence, on the annihilation or, at the very least, the immobilizing containment of anarchic impulses."[13] However, the often-elaborate procedure of expulsion may last the entirety of the novel.

In a quest to define new archetypes of female behavior and identity, Austen's *Northanger Abbey* (1818) and Brontë's *Villette* (1853) must diminish the fictional power of the eighteenth-century flirt. However, these novelists succeed only in partly displacing her from the novel's domain. By granting their coquettes a simultaneously central and liminal status in their novels, Austen and Brontë intimate that Isabella of *Northanger Abbey,* Kitty of *Pride and Prejudice* (1813), and Ginevra of *Villette* are stumbling blocks to the emergence of protofeminist ideals. Even while they punish these coquettish females, however, both Austen and Brontë depict Isabella and Ginevra as crucial to the smooth functioning of social relations and the advancement of female interests. Isabella and Ginevra emerge as weightless doppelgängers against whom Austenian and Brontëan heroines such as Catherine Morland and Lucy Snowe—wise, intelligent, but unworldly—struggle to define themselves. Significantly, in both *Northanger Abbey* and *Villette* it is invariably the male suitor who imparts pragmatic lessons in flirting while remaining free from accusations of playing at coquetry, whereas Isabella and Ginevra are socially ostracized for their flirtatious behavior. However much Austen and Brontë insist on the uncontrollable nature of Isabella's, Ginevra's, and Kitty's manipulative deportment, both authors repeatedly imply that female coquetry is an aspect of literary performance itself—specifically, female literary performance. In order to understand the coquette's devolution from a state of potent feminine majesty, we must appreciate her at the pinnacle of her authority in eighteenth-century Restoration theater and in popular narrative of the same period.

CONGREVE'S "THE WAY OF THE WORLD": THE EIGHTEENTH-CENTURY COQUETTE AS FEMININE EXEMPLUM

Before considering in greater detail the coquettish female in the work of Austen, Charlotte Brontë, and Thackeray, I want to consider a notable representation of the eighteenth-century coquette: William Congreve's *The Way of the World* (1700). While other eighteenth-century literary archetypes suggest themselves as key precedents for the Victorian coquette—notably, Pope's Belinda from "The Rape of the Lock" (1714)—the case of Congreve's Millamant highlights Victorian coquetry's crucial theatrical affinities. It was in response to an array of popular representations of the coquette that both Austen and Brontë fashioned their own versions. They participated in a widespread cultural fascination with the flirt that depicted her at once as a creature of exotic interest and a widely recognizable type. That the coquette should have thrived in Restoration comedy was determined largely by issues related to genre. Given the limitations on the representation of sexuality in the theater generally, the stage was the ideal setting for the depiction of an unfettered feminine sexuality that could be alluded to but not depicted too overtly. The coquette's increasing significance, moreover, is linked to contemporary debates concerning the struggle for dominance in a ferocious battle of wills dividing the sexes. Thus, the quintessential coquette of the era appears in Congreve's final work, *The Way of the World*. First produced in 1700, the play is one of the earliest literary texts in English to deal in explicit terms with relations between the sexes as a struggle of power.[14]

Probably no other English author presents a more pronounced version of the female flirt in pure form than does Congreve in the figure of Millamant. Meredith deemed her a "perfect portrait of the coquette, both in her resistance to Mirabell and the manner of her surrender, and also in her tongue."[15] In Millamant we witness the coquette as at once culturally emblematic of exemplary womanhood and as markedly individual in temperament. But even more than a dazzling female icon, she represents womanhood as a discretely organized class. Millamant implicitly defends the interests of this politically self-aware sect when she speaks to Mirabell in the first-person plural ("If they did not command us"). Beyond her role as a coquettish archetype, Millamant is an idealized woman, first introduced on stage as arriving (appropriately, tardily) as if she were an armada; according to her smitten suitor, she comes in "full sail, with her fan spread and her streamer out and a shoal of fools for tenders." Her unpunctual arrival sets the tone for her subsequent erotic deferrals. Immediately upon her entrance, we are alerted to her as a unique combination of sexual self-assurance, linguistic prowess, and polished aesthetic judgment. Before those gathered, Millamant asks her maid to remind her why her ladyship has been late:

> Mincing: Oh mem, your La'ship stayed to peruse a pequet of letters.
> Millamant: Oh, ay, letters—I had letters—I am persecuted with letters— I hate letters. Nobody knows how to write letters; and yet one has 'em, one does not know why. They serve one to pin up one's hair.
> Witwoud: Is that the way? Pray, madam, do you pin up you hair with all of your letters? I find I must keep copies.
> Millamant: Only with those in verse, Mr. Witwoud. I never pin up my hair with prose. I fancy one's hair would not curl if it were pinned up with prose. I think I tried once, Mincing.[16]

Millamant's boast of knowledge of the composition of letters (along with her preference for poetry over prose) is a declaration of aesthetic prowess. That aesthetic acumen is entangled with Millamant's role as fastidious erotic chooser. Her consciousness of the beautiful is more than finely, fully wrought; it is so completely a part of Millamant's being that poetry lends her hair the curls necessary for her everyday deportment. Millamant's comments encapsulate the familiar eighteenth-century debate concerning art versus nature, collapsing the two categories as the coquette's artificial traits are naturalized. Mirabell notes her follies are "so natural, or so artful, that they become her," while Millamant herself repeatedly implies that a ceaseless parading of artifice has its source in an unfathomable nature.

Not only does Millamant's aesthetic sense confound ordinary principles of feminine deportment, it comprises her very being. As Mirabell observes: "I like her with all her faults; nay, I like her for her faults. Her follies are so natural, or so artful, that they become her; and those affections which in another woman would be odious, serve but to make her more agreeable." As Julie Peters argues, Congreve here "suggests repeatedly that artifice is so multilayered that nature and art are indistinguishable in the end . . . the artificial forms that surrounded culture, and the pedantry arising from a culture of machine-made pages, called attention to the power of art over nature and over humans." The coquette's artifices represent nature rendered impotent. The "artificial" Millamant is infinitely complicated, as suggestive of depth as are her moments of sincerity; indeed, her verbal feats effectively collapse the distinction. Millamant additionally represents coquetry's triumph over a too-swift exhaustion of erotic desire supposedly grounded in the natural realm. In an advance of civilized behavior over nature, she adeptly eclipses the brutish state of marriage into which women, as she famously declares, "dwindle." The social and generic assumptions underpinning Restoration comedy allowed for such a resistance. As Kenneth Muir has noted, "in the world of the Restoration comedy—and to some extent in the society reflected by that comedy—it was assumed that men and women were naturally promiscuous." [17]

In the face of such a libertine sexual ethos, Millamant's witty defense of deferred erotic gratification is a comic assimilation of the wisdom of the Cavalier poets of a generation before, who intimated that absolute sexual freedom spoils true eros. Millamant, quoting the lines of a Suckling poem ("Like Phoebus the no less amorous boy"), is answered by Mirabell, who finishes the poem for her on entering the stage: "Like Daphne she, so lovely and as coy." [18] Here the flirtation linking Millamant and Mirabell encompasses a secret rhetoric, a recondite system of communication embedded within the larger theatrical structure of Congreve's text. Millamant's conversational jousting with Mirabell places both of them outside of the wanton amorous carnival that encompasses nearly all other characters in Congreve's play. Hazlitt saw the encounter in this scene as a decisive moment in the play, the "height of careless and voluptuous elegance, as if [Millamant and Mirabell] moved in air, and drank a finer spirit of humanity." [19] Significantly, they do not join in the dance at the play's conclusion, as if the flirtatious prologue to their marriage (the verbal high point of Congreve's play) marked them as a separate connubial species.

Although Millamant is the embodiment of womanhood at its peak, she looms over other figures in the play as a social dissident who chastely refuses to indulge in the libertine rituals that Congreve taxonomizes as the very signature of London's high society. Her absolute investment in coquetry allows for her role of eagle-eyed "outsider." Seemingly unencumbered by lust, Millamant is a masculine fantasy of what motivates women in a state of love; it is undiluted power, rather than erotic need, that drives her. In a typically self-confident declaration, she breezily explains what prompts her and her entire sex:

> Millamant: O, the vanity of these men! Fainall, d'ye hear him? If they did not commend us, we were not handsome! Now you must know they could not commend one, if one was not handsome. Beauty the lover's gift! Lord, what is a lover, that it can give? Why, one makes lovers as fast as one pleases, and they live as long as one pleases, and they die as soon as one pleases; and then, if one pleases, one makes more.

Enhancing the link between aesthetic concerns and coquettish amours, Millamant employs the terms of a specifically female creator. The verbally adept woman "artist," denied an egalitarian social role, discovers her true self through the imperial exercising of her erotic will.[20]

In such a way are Millamant's speeches a dress rehearsal for a sexual libertinism that cannot be fully staged. She does not so much generate new plots (as does, for example, Thackeray's Becky Sharp) as brilliantly conjure up other individuals. Her self-confident declarations of female license thus constitute an intense articulation of isolate, feminine subjectivity. In her declaration above, Millamant's comic power is bound up with her failure to imagine other lives, especially Mirabell's. Millamant's meditative reminiscences, as Edward Burns notes, "internalize the pastoral fictions of courtship."[21] Coquetry is here primarily verbal flair, a linguistic act in lieu of amorous action. What makes Congreve's conception of Millamant's coquetry so substantial is that her remarks, in this scene and in the celebrated "proviso" sequence, map a place for coquetry as a separate, intellectually defensible arena of feminine authority. That authority has its source not only in Millamant's striking self-sufficiency but in sadistic gamesmanship as well. As Edward Burns has noted, the proviso scene is a "ceremonial expansion of artifice, seamless with mock-pastoral 'chase.'"[22] Although it becomes evident that Millamant and Mirabell genuinely do desire each other, her insistence on the coquette's sovereignty makes her weightier than other characters in Congreve's play. In revealing contrast to her protracted, detailed defenses of flirtation is Millamant's admission of love for Mirabell in act 4, a revelation that is comic in its terse urgency and (offhandedly delivered) emotional extravagance: "Well, if Mirabell should not make a good husband, I am a lost thing, for I find I love him violently."

Congreve suggests that linguistic extravagance is suited to the expression of coquetry, while romantic love is served by a trite conciseness of verbal expression.

The frequently noted historical transition between Jacobean drama and Restoration theater is one in which comedies of situation are replaced by those of character; *The Way of the World* encapsulates this transition. As a man lacking money and infatuated with a woman who stands to inherit a substantial fortune, Mirabell is situationally comic; but Millamant is comic entirely because of what comprises her character—her queenly use of men, her masking of her love for Mirabell, her proto-camp (hair)styling in verse. Immune to the amorous attentions of others, her deferrals are a disavowal of all action and a disengagement from any situation that might even momentarily undermine her stature. This crucial obliviousness to changeable circumstance was noted by Hazlitt when he argued that "all her airs and affectation would be blown with the first breath of misfortune."[23] Such postponements of desire are the very foundation of her identity.[24]

TWISTED SISTERS: JANE AUSTEN, CHARLOTTE BRONTë, AND WILLIAM MAKEPEACE THACKERAY

The coquette reached her zenith in the eighteenth century as a figure of resplendent theatricality and aristocratic feminine power, yet when removed from her primary domains of the stage, the court, and the salon, she reemerges in the nineteenth century as a specter haunting fictional discourse. Austen, Brontë, and Thackeray import the French-identified coquette into nineteenth-century British fiction, thereby installing a built-in dialectic within the structure of their novels, one that centers on the matter of proper feminine behavior. In *Northanger Abbey,* Austen strives to contain the erotic mayhem unleashed by Isabella even as Isabella, like the gothic conventions satirized in the novel, is comically spoofed. In *Villette,* Brontë creates in Ginevra a flirt whose continual physical proximity to the heroine indicates that she is the projection of Lucy's fantasy life, an *ennemie-soeur* as well as an unconscious force made corporeal. Narrating the duplicities of Thackeray's Becky Sharp becomes isomorphic with the very enterprise of novelistic craft.

Significantly (and this differentiates the coquette from the figure of the courtesan as exemplified in Daniel Defoe's 1724 *Roxana*), Lady Susan is motivated by far more than financial gain. While Austen's antiheroine has become financially hard-pressed after her husband's death (and is perceived by her upper-class adversaries as motivated by the promise of monetary gain), material improvement is by no means her chief incentive. "I must own myself rather romantic," she tells her friend Mrs. Johnson as she explains why she could never have married Sir James Martin, a dullard whom she foists on the daughter she finds insipid, adding that "riches only . . . will not satisfy me." [25] More precisely, her economic needs stand in continual tension with her role as an aesthetic "connoisseur" of male allurements. "I have made him sensible of my power," Lady Susan boasts of her wooing of Reginald de Courcy, "and can now enjoy the pleasure of triumphing over a mind prepared to dislike me." [26] That coquetry denotes a more obdurate aspect of her character, independent of economic status, is suggested by Sir Reginald de Courcy, who speaks of her "encouragement of other men" while married. Similarly, neither Isabella Thorpe nor Ginevra Fanshawe is motivated by merely material aspirations (although Ginevra does win her nobleman at the end of *Villette*).

Like Austen's Lady Susan, Ginevra always threatens to take away narrative control from Lucy. Indeed, she often seems poised to seize possession of the entire narrative, replacing the heroine's tale of frustrated (soul-revealing) contentment with one of seemingly endless, meaningless pleasure. Again, as with Austen's Lady Susan, Brontë's determined disciplining of the coquette is too richly comic to suggest merely a moralizing aim on the part of the novelist. The indeterminate endings of both these novels insist that the coquette cannot be routed easily; the correspondence that constitutes *Lady Susan* must come to an end, we are told, because Lady Susan is suspected by her daughter-in-law of reading and even writing her daughter's letters. A merry widow with an unlimited libido, Lady Susan goes so far as to toy with the affections of her sister-in-law's youngsters. "I meant to win my sister-in-law's heart through her children," she reveals to a friend. "I know all their names already, and am going to attach myself with the greatest sensibility to one in particular, a young Frederic, whom I take on my lap and sigh over for his dear uncle's sake." [27] Both Isabella and Ginevra, meanwhile, disappear from their narratives in ghostlike fashion, as if their ultimate destinies were beyond fictional disclosure.

Although coquetry evokes theatricality, the defining traits of Isabella and Ginevra render them more fundamentally elusive than the actress: the coquette's inordinate pleasure in simultaneously raising erotic expectations and frustrating them become analogous to literary creation — specifically, to the novelist's refusal to execute a plot in a particular fashion. In

Northanger Abbey, the implied romantic reader is led by Austen's narrator
to expect, like the heroine herself, a "gothic" resolution of the plot. Such
expectations are undermined, however, as both gothic tropes and unbridled coquetry are left by the wayside on behalf of a more restrained connubial resolution for Catherine and Tilney. That the coquette Isabella is an
ardent reader of the gothic fictions of Radcliffe suggests that Austen wishes
to collapse—all the better to dismantle—these two strains of eighteenth-
century literary discourse.

Similarly, in *Villette* the implied reader is induced by Brontë to expect
a happily resolved marital accord for M. Paul and Lucy only to witness
M. Paul drown in a peculiarly shrouded finale. And because Catherine and
Lucy must ponder endlessly what drives their coquette-doppelgängers in
their devilish behavior, these coquettish females become synonymous
with the female eroticism that cannot be contained or repressed. In the
midst of her contempt for Ginevra's multiplication of lovers, Lucy continually allows herself to be positioned in close proximity to a woman she
would have the reader believe she loathes. Thus, in the much-discussed
scene in *Villette* in which Ginevra and Lucy appear in a play, Lucy is willing to be depicted as Ginevra's lover. Throughout *Villette,* Brontë seems to
require such "shadow" coquettes as Ginevra not so much to serve as the
embodiments of her hero's and heroine's repressed desires (although they
serve in this way, too) but as *idealized* versions of a repressed self.

Brontë's rendering of Ginevra as partially Gallic and Thackeray's presentation of Becky Sharp as the French-proficient daughter of a Parisian
opera performer (which Becky fraudulently presents as an aristocratic
"lineage") suggest that both novelists are importing to the English novel
—even as they keep in marked check—the French and aristocratic energies associated with coquetry. If there is a process of "democratization" in
the importation of these figures to these novels, it is only partly successful.
Ginevra has smuggled a volatile admixture of French aristocratic social
manners and an unrepressed sensuality to the middle-class domestic
realm symbolized by the girls' school where she works. Much of the alarm
inspired by the unstoppable coquetries of Austen's widowed and financially strapped Lady Susan stems from her retention, exaggeration, and refinement of techniques of coquetry that are perceived by others as distinctly upper-class in kind. (Indeed, Lady Susan's enemies repeatedly
question her legal right to retain the titular authority she won from her de-
ceased husband.) In a far more muted way, the coquettish gambits of the

wellborn Rosamond Vincy in George Eliot's *Middlemarch* are initially employed to secure the financially promising Tertius Lydgate as a husband. When Lydgate's poor business dealings jeopardize Rosamond's middle-class comforts, the woman described by Eliot's narrator as not knowing the difference between love and flirtation seeks other erotic "conquests." Like Becky Sharp's "victims"—Jos Sedley, Osborne—Lydgate has a "weakness" that makes him an ideal target for the Rosamonds of this world. (Lydgate previously has been deluded by the insincere coquetries of Mme. Laure during a French sojourn, proving himself as easily hoodwinked as those who succumb to Becky's French poses.)

Austen's and Brontë's coquette antiheroines regularly frustrate their own interests even as their sphere of influence expands. Isabella Thorpe of *Northanger Abbey* sabotages her own projected marriage to Catherine Morland's brother by toying with Captain Tilney, while Austen's Lady Susan, the "most accomplished coquette in England," encourages her daughter's alliance with a man whom Lady Susan finds repellent, then herself flirts with the eligible, young Reginald de Courcy, who later marries Lady Susan's daughter. The coquette's powers are unrestrained, her field of activity boundless, owing partly to her aristocratic origins. She seems detached from any single institutional sphere, constituting a teasing peril to individuals and the family unit as she takes everyday, socially acceptable flirtation to extremes. "[S]he does not confine herself to that sort of honest flirtation which satisfies most people," notes Reginald de Courcy of Lady Susan, "but aspires to the more delicious gratification of making a whole family miserable."[28]

The coquette's insurgency is related to what I have already called her power to disrupt the normal contours of time. In Balzac's "La Duchesse de Langeais" the narrator notes that the "secret conversations" between the protagonists Antoinette and Armand are "speeded up or slowed down at a woman's whim, through a dispute over words when feeling moves too fast, or through a complaint over feeling when words no longer respond to thought."[29] Such toying with temporality affects the representation of narrative time. In English fiction, the coquette sustains a contradictory role, for while she subverts the unfolding of marital plots, she also allows for emotionally gratifying (as opposed to merely socially feasible) marriages to take their course. Collapsing narrative time, Rosamond's coquettish kneeling before Ladislaw, traumatically misconstrued by Dorothea Brooke in chapter 77 of *Middlemarch,* at last forces a crisis and then a resolution of the too-long-deferred romance between Dorothea and Ladislaw. Similarly, in a protraction of temporality in Brontë's *Villette,* Ginevra Fanshawe, flirting with Lucy Snowe's on-again, off-again suitor, Dr. John, inadvertently provides Lucy the opportunity to recognize Dr. John's emotional aloofness and thus his unsuitability as a husband. Ginevra's role as an accidental gauge of masculine sincerity is acknowledged by Lucy even as she condemns Ginevra as hopelessly mercurial. "My patience would often have failed, and my interest flagged in listening to her, but for one thing," observes Lucy. "All the hints she dropped, all the details she gave, went unconsciously to prove, with great delicacy and respect, that M. Isidore's homage was offered with great delicacy and respect." (One sentence later, however, Lucy discloses how she informed Ginevra "very plainly that I believed him much too good for her, and intimated with equal plainness my impression that she was a vain coquette."[30])

Typically, flirtation in *Middlemarch* and *Villette* signifies a coded language within society's larger cultural code. However, the hidden laws of flirting operate on a less predictable "temporal clock" than that dominating the rites of courtship. The heroine must master this veiled system—as her coquettish double has—if she is to fit into the rhythms of society. As a teacher and colleague of the French-speaking Paul Emanuel, Lucy must be fluent in the French language; like the French linguistic tropes that operate as an internal system of communication throughout *Villette,* coquetry operates as a set of codes. Likewise, Lucy comes to grasp the additionally "private" rhetoric of coquetry required to woo M. Paul, who will emerge as her true match. Catherine and Lucy are ingenues poised for the education only experience affords. But Isabella and Ginevra represent the existence of competing narratives, alternative romantic strategies, voyeuristic pleasure, and perverse plotting. They assimilate self-improvement as "dark knowledge," which then must be banished from the narrative as unnarratable. Austen's narrator notes Catherine's disillusionment: "She was ashamed of Isabella, and ashamed of having ever loved her," notes Austen of Catherine after the revelation that Isabella has flirted with both Captain Tilney and Catherine's brother, James. Still, the coquette has left a palpable trace; by banishing Isabella, Catherine hypocritically demonstrates her own fickleness of temperament, as she concludes that James "should never hear Isabella's name mentioned by her again."[31] In a realization of Catherine's wish, Isabella soon disappears from *Northanger Abbey* and the details of her fate are undisclosed. Similarly, Ginevra

Fanshawe fades from *Villette* as if she had become a ghostly presence or a spectral force of nature. When Ginevra vanishes from the Rue Fossette, where she and Lucy have been sisterly enemies, Brontë informs us that "the nymph was vanished, engulfed in the past night light, like a shooting star swallowed up by darkness."[32]

Ghostly presences have a long history of identification with the sexually ignominious, and the coquette leaves a palpably perverse trace on the narrative even after disappearing. Having herself become identified with the animated continuation of narrative in Brontë and Austen, she becomes synonymous with the very antithesis of plotting, the cessation of storytelling. In the final pages of *Lady Susan* and *Villette,* we are informed that Susan and Ginevra are married, but these events are not depicted as transformative. Having wooed two men at once, Isabella finally is left emptyhanded. Only retrospectively do the actions of Ginevra and Isabella resemble a protracted distraction from the central plots of *Villette* and *Northanger Abbey.*

Refusing to develop or even to change significantly, Susan, Isabella, and Ginevra challenge what has been called the "cult of interiority" cultivated by the Victorian novel.[33] These coquette-demons respond to multidimensionality, in dialectical fashion, by affirming a delimited twodimensionality of self. What Austen calls Isabella's "boasted absence of mind" is as much a theory of individual character as it is a description of Isabella's proud empty-headedness. Since the reader has witnessed Isabella's cunning (she has, of course, fooled Catherine for the large part of Austen's narrative), Catherine's remark refers not so much to an absence of intellectual acumen as the absence of fictive depth. Similarly, Lucy Snowe notes of her arch rival Ginevra that "her liking and disliking, her love and hate, were mere cobweb and gossamer." And yet both Isabella and Ginevra are intelligent and often as acute in their observations as Catherine and Lucy. In a suggestive formulation, Georg Lukács once characterized this quality as "intellectual physiognomy," by which Lukács meant the novelist's establishment of fictive weight, whereby unintelligent characters are rendered fictionally compelling. According to Lukács, a "character's awareness will appear abstract and bloodless . . . to the extent that it is divorced from his concrete potentialities—unless it is founded on rich, concrete human passions" and "multifarious interrelationships."[34] The imposition of Isabella and Ginevra into *Northanger Abbey* and *Villette* is a reversal of this literary principle, because both of these figures refuse to channel their impulses into appropriate relationships. Instead, Isabella and Ginevra repeatedly demonstrate an austere management of the self in lieu of identity-transforming relations with men. The one characteristic of Ginevra that was "strong and durable," according to Lucy, is her "selfishness." As embodied by Ginevra and Isabella, coquetry depends on the deployment of an aesthetic of superficial character, what Simmel described as coquetry's "surface dialectic."[35] There can be no depth where there is mere artifice.

If this concept can be extended to the cultural meaning of plots, then the binary dynamic of flirting concerns not so much the visible and the invisible but rather the narratable versus the unnarratable. Again and again in *Lady Susan, Northanger Abbey,* and *Villette,* the details of the coquette's behavior are narrated indirectly, told by others and recounted either before or after the fact. While the epistolary form of *Lady Susan* frustrates direct depiction as it heightens subjective perspective, in *Northanger Abbey* and *Villette* the unnarratable nature of Isabella's and Ginevra's coquetries stands in contrast to a more direct representation of Catherine's and Lucy's activities. Ultimately functioning outside the orbit of novelistic realism, the coquette's basic unnarratability suggests a vaguely disreputable desire. When Reginald de Courcy turns against Lady Susan, for example, it is because of indirect hearsay of her activities, none of which he himself has witnessed. He writes: "I am obliged to declare that all the accounts of your misconduct during the life and since the death of Mr. Vernon which had reached me in common with the world in general, and gained my entire belief before I saw you, but which you by the exertion of your perverted abilities had made me resolve to disallow, have been unanswerably proved to me."[36] Notes Austen's narrator of Isabella in *Northanger Abbey:* "Her professions of attachment were now as disgusting as her excuses were empty, and her demands impudent." On receiving a self-exculpating letter from Isabella (asking Catherine to write to her brother James to explain Isabella's actions), Catherine is indignant: "'Write to James on her behalf!—No, James would never hear Isabella's name mentioned by her again.'" Because of her "disgusting" emptiness, Isabella must be banished from Catherine's circle of associates and, indeed, from the novel itself.[37]

Ostensibly so different in authorial temperament, Austen and Brontë have a number of similarities that literary critics seldom have explored. Readers have perhaps been too eager to accept at face value Brontë's much-quoted appraisal of Austen as evincing a want of passion in her fiction. Tony Tanner, for example, begins his book-length study of Austen by stressing the differences between Bronte's "almost obsessive life and intensity" and Austen's cool-tempered prose. "For Jane Austen, the social world was the ultimate realm of reality, no matter what internal miseries and struggles and isolations may be experienced within it," notes Tanner in an essay on *Villette*. "For Charlotte Brontë this social reality with its authoritative norms and finally acceptable values had gone, and metaphors take the place of this lost society. Particularly for Lucy Snowe in her displaced situation in Madame Beck's 'hollow system,' where all is stealth uncertainty and latent hostility, there are not only no ordained values structured into the environment, there are not even any epistemological certainties." [38]

This captures an essential disjunction between the work of these two novelists, but it also downplays the way in which Austen remains fascinated by how certain figures threaten the social world as an ultimate realm of reality. Expressed another way, *Lady Susan* and *Northanger Abbey* continually suggest that society may be supplanted on behalf of sinister characters with venal aims, figures whose very presence acts to undermine society as the locale of virtuous acts and romantic happiness. The social sphere in Austen's novels indeed may be the ultimate source of meaning, as Tanner notes, but Susan, Isabella, and Ginevra continually threaten integrity of that realm with their polished feats of duplicity and their transformation of sociability into a perverse form of gamesmanship. In Lucy Snowe's ongoing reaction to her adversary Ginevra Fanshawe and in Catherine Morland's growing distaste for Isabella Thorpe, one observes a strident response to a female rival. The peculiar fictional reprimands suffered by Ginevra and Isabella represent more than the disciplining of a bad girl as a prototypical "evil twin." The vibrant eighteenth-century coquette becomes disciplined by a more rigorously managed notion of the self. Before she is chastised and exorcised from the narrative, the coquettish tease in Austen and Brontë is granted a power and a force unlike any other character in nineteenth-century fiction.

Austen was drawn to the character of the female flirt in one of her earliest fictional efforts, *Lady Susan*. Given the coquette's impressive stature in Restoration theater, recasting her in convincingly negative terms was by no means an easy task for Austen, yet there was a contradictory power in the Millamants of eighteenth-century writing that Austen needed to resolve. The coquette threatens Austenian paradigms in that unwholesome as she is, she successfully embodies those traits that the novelist valued most highly in her heroines: wit, the absence of self-delusion, the philanthropic impulse to destroy the illusions of others, a heightened rationality, and emotional self-mastery. Critics have viewed *Lady Susan* in decidedly contradictory terms, refusing to assimilate the novel into prevailing histories of the novelist's literary career. They have variously described this early work as a "masterpiece" and a "failure." Marvin Mudrick sees the novel's heroine as a tragic figure, a victim of a narrow-minded society, a view that miscalculates the antic tone of *Lady Susan*. A. Walton Litz deems her a wholly idealized creature, one as remote from reality as the Man of Feeling. More recently, Warren Roberts has identified her with the marquise of Laclos's *Les liaisons dangereuses*. Some critics have sought models amongst Austen's relatives, while others have even come to view Lady Susan as a clinical case. Beatrice Anderson views her as a prototype of a personality disorder that has been documented in psychological literature for more than 150 years, part of a phenomenon she characterizes as "sociopathy" in that unlike schizophrenia and other psychoses, it is often not readily discernible. Clearly, with Lady Susan, Austen had invented a figure as complicated as Emma or Anne Elliot, characters usually regarded as the culmination of the novelist's artistic achievement.

The continual exclusion of *Lady Susan* from the Austen canon suggests less a set of reasoned aesthetic choices than a willful attachment to a single view of Austen's accomplishments as an author who, as Ronald Blythe maintains, was able "to advance the eighteenth-century novel along the road which led to Henry James and Proust."[39] *Lady Susan* plays havoc with two of the more important developments in criticism of the novelist's work, both of them intertwined: one, Austen's intellectual affiliations and political allegiances; and the other, the extent of her feminist critique of patriarchal social structures. In *Jane Austen and the War of Ideas,* Marilyn Butler contends that Austen largely created her fictions in a spirit of anti-Jacobin quietism as a considered reaction against the sentimental novel as exemplified by Henry MacKenzie. Claudia Johnson, however, claims that *Northanger Abbey* "domesticates the gothic," and that Austen's "interrogative, rather than declarative narrative methods" are part of a career devoted to refining techniques that "serve moderately progressive rather than reactionary political outlooks."[40] An attentive examination of the figures of Lady Susan and Isabella suggests that Austen is responding to another set of literary conventions with which she would have been familiar: the figures of Restoration theater. At the deeper level of what might be termed *Lady Susan's* and *Northanger Abbey's* social and even political unconscious, the conception of character—and specifically female character engendered by Restoration drama—is more threatening to the unfolding ideological credo of the realist novel. Austen resembles less the self-assured conservative of Butler's framework or the shrewd critic of a prevailing patriarchal ethos posited by Johnson than a writer who registers the accumulating tensions between a seductive feminine artifice and mature, female restraint. Having begun her career by celebrating, in *Lady Susan,* the coquette-demons of eighteenth-century literature, Austen ultimately exorcises such figures in *Northanger Abbey* on behalf of a canny womanhood.

Penned when Austen was probably about twenty years old, the epistolary *Lady Susan* concerns a widow who continues to seek out male admirers. Austen's irony throughout is tangible, since it is her social destructiveness of Lady Susan's sociability, what her sister-in-law, Mrs. Catherine Vernon, calls Lady Susan's "absolute coquetry," that is illustrated at every instant in Austen's novel. That the "merry widow" Susan Vernon is revealed to us through a series of letters (her own as well as those of her relatives and friends) heightens our sense of this coquette's comic dishonesty and unreliability. (In *Northanger Abbey,* Isabella's only attempt at defending herself comes in the form of a lengthy missive to Catherine, one of two pieces of correspondence reproduced in their entirety in the novel, a defensive maneuver that Catherine immediately dismisses for its "inconsistencies, contradictions and falsehood."[41]) Yet as the letters of Lady Susan's relations accumulate in their undisguised consternation at the havoc she may wreak, the epistolary form also intensifies our sense of Lady Susan as an opaque, formidable center of narrative interest. That she is revealed to us through her correspondence only lends formal logic to what Lady Susan herself makes explicit; namely, that her power stems from her linguistic skills. Letters, through which Lady Susan may present an idealized self-image, are the best literary vehicle for the narration of Susan's coquetry. Explaining to a friend why she expects to have her way with the Vernons and Sir Reginald, she insists it is her possession of a "command of Language."

Articulate, dynamic, contemptuous of marriage, Lady Susan in many ways is a worthy descendent of Millamant, whose flirtations also harbored a distinctly political character: duping men as a protofeminist activity.

Here coquetry allows for the spirited trafficking in men, who are represented as a mentally deficient class wholly incognizant of feminine wili-
ness. "Keep him therefore I entreat you in Edward St.," Lady Susan tells
Mrs. Johnson in asking her friend to entertain Reginald, whose attentions
have begun to tire Lady Susan. "You will not find him a heavy companion,
and I allow you to flirt with him as much as you like." [42] Yet whereas Millamant is herself for a time the naïve target of ruthless schemers, in *Lady
Susan* one finds a diametrically reversed role for the heroine. The widowed mother Lady Susan energetically hatches numerous plots, always behind the veil of social decorum. Susan's aristocratic relatives by marriage,
meanwhile, choose to protect their eligible sons from her erotic encroach-
ment. Sir Reginald catalogues Lady Susan's wrongs in a cautionary letter:
"Her neglect of her husband, her encouragement of other men, her extravagance and dissipation were so gross and notorious, that no one could
be ignorant of them at the time, nor can now have forgotten them." [43]
With satirical pleasure in her antiheroine's social triumphs, Austen demonstrates how easily mere sociability can be employed for unscrupulous
aims. Lady Susan's daughter-in-law warns her brother Reginald of falling
for "this dangerous creature":

> She is really excessively pretty. However you may choose to question the al-
> lurements of a lady no longer young, I must for my own part declare that I've
> seldom seen so lovely a woman as Lady Susan. She is delicately fair, with fine
> gray eyes and dark eyelashes; and from her appearance one would not sup-
> pose her more than five and twenty, though she must in fact be ten years
> older. I was certainly not disposed to admire her, though always hearing she
> was beautiful; but I cannot help feeling that she possesses an uncommon
> union of symmetry, brilliancy and grace. Her address to me was so gentle,
> frank and even affectionate, that if I had not known how much she has always
> disliked me for marrying Mr. Vernon, and that we had never met before, I
> should have imagined her an attached friend. One is apt I believe to connect
> assurance of manner with coquetry, and to expect that an impudent address
> will necessarily attend an impudent mind; at least I was myself prepared for
> an improper degree of confidence in Lady Susan; but her countenance is ab-
> solutely sweet, and her voice and manner winningly mild. I am sorry it is so,
> for what is this but deceit? Unfortunately one knows her too well. She is
> clever and agreeable, has all that knowledge of the world which makes con-
> versation easy, and talks very well, with a happy command of language,
> which is too often used I believe to make black appear white. [44]

Lady Susan has so mastered coquetry that artifice is rendered natural. Her
daughter-in-law's skepticism about a possible deception has given way

to evident awe before the "symmetry" of cohesive female artistic ac-
complishment. Mrs. Vernon's description, though designed to warn her
brother of the devious widow's charms, nonetheless keenly conveys Lady
Susan's erotic power. Most compellingly, this letter evokes Lady Susan's
worldly appeal, a magnetism of social effects that masks a venal character.
The document testifies to the authority of feminine artifice. Intriguingly,
exactly how Mrs. Vernon knows that Lady Susan dislikes her is nowhere
made intelligible in the text, and therefore Mrs. Vernon's animosity is
granted little validity. Clearly, Lady Susan thwarts common modes of understanding. By the time one has reached the last line of her daughter-in-
law's letter—in which Mrs. Vernon wonders how "it is scarcely possible
that two men should be so grossly deceived" by Lady Susan—the reader
may have been taken in by Lady Susan's charms. Determined that her
daughter should wed a man she herself finds repugnant, Lady Susan
strives to win the affection of her sister-in-law's brother even as she aims
to rekindle the romantic interest of a previous lover. Ultimately, Susan
Vernon is defeated in her machinations, forced to marry her daughter's
wealthy, although drearily conventional, former suitor.

Lady Susan anticipates a number of Victorian "bad mother" texts that
sought to define the parameters of motherhood.[45] But whereas these other
works unambiguously functioned as cautionary conduct books for future
mothers, Austen constantly spoofs the "naturalness" of mother-child relations. Lady Susan's fourth letter begins with a startlingly harsh judgment
of her own daughter:

> You are very good in taking notice of Frederica, and I am grateful for it as a
> mark of your friendship; but as I cannot have a doubt of the warmth of that
> friendship, I am far from exacting so heavy a sacrifice. She is a stupid girl, and
> has nothing to recommend her. I would not therefore on any account have
> you encumber one moment of your precious time by sending her to Edward
> St., especially as every visit is so many hours deducted from the grand affair
> of education.[46]

Unkind, shocking in the absoluteness of its estimation, this letter is perhaps the greatest indictment provided by Austen of her irascible antiheroine. Nonetheless, the reader is left with a question concerning Lady
Susan's ruthless judgment of her own offspring: on the basis of the evidence provided, is that judgment not true? While Lady Susan not-so-
secretly seems to consider Frederica as a romantic rival—and, indeed,
Frederica will win the hand of Reginald de Courcy—this handsome

thirty-five-year-old widow emerges as not wholly unjustified in her un-sparing judgment of her daughter. Lady Susan recognizes the unfairness of a scenario where a less accomplished woman secures the devotion of a man. There is a sense, too, that Austen's literary allegiances lie with Lady Susan; Frederica Vernon is permitted only a single letter in *Lady Susan,* a short, unremarkable, complaining missive that demonstrates she is alto-gether without her mother's inspired epistolarity.

The frivolous display of affection, the inconstant expression of feigned emotion, the vacuous toying with men's hearts, the deliberate cultivation of artifice, what might be described as the accoutrements of a female car-nivalesque—all are required to give way to a more decorously main-tained conception of flirting. In the battleground of courtship, Catherine and Lucy do not so much dismiss coquetry as repellent as they invent, through the process of self-education, an updated, more functional (in social terms) version of flirtation, one that may be justified on moral grounds. These two competing forms of coquettish behavior take place on a heated terrain that constitutes the fissures between eighteenth-century and nineteenth-century fictional forms. Both *Villette* and *Northanger Abbey* are novels of female education in which the protagonist learns not only to flirt but to do so in a specific manner. The heroines of both novels learn to flirt properly, while antiheroines, depicted as changeable doubles, are denigrated precisely for flirting. In this way, a new feminine ideal may be asserted. What unites the Austen of *Northanger Abbey* (but not *Lady Susan*) and the Brontë of *Villette* is not only their depiction of these two opposing archetypes of feminine behavior but their interest in persuading the reader, through an argument cast in moral terms, of the superiority of multidimensionality of self, one that is mutable but without being wholly destructive of consistent identity. Catherine and Lucy are fascinated by Isabella and Ginevra because these coquettes lack an additional dimension of character. They perform the repressed desires that good women must learn to redirect toward socially positive ends.

Coquetry haunts *Northanger Abbey* as much as the gothic tropes that Austen famously parodies. While Austen satirizes gothic conventions quite forcefully in *Northanger Abbey* as a conflict between Catherine's es-capist reading and the more complex, shifting nature of actual experience, the tension between comically rendered gothic sensibility and a mor-dantly ironized realist style is not deeply imbedded in the novel's structure or its deeper psychology. Rather, gothic is a largely comic means by which

Austen establishes the value of a more rationally based realism. Gothic tropes allude to an essentially supernatural reality that Austen, seeing that reality as having no empirical foundation, can fruitfully mock as she satirizes the reading audience for gothic. On a deeper level of what might be termed the "unconscious" structure of *Northanger Abbey,* the conception of female character engendered by Restoration drama is still more threatening to the unfolding ideological credo of Austen's proto-Victorian text.

In a shift in authorial sympathy as well as narrative approach, Austen in *Northanger Abbey* recasts Lady Susan as Isabella Thorpe, a coquette whose equivocating nature only becomes evident in the novel's last pages. If Lady Susan was the "most accomplished coquette in England," then Isabella is far more ferociously accomplished in deceiving Catherine and the reader for so long; unlike Lady Susan, she is not revealed as conniving until the novel's penultimate pages. For if we choose to consider *Northanger Abbey* not as an uncomplicated satire on gothic tropes (as the work is usually treated) but as a highly conflicted treatment of anxiety and disjuncture, then Austen seems neither the ironic conservative posited by Marilyn Butler nor the shrewd critic of a patriarchal ethos emphasized by Claudia Johnson. She emerges as a less ideologically resolved writer who, in the interest of an elevated but canny womanhood, struggles to exorcise the demons of Restoration coquetry in order to establish her independent literary credentials.

In expressing novelistic interest in the figure of the sinister mother and conniving coquette Lady Susan, Austen disrupts the smooth-running lines of the marriage plot, as she adopts not only elements of Restoration theater but also such eighteenth-century fictions of female rakishness as *Moll Flanders* and *Roxana.* Catherine's education depends not merely on the disciplining of Isabella Thorpe but on the depiction of Isabella's very character as two-dimensionally constituted and ultimately outside the realist novel's purview. If Millamant signifies the coquette as a feminine ideal, then Isabella is introduced into Austen's female bildungsroman to present the coquette as unnatural, negative exemplum. The matter of Isabella's fictive "weight" is related to a discussion that has dominated critical exegesis concerning both the eighteenth-century and nineteenth-century novel. Gothic thematizes that which is irrational and spectral, but "Restoration character" suggests an alternative moral framework, a countervailing set of social rules, and a competing conception of identity. A key conversation in *Northanger Abbey* occurs when, upon discovering that

Isabella, although engaged to Catherine's brother, is flirting with Frederick, Catherine questions Henry Tilney:

> "Is it my brother's attentions to Miss Thorpe, or Miss Thorpe's admission
> of them, that gives the pain?"
>
> "Is not it the same thing?"
>
> "I think Mr. Morland would acknowledge a difference. No man is of-
> fended by another man's admiration of the woman he loves; it is the woman
> only who can make it a torment."
>
> Catherine blushed for her friend, and said, "Isabella is wrong. But I
> am sure she cannot mean to torment, for she is very much attached to my
> brother. She has been in love with him ever since they first met, and while
> my father's consent was uncertain, she fretted herself almost into a fever. You
> know she must be attached to him."
>
> "I understand: she is in love with James, and flirts with Frederick."
>
> "O! no, not flirts. A woman in love with one man cannot flirt with
> another."
>
> "It is probable that she will neither love so well, nor flirt so well, as she
> might do either singly. The gentlemen must each give up a little."
>
> After a short pause, Catherine resumed with "Then you do not believe
> Isabella so very much attached to my brother?"
>
> "I can have no opinion on that subject." [47]

The open-minded Henry Tilney coolly expresses a conception of female
flirtation not only as compatible with an exalted romantic desire but as in-
tegrally intertwined with romantic ardor; indeed, one facilitates the other.
Catherine, meanwhile, naïvely questions the possibility that a residual eros
might supplant love as she defends, in sisterly fashion, the intentions
of her friend. Both Catherine's and Henry's theories of flirtation, however, minimize and thus misconstrue the depth of Isabella's deceitfulness;
Henry does so by assuming that feminine coquetry merely constitutes an
innocently offered, flattering compliment to men, while Catherine imagines that a plot of courtship in itself satiates female eros.

That the urbane Henry and not simply the unworldly Catherine should
so miscalculate Isabella's character indicates that mere knowledge of recognizable social types is required to comprehend coquetry's manifestations. In actuality, Isabella is solely preoccupied with flirting for its own
sake, and as such she defies Catherine's too-limited conception of the parameters of female behavior. The revelation that Isabella simultaneously
has pursued both James and Frederick itself at last establishes her role in
the novel as a two-faced vixen. That Austen effectively "punishes" Isabella

by denying her either man is, in the novel's terms, an empty retribution. For it is a mysterious, albeit basic, aspect of Isabella's character that she does not seem to want—or really to require—a suitor. What lends the exchange between Catherine and Isabella quoted earlier an enhanced fascination is that the heroine momentarily assumes the role of her coquette-friend. Just as Catherine mistakenly imagines that Isabella is virtuous, so too does the heroine assume the physical expression of embarrassment—a blush—which Isabella herself is incapable of registering. The disciplining of Isabella here occurs when Catherine is briefly transformed into Isabella, but an Isabella rendered civilized through a shame-indicating blush.

The "mature" Austen so beloved of the novelist's critics and many of her readers came to disavow an absorption in coquette-demons and their pedagogical value for wide-eyed ingenues. In *Emma* (1816), for example, the learning process has been reversed and the heroine's sisterly acquaintance is far more naïve, herself in need of tutorial advice. Harriet Smith is selected by Emma as an ideal companion because she is even less versed in games of coquetry than Emma herself. In the scenes in which Emma and Knightley battle over the rules of attraction between the sexes, Harriet is useful chiefly as a foil for Jane to play up her own cleverness with Knightley:

> "I am very much mistaken if your sex in general would not think such beauty, and such temper, the highest claims a woman could possess."
>
> "Upon my word, Emma, to hear you abusing the reason you have, is almost enough to make me think so too. Better be without sense, then misapply it as you do."
>
> "To be sure," cried she playfully. "I know *that* is the feeling of you all. I know that such a girl as Harriet is what every man delights in—what at once bewitches his senses and satisfies his judgment."[48]

Eager to lend psychological opacity to Emma's character, Austen keeps the reader from knowing whether her heroine is aware of the extent to which she is testing Knightley. The figure who will mostly forcibly test Knightley's devotion—as well as Emma's understanding of authentic romantic ardor—is undoubtedly Frank Churchill, whose arrival in Highbury is endlessly delayed. (When he finally appears, he abruptly takes off for London.)

In the triangular diagrammatics of flirting that permeate *Emma* and that reach their apotheosis in the celebrated Box Hill episode in the novel, Frank Churchill becomes the passive object of Emma's attentions. Unbeknownst to Emma, Frank is secretly engaged to her rival Jane Fairfax. Before the gathering at Box Hill turns disastrous, Emma finds in Frank Churchill an ideal partner in frisky, purposeless badinage:

> To amuse her, and be agreeable in her eyes, seemed all that he cared for— and Emma, glad to be enlivened, not sorry to be flattered, was gay and easy too, and gave him all the friendly encouragement, the admission to be gallant, which she had ever given in the first and most animating period of their acquaintance; but which now, in her own estimation, meant nothing, though in the judgment of most people looking on it must have had such an appearance as no English word but flirtation could very well describe. "Mr. Frank Churchill and Miss Woodhouse flirted together excessively." They were laying themselves open to that very phrase—and to having it sent off in a letter to Maple Grove by one lady, to Ireland by another.[49]

Austen saturates this scene in ironies: at the precise moment when Emma realizes that her actual relation with Frank means "nothing" (although Austen tells us that she "still intended him for her friend"), an ever-widening public opprobrium has it that she is flirting "excessively." That Emma only increases her flirting with Frank after seeing that a "nothing" divides them paradoxically brings her closer to Frank. For as the reader learns retrospectively, Frank's hidden betrothal to Jane Fairfax has allowed him to submit to Emma's flirtations in public. Like Frank, Emma is already "committed" to another, Knightley, although she has yet to perceive either of these commitments. Before all of this can manifest itself, however, Emma must be roundly humiliated first for flirting with Frank, then for insulting Miss Bates—while Knightley, misreading Emma's attention to Frank, is reduced to the role of jealous rival. Ultimately, Frank himself is redeemed at the conclusion of *Emma* because his love for Jane is genuine but also because he is the inadvertent conduit, like Harriet early in the novel, for Emma and Knightley's "courtship."

All of Charlotte Brontë's writing reveals an absorption in coquettes, an intensifying interest that may have had as one of its sources Brontë's impassioned reading of *Ranthorpe* (1847) by George Henry Lewes, the companion of George Eliot. The hero of Lewes's novel, an aspiring poet and playwright, seeks his literary fortune in a bohemian London that gradually turns treacherous. Although Ranthorpe has a number of catastrophic literary failures (a tragedy he authors is booed off the London stage), the climax of the novel turns on the protagonist's rescue from a near-betrothal to the flirt Florence Wilmington—a decision averted only when a close male friend, Wynston, warns him of her dishonest nature. (Wynston witnesses Florence flattering a wealthy nobleman with the same intensity she once directed toward him.) In a long monologue delivered to Ranthorpe, Wynston explains how Florence bewitched him:

> She was like the chameleon reflecting the color of every tree under which it reposes; she passed from the most contradictory ideas, and antagonistical sympathies, in the same evening—the same hour—with unparalleled ease. She flattered every body, and cared for none. For none—no, not even for me; beyond the gratification of her vanity, which was pleased with the idea of the cleverest man in the county being her slave. I did not know this at the time—I did not suspect it. She was all enthusiasm, tenderness, and melancholy grace; the tears would come into her eyes if I recited verses to her, or if I complained of a headache. She seemed "wrapt in adoration." I believed all this; the fumes of vanity intoxicated me—delirious presumption distorted my judgment.[50]

Lewes presents the problem of female coquetry as a challenge to male cognition; its resolution occurs when men share their discoveries concerning the perfidy of the coquette and her fast-changing mutations. That Wynston says of Florence that she initially "seemed 'wrapt in adoration'" indicates Wynston's self-conscious detachment from a hackneyed literary vocabulary, the coquette's powers of assuming the guise of romantic passion, and the bitter rewards of masculine gullibility. Clearly, the challenge for the new fictionalist, as well as for the male suitor, is to discover improved modes for the detection of feminine duplicity.[51]

The effect of *Ranthorpe* on Brontë could not have been more arresting. "I have read a new book," she exulted in a letter to Lewes, "—not a reprint—not a reflection of any other book, but a *new book*. I did not know such books were written now. It is very different to any of the popular works of fiction; it fills the mind with fresh knowledge." That "fresh knowledge" undoubtedly inspired Brontë in a work that demonstrated her most sustained absorption in taxonomizing coquettish female conduct, *Villette*.[52] Unlike *Northanger Abbey*, where Catherine only learns of Isabella's deviousness at the end of the novel, Lucy, the heroine of *Villette*, finds herself living in close proximity to an antiheroine whose deceitfulness she continually claims to despise. Yet whereas Isabella represents the possibility that intimates might be two-faced, Ginevra in fact is less underhanded than cheerfully avaricious. She may deceive her male suitors, but like Millamant, who symbolized female "class" solidarity, Ginevra is generally frank with her confidante Lucy. Indeed, it is curious that while Lucy Snowe's "autobiography" as outlined in *Villette* has been characterized as a hysterical narrative by numerous critics of the novel, these discussions fail to explain the most irrational (that is, hysterical) aspect of her narrative: Lucy's intensely vocalized loathing of Ginevra, a hatred that is out of proportion to Ginevra's "wrongs."

Ginevra represents unrestrained desire, eros fulfilled without regard to the codes of correct behavior. She is a galling reminder that Lucy's training may have been misguided: bad girls *do* triumph. Ginevra is a constant reprimand to Lucy's education, and she inspires Lucy to comic moments of envy. At one point Lucy cattily notes that "Miss Fanshawe's travels, gaieties, and flirtations agreed with her mightily; she had become quite plump, her cheeks looked as round as apples." Not only does Lucy demonstrate an uncontrollable physical revulsion when in the same room as Ginevra, she is haunted by her even in the midst of happy thoughts:

> That morning I was disposed for silence: the austere fury of the winter-day had on me an awing, hushing influence. The passion of January, so white and so bloodless, was not yet spent: the storm had raged itself hoarse. . . . Had Ginevra Fanshawe been my companion in the morning-room, she would not have suffered me to muse and listen undisturbed. . . . and how she would have rung the changes on one topic! How she would have pursued and pestered me with questions and surmises—worried and oppressed me with comments and confidences I did not want, and longed to avoid.[53]

In passages such as this, Ginevra is less a thoroughly conceived character than a besetting unconscious force. The questions Ginevra asks are ones that Lucy must answer to achieve spiritual and romantic enlightenment.

Ginevra, continually reprimanded by Lucy, seems unable to feel "ordinary" emotions such as jealousy or animosity. "Indignant at last with her teasing peevishness, I curtly requested her to 'hold her tongue'," Lucy informs the reader on one of the numerous occasions when she scolds Ginevra. "The rebuff did her good, and it was observable that she liked me no worse for it."[54] At no point in *Villette* is Ginevra—who, according to Lucy, is of "light, careless temperament"—depicted as in any way discomfited by such actions. Male affection and homage, which she continually seeks, please her no more or no less than male rejection. It is not merely that she is unrepressed; her desire seems to exist beyond a realm of

disappointment and satisfaction. Much less an ontologically distinct character than one character's fantasized projection of another's happiness,
Ginevra is a goading embodiment of the essential associability of Lucy's
concealed romantic cravings.

Fiercely intimate yet opposed in temperament, Lucy and Ginevra seem
to be opposite figures gazing at each other in a mirror. As John Kucich
notes, the two women share several defining traits: "Both resent being fet-
tered; both disdain the complacency of the 'bourgeois' marriage; both sustain romantic relationships to John Graham; both are excellent actresses,"
and most importantly, both have "reversible capacities for rivalry."[55] Despite their anxiety-ridden acquaintance, at moments these women seem to
serve as mirror images of each other. "Ginevra seemed to me the happiest," observes Lucy in a startlingly lyrical aside to the reader.

> She was on the route of beautiful scenery; these September suns shine for
> her on fertile plains, where harvest and vintage matured under their mellow
> beam. Those gold and crystal moons rose on her vision over blue horizons
> waved in mountain lines.
>
> But all this was nothing; I too felt those autumn suns and saw those har-
> vest moons, and I almost wished to be covered in with earth and turf, deep
> out of their influence; for I could not live on their light, nor make them com-
> rades, nor yield them affection. But Ginevra had a kind of spirit with her,
> empowered to give constant strength and comfort, to gladden daylight and
> embalm darkness; the best of the good genii that guard humanity curtained
> her with his wings, and canopied her head with his bending form. By True
> Love was Ginevra followed: never could she be alone. Was she insensible to
> this presence? It seemed to me impossible.[56]

While Ginevra is the heroine's unconsciously desired love object, she is
also Lucy's idealized conception of femininity. If, as Nina Auerbach has argued, Lucy's "hallucinated struggles seem almost independent of" her two
suitors and her feelings "ebb and swell with only a slight connection to external events," her responses nevertheless are intimately entangled with
Ginevra.[57] Ginevra stands for what can and cannot be evoked, what may
be introduced into the text but must be left unresolved.

This question of "narratability" is basic to the entire logic of *Vanity
Fair*. What the narrator knows (and so can narrate) is fundamental to
Thackeray's evocation of Becky's (and to a lesser degree, Amelia's) flirting
with men. As soon as Becky leaves the world of Pinkerton's school in the
first chapter of the novel, her behavior presents challenges to narration.
Here, for example, Becky woos a slow-witted Jos Sedley:

"By Gad, Miss Rebecca, I wouldn't hurt you for the world."

"No," said she. "I *know* you wouldn't;" and then she gave him ever so gentle a pressure with her little hand, and drew it back quite frightened, and looked first for one instant in his face, and then down at the carpet-rods; and I am not prepared to say that Joe's heart did not thump at this little involuntary, timid, gentle motion of regard on the part of the simple girl.

It was an advance, and as such, perhaps, some ladies of indisputable correctness and gentility will condemn the action as immodest; but, you see, poor dear Rebecca had all this work to do for herself.[58]

Here the shift in perspective highlights narration as a series of artificial literary conceits, drawing attention to Becky's exact physical moves as she makes her military-style "advance" and "retreat." Further, Thackeray coyly offers an "I am not prepared to say" regarding Sedley's inner feelings; thus, acts of coquetry allow Thackeray the opportunity to publicize both the powers and limits of his distinctive narrative "omniscience."

Indeed, the two key, all-determining events protracting the plot in Thackeray's novel involve questions of narrative verification surrounding acts of flirtation. The first of these scenes involves Becky's toying with Lord Steyne, the exposure of which leads to a spiraling series of representations and misrepresentations culminating in Rawdon's final disillusionment with his wife. The second crucial incident is the flirtation between George Osborne and Becky, an incident of such crucial narrative significance in *Vanity Fair* that it coincides and competes with cataclysmic historical events of Napoleonic scale in its power to affect lives of Thackeray's characters. At Quatre Bras on the morning of the Battle of Waterloo, in a confrontation that will cost him his life, George confesses to his friend and comrade Dobbin, as they survey the "black masses of Frenchmen who crowned the opposite heights," his guilt over the episode with Becky: "'I have been mixing in a foolish intrigue with a woman,' George said. . . . 'If I drop, I hope Emmy will never know of that business. I wish to God it had never begun!'"[59] The disclosure of this dalliance by Becky, years after the fact, serves to liberate Amelia from the state of comatose bereavement that has prevented her betrothal to Dobbin. As in *Villette* and *Northanger Abbey*, the actions of the coquette tend to mute the flirtations of the good girl; Amelia's rapport with the sweet-natured Dobbin is always a romantic subplot. Shortly before Becky's blunt disillusionment of Amelia, Thackeray offers a droll revisionary gloss on literary history. The puppeteer hints that flirtations have eluded the perceptual acumen of a writer of Shakespeare's perspicacity. Noting Amelia's on-again, off-again encouragement of Dobbin, Thackeray offers a typically expansive narrative tangent:

> Not that Emmy, being made aware of the honest major's passion, rebuffed him in any way, or felt displeased with him. Such an attachment from so true and loyal a gentleman could make no woman angry. Desdemona was not angry with Cassio, though there is very little doubt she saw the lieutenant's partiality for her (and I for my part believe that many more things took place in that sad affair than the wealthy Moorish officer ever heard of); why, Miranda was even very kind to Caliban, and we may be pretty sure for the same reason. Not that she would encourage him in the least,—the poor, uncouth monster—of course not. No more would Emmy by any means encourage her admirer, the major. She would give him that friendly regard, which so much excellence and fidelity merited; she would treat him with perfect cordiality and frankness until he made proposals: and *then* it would be time enough for her to speak, and to put an end to hopes which never could be realized.[60]

Providing a winking first-person interjection insinuating that Othello's irrational jealousy may not have been so baseless after all and that Miranda's magnanimity toward the misshapen monster of "The Tempest" may have had lust as a motive, the narrator of *Vanity Fair* hints that coquetry eludes the conventions of theatrical mimesis. The complicating rhetoric of the realist novel, we are instructed, is superior to that of merely dramatic venues. The satirical novelist provides what a playwright cannot—namely, an updated, enhanced female psychology, which, paradoxically in *Vanity Fair,* is on close scrutiny actually less individuated than the male psyche in that, as the passage above suggests, all women are inherently flirtatious. (Elsewhere in *Vanity Fair,* Thackeray's narrator, describing Becky's toying with Jos Sedley, is less schematic, noting that "The bearded creatures are quite as eager for praise, quite as finikin over their toilets, quite as proud of their personal advantages, quite as conscious of their powers of fascination, as any coquette in the world."[61]) In the paragraph above, Amelia, seemingly so simple and earnest, demonstrates a more complex psychology than that which might be captured on stage, while her ability to raise and shatter male hopes is not all that unlike the stratagems of the duplicitous Becky. Once again, it is through coquetry that the nineteenth-century novel announces its evolutionary "advance" as a genre. Through the probing exploration of the teeming, abstruse inner life of the flirting female, the Victorian novelist supplants earlier literary discourses that shape the representation of the self.

🏵 2 🏵

The Flirtation of Species
Darwinian Sexual Selection
and Victorian Narrative

DARWIN'S REVISIONISM IN "THE DESCENT OF MAN"

A deeper student of Science than his rivals, he appreciated Nature's
compliment in the fair one's choice of you. We now scientifically know
that in this department of the universal struggle, success is awarded to
the bettermost. You spread a handsomer tail than your fellows, you
dress a finer top-knot, you pipe a newer note, have a longer stride; she
reviews you in competition, and selects you. The superlative is magnetic
to her. She may be looking elsewhere, and you will see—the superlative
will simply have to beckon, away she glides. She cannot help herself; it is
her nature.
—George Meredith, *The Egotist* (1879)

Our great Mikado, virtuous man,
When he to rule our land began,
  Resolved to try
  A plan whereby
 Young men might best be steadied.
So he decreed, in words succinct,
That all who flirted, leered or winked
(Unless connubially linked),
  Should forthwith be beheaded.
—Gilbert and Sullivan, *The Mikado* (1885)

Of the many propositions advanced by Charles Darwin, that which has
endured as the most controversial, although until recently the least explored by literary critics and cultural theorists, addresses the question of
"sexual selection" in the natural world. First presented at length in *The
Descent of Man and Selection in Relation to Sex* (1871), Darwin's theory of
sexual selection (a term he initially introduced in his 1859 *The Origin of
Species*) detailed how throughout the animal kingdom, such features as

the antlers of a buck, the spurs of a cock, or the pincers of a lobster allowed the male to defeat his rivals for the attention of females. But even secondary sexual characteristics, such as the singing or plumage of birds, which held no obvious utilitarian function, now acquired a new importance. Darwin's colleague Alfred Wallace had wondered why male adornments, potentially perilous in that they presumably enabled predators to locate male prey, were so pervasive throughout the animal kingdom. As outlined in *The Descent of Man,* brilliant color, a handsome plumage, even the sound of a male animal's voice, all had to be figured into the intricate calculus of sexual mating.

Since publishing his theory of evolution, Darwin had struggled to fathom how its mechanisms could account for such apparently extravagant traits as peacocks' tails and turkey cocks' wattles, mainly male excrescences that were without obvious utility or survival value. Darwin came to view such features, what he termed "sexual dimorphism," as pivotal in the perpetuation of a given species. Because a chosen male would have a greater chance of propagating his genes, such genetically transmissible features as made him attractive would spread in the next generation. Sexual selection sought to explain competition among creatures of the same species for access to reproduction, serving as the procreative version within a single species of "natural selection" among different species.

If the author of *The Origin of Species* often seemed to present the natural world as driven by impersonal forces that may or may not have an evident teleological design, the theory of sexual selection tempered such implications by appearing to reintroduce choice as a crucial element in the natural universe. With the set of ideas embodied in the theory of sexual selection, Tennyson's image of "nature red in tooth and claw" yielded to recognizably human narratives in which mates were cyclically wooed, pursued, courted, and won. At one level, then, *The Descent of Man* confirmed the prevailing Victorian faith that the "courtship plot" was so universal as to possess a basis in nature. Just as Darwin himself was both an ideological conservative and a radical upstart, *The Descent* provided a bridge for seemingly contradictory strains within Victorian culture: the divide separating Victorian ethical strenuousness, high-minded and "purposive," and an incipient aestheticism built on a belief in the randomness of "sensations" and "impressions." Darwin's depiction of a powerful female in command of what amounted to an elaborate male beauty contest laid the philosophical groundwork for an aestheticism of purposeless, "unnat-

ural" dimensions. In a courtship plot now sanctioned by Darwinian nature, the marriage-postponing New Woman and the self-primping dandy
were suddenly united in their shared roles not so much as denaturalized
subjects (for Darwin the scientific empiricist, an impossibility) but as
figures who simply took nature's "laws" to extreme conclusions. Just as the
female might come to savor the erotic power accorded to her in nature's
scheme, so too did a love of blue china, Oriental bric-a-brac, or peacock
feathers reveal a thoroughgoing devotion to the accoutrements invaluable
to nature's courtship laws. Embedded in the theory of sexual selection was
the suggestion that both the New Woman and the aesthete-dandy might
relish their identities in the absence of courtship itself.

Although Darwin's critics would have balked at the suggestion, it is clear
that those aspects of *The Descent of Man* that provided an intellectual
foundation to Victorian feminist aspirations and aestheticist ideology allowed the evolutionist's colleagues to dismiss his ideas as scientifically
unsound. Among those sharply dissenting from the propositions of *The
Descent* were such otherwise sympathetic coevolutionists as Alfred Wallace, Julian Huxley and Darwinism's fellow-traveling German ethnolo-
gists. Most of Darwin's contemporaries strenuously rejected his theory of
sexual selection, dismissing its basic argument out of hand or choosing to
ignore it altogether. The theory of sexual selection, after all, posited narratives of courtship in which females were the ultimate decision makers
and males competed for female approval in order for procreation to occur. Still, while located in a natural matrix as an archetypal, apparently
preordained "courtship plot," Darwin's delineation of sexual selection invited speculation as to what might occur if courtship were stalled, abandoned, or for some reason failed to occur.

To be sure, Darwin's *The Descent of Man* could also be enlisted to mimic
the period's conventional wisdom. After all, Darwin had highlighted male
sexual drive, even noting at one point that the female is "less eager than
the male . . . she is coy, and may often be seen endeavoring to escape from
the male."[1] Nonetheless, even this emphasis on female "coyness" and aggressive male behavior raised disturbing possibilities. By refusing to allow
for feminine motivation to participate in sexual selection, Darwin hinted
at narratives of never consummated coquetry that females could engineer.
Such scenarios, in which nature itself seemed to give sanction to "useless"
desire, would find the female of the species prolonging procreation indefi-
nitely as the male self-preeningly competed for a perpetually proffered but
never delivered female approval.

Despite its poor reception during Darwin's day, the idea of sexual selection has proven of considerable, enduring interest to evolutionary theorists in recent years, who increasingly have returned to the basic assumptions informing Darwin's once-disputed arguments. Some evolutionary theorists have taken Darwin's theory of sexual selection a good deal further than Darwin himself, seeing in the biological dynamics of reproduction, for example, a confirmation of the postulates of sexual selection theory, claiming to have discovered that the females of certain species seem to have a mechanism to choose between different sperm—perhaps to select the sperm most compatible with their own DNA.[2] To the extent that the theory of sexual selection has been revised by evolutionary scientists, it is toward the idea that because an extravagant tail or seductive wattle has costs, in energy and survival chances, their splendor is an indicator that he who bears them must have "good genes" to enable him to withstand those costs.[3]

Literary critics attending to Darwin's writing within the context of Victorian literature and culture, meanwhile, have continued to skirt, misconstrue, or fail to consider the full implications of *The Descent of Man*. In *Darwin and the Novelists: Patterns of Science in Victorian Fiction* (1988), a brilliant exploration of the common cognate patterns of science that Dickens, Trollope, and Joseph Conrad shared with Darwin, George Levine altogether avoids the subject of sexual selection.[4] In her landmark study of Darwinian narrative, *Darwin's Plots* (1983), Gillian Beer devotes a single chapter to the theory of sexual selection as it informs the late fiction of George Eliot and the novels of Thomas Hardy. According to Beer, Darwin is "telling a new story, against the grain of the language available to tell it in." For Beer, the author of *The Descent of Man* is arguing that "women are on the scale of development with a less developed race, inevitably lagging behind European manhood"—part of a thesis, *Darwin's Plots* concludes, that Eliot subtly refined in her fiction and that in his novels Hardy more or less wholly retained.[5]

Like Beer, other recent theorists examining Darwin's work have underlined the close contiguity between Darwinian thought and conventional —indeed, hide-bound—Victorian belief. Nancy Armstrong, in her examination of Victorian domestic fiction, contends that Darwin emphasized the female domestication of male competitive instincts in *The Descent* in order to replace sexual exchange for competition as the foundation of natural order.[6] Philip Barrish, noting the exceptional power afforded females in Darwin's theory of sexual selection, nonetheless sketches a Darwin animated by thoroughly patriarchal imperatives: "Women are indeed granted a certain 'power' in such models, but at best it is only a version of the power which they have always been accorded: to produce and tend male subjects."[7] Observing a univocal narrative where Beer saw multivocal plots, Ruth Bernard Yeazell has suggested that Darwin's theory of sexual selection was formed substantially by the evolutionist's fondness for the "happy" endings he gleaned from his readings of Victorian novels, leading Darwin not only to anthropomorphize nature but, according to Yeazell, to retell a single story of species mating that always "appears to end, and end happily."[8] Such a perspective may be gleaned from the scientist's own autobiography, where the evolutionist revealed that he confined his leisure-time reading to satisfyingly resolved novels, the central character of which should be, he opined, "some person whom one can thoroughly love, and if it be a pretty woman all the better."[9] Darwin, Yeazell suggests, simply planted such designs in his own empirical investigations.

Most recently, Rosemary Jahn has called for an even more skeptical estimation of Darwin's theorizing regarding sexual selection. Arguing that accounts such as Yeazell's "do not fully acknowledge the arguments for women's biological and intellectual inferiority and for male agency and choice" in the evolutionary thinker's work, Jahn explores Darwin's reliance on Victorian anthropological narratives. She maintains that although female choice is an important part of domestic courtship fictions and animal mating behavior, in *The Descent of Man* it is of subordinate importance to the "role played by male discrimination in shaping the power relations of modern human culture." Writes Jahn: "[Darwin] could only conceive of sexual choice by women as operating within the constraints of the patriarchal gender relations his account of human evolution had deemed necessary."[10] Darwin's evolutionary "discoveries" were indeed complex reconstitutions of earlier Victorian discursive practices. As Yeazell and Jahn usefully remind us, Darwin possessed his own distinct and traceable origins.[11] Just how snugly his paradigms fit into earlier narratives is suggested by T. H. Huxley's celebrated statement upon completing *The Origin:* "How extremely stupid not to have thought of that." George Eliot (who on one occasion criticized Darwin as a Johnny-come-lately to the ranks of evolutionary thinkers) assumed a similar attitude in her remark that "at first sight" Darwin's ideas in *The Origin of Species* were "implausible," but later one arrives at "something like an actual belief in it."[12]

Still, critics of Darwin as overly complicit in rigid Victorian *doxa* on the relations between the sexes simplify the complexity of *The Descent*. Yeazell's argument, notably, relies too strictly on an understanding of "endings" as exposing a given plot's ideological import. More importantly, by viewing Darwin as in collusion with the most essentialist sexual ideologies animating Victorian systems of belief, critics of *The Descent of Man* minimize Darwin's sustained attention to sexual "variations" as much as to purposive concepts of sex.[13] The Charles Darwin inhabiting such critiques is generally the cautious Victorian clubman, a scientific genius yet also a philistine of crushingly middlebrow tastes. No doubt Darwin was temperamentally and ideologically predisposed to find "happy designs" and therefore may have preferred novels—and empirical experiments—that appeared to embody them. Yet there is a multiplicity of contradictory narratives embedded in Darwin's major texts, none of them explained by the "courtship" endings that seem to cap such trajectories. If Darwin was affected by other nineteenth-century narratives and by myths of female agency, he was beholden to them in all of their complication and contradiction.

Indeed, *The Descent of Man* encompassed a number of "unhappy" endings, peculiar anomalies, and disturbingly inassimilable and strange cases in nature. While Darwin always stressed patterns of coherence, it was the "variations in nature" that became his prime locus in *The Origin of Species,* where he noted in a typical passage that "the number and diversity of inheritable deviations of structure, both those of slight and those of considerable physiological importance, is endless."[14] Always in Darwin's writings there is an alert attention to deviations in nature. In a letter to Charles Lyell, for example, Darwin wrote excitedly of his discoveries with cirrepedes, or barnacles, which became the subject of an 1854 monograph he authored, observing that "the other day I got the curious case of a unisexual, instead of hermaphrodite, cirripede, in which the female had the common cirrepedal character, and in two of the valves of her shell had two little pockets, in each of which she kept a little husband; I do not know of any other case where a female invariably has two husbands.[15] In another barnacle he discovered fourteen "little husbands" inside a single female. The linguistic anthropomorphizing evident in Darwin's choice of the word "husband" quite aside, Darwin's delight in the discovery of female erotic dominance and vigor in nature is palpable. *The Descent of Man* evokes similar images of female potency and an attendant atypical sexuality in a text that accommodates a number of counternarratives of "purposeless" desire. As we shall see, Darwin's theory of sexual selection provided a model of courtship that implicitly questioned prevailing Victorian conceptions of the passive female and that rendered the conventional Victorian male, with his austere, well-managed attire, an aberration in history.

Historically, those late-Victorian and Edwardian writers who strove to win public acceptance for homosexual eros were reluctant to rely on Darwinian thought, preferring, as was the case with writers linked to the Aestheticist Movement, to link same-sex eros with earlier, "advanced" civilizations such as classical Rome and Greece. Perhaps for this reason, current histories of the origins of "homosexuality" as a unified conceptual term in the nineteenth century pay scant attention to Darwin's sexual theories. That the leading scientific figure of the Victorian period should have harbored no conception of the "unnatural" is an aspect of Darwin's lifelong intellectual project that deserves to be noted. He was a thoroughgoing empiricist, whose "hypothetico-deductive" method understood any phenomenon occurring in nature as, ipso facto, "natural." As Levine has noted of the general terms of Darwin's scientific methodology, the evolutionist diverges from his natural theological predecessors in large part because of his preoccupation with anomalies and aberrations.[16]

Such a methodology meant that strains of teleological "progressivism" in Darwinian thought were tempered by a countervailing attention to observable fact, relating events to cause and effect rather than to ultimate goals. In Darwin, notes Beer, "deviation, not truth to type, is the creative principle."[17] It therefore seems curious that while the theoretical propositions regarding sexuality informing *The Descent of Man* were receiving extraordinary attention at the precise moment when one finds a new conceptualization of sexual "deviance" in the medical sciences, Darwin himself never seems to have concerned himself with the possibilities of homosexual eros. Darwin's silence on the subject goes far in explaining the near-total neglect with which recent theorists of homosexuality have treated Darwin's ideas even as they extensively have attended to late-Victorian sexologists such as Havelock Ellis, Richard von Krafft-Ebing, and Edward Carpenter.[18] In marked contrast to Darwin, these turn-of-the-century sexologists found a human macrocosm in nature teeming with "deviant" phenomena. Yet it would be wrong to allow Darwin's apparent silence on the subject of "aberrant" eros to discourage us from extrapolating from his formulations what in fact comprises a telling (if obliquely conveyed) dimension in the history of same-sex desire.

Darwin's accent on protracted erotic play (broadly defined in *The De-*

scent to include all who strayed from the path of sexual selection) provides a link to late-Victorian aestheticism and its semi-covert dissident sexual politics. Through the potential for female misbehavior in deciding to prolong courtship or else *not* to choose a mate at all, Darwin implicitly located in sexual relations a dynamic whereby men and women might suspend or else altogether resist their evidently preordained roles in sexual courtship. Most importantly, the female arbitrators and dandified males posited in Darwin's scheme provide a vivid counternarrative to the shrunken, often diminished "cases" repeatedly taxonomized by Ellis and Krafft-Ebing, as well as by Freud later in the century, even though all of these figures were more progressive—and, in Ellis's case, activist—in their stated social positions than Darwin. In his philosophical relativism, in which a multiplicity of plots compete for attention, Darwin's depiction of a sexually varied natural kingdom strikes a distinctly postmodern chord.[19] Whereas nature in *The Origin* has been a series of struggles for dominance, in *The Descent* it had become a series of shifting weights and balances. Power not granted in the male economic domain is granted in the sweepstakes of courtship.[20]

If most scientists strove to relegate Darwin's theory of sexual selection to the intellectual dustbin, late-Victorian writers had anticipated and carefully calibrated the imaginative prospects of "dissident desire" through the constitution of coquetting males and females. Most importantly, in *The Descent of Man,* erotic coyness is linked to an overly developed aesthetic sense, in what proved for Darwin's readers one of the book's most troubling claims. In speculating as to why, say, a peahen should initially demonstrate a preference for particular colors or patterns on her prospective partner's tail, Darwin suggested that all such creatures had an inborn appreciation of beauty that (this Darwin could only imply) they shared with humans. Although, confronted with the ugliness of the turkey cock's waddle and the growing uproar over his suggestion of aesthetic impulses in animals, he later rejected the idea of a nonhuman "aesthetic," Darwin's enduring image of a natural realm informed by aesthetic determinations tapped into other ascendant Victorian intellectual currents.

Sexual selection's emergence as a scientific argument coincided with the rise of Paterian aestheticism. Two years after the publication of *The Descent of Man,* Walter Pater's *The Renaissance* (1873) had its own incendiary effect on contemporary audiences. Like Darwin, Pater conceived of evolutionary rises and falls in nature, expressed as a sustained, subjective conception of art history, in part derived from Johann Joachim Winckelmann, in which Western culture reveals distinct highs and lows, "phases" of creative "development" not unlike Darwinian evolutionary stages. The preface to *The Renaissance* offered a corollary between the phenomenon meriting aesthetic attention and nature's creation by asserting that the "objects with which aesthetic criticism deals . . . possess, like the output of nature, so many virtues or qualities."[21] Moreover, the originality of Pater's analysis lay in its insistence that aesthetic works produce sensations in individual *natures*, in a process that emphasized measurable physical reactions and ever-shifting natural forces. "What is this song or picture, this engaging personality, presented in a life or in a book, to *me?*" he asked in a series of rhetorical queries that opened *The Renaissance.* "What effect does it really produce on me? Does it give me pleasure? How is my nature modified by its presence, and under its influence?"[22] No doubt to protect himself against charges of emotionally charged hedonism, Pater's sensualism is expressed in the terms of a detached scientist seeking the natural principles by which pleasure was produced in an aesthetically sensitive individual. By the late 1800s, Pater's aestheticist principles had coalesced not only into a widely embraced philosophical system but, with Wilde's mounting fame, a politics of heterosexual renunciation and a concomitant subcultural homosexual enterprise across Europe.[23]

Some of these connections are evident in the opening pages of Marcel Proust's *Sodome et Gomorrhe* (1921) from *A la recherche du temp perdu,* where the narrator draws an explicit connection between Darwin's scenarios of cross-species courtship and homosexual flirting in describing the coded relations between Charlus and the tailor-turned-secretary Jupien: "I found the pantomime, incomprehensible to me at first, of Jupien and M. De Charlus as curious as those seductive gestures addressed, Darwin tells us, to insects by the flowers called composite which erect the florets of their capitula so as to be seen from a greater distance, like certain heterostyled flowers which turn back their stamens and bend them to open the way for the insect."[24] The contiguous bonds linking delayed eroticism, turn-of-the-century aestheticism, and homoerotic dandyism reach their apotheosis in the ostentatiously staged aloofness of Lord Henry in Wilde's *The Picture of Dorian Gray.* Darwin's theory of male self-fashioning in *The Descent* provided an inadvertent basis for this Wildean credo of a life luxuriously devoted to artifice, of sexuality emancipated from "purposeful" predilections. Although Oxford-based aesthetes clamorously eschewed Nature, Nature itself—or so *The Descent of Man* implied—offered a foundation for aestheticism.

As a tacit theorist of a naturalized aestheticism of consciously managed deferrals, Darwin relied on a matrix of nineteenth-century fictive texts in which protracted female desire, as well as a "feminine aesthetic," held sway. Not only did sexual selection as a scientific proposition date back to the work of Darwin's grandfather, Erasmus Darwin, but *The Descent of Man* simply lent scientific credence to a formulation that Victorian fictionalists long had made the central focus of their novelistic enterprises. That female choice might comprise a supercommanding element in courtship—and, more provocatively, that the female's power of choosing might endure after the successful completion of courtship and marriage—were notions that permeated the novels of a wide range of novelists of the 1870s and 1880s, not only in George Meredith's protofeminist works *The Egotist* (1876), *Diana of the Crossways* (1879), and *Beauchamp's Career* (1885), but in the more socially conservative novels of Trollope. As Beer comments in her discussion of Darwin's transformative cultural effects in the Victorian period, suddenly "topics traditional to the novel—courtship, sensibility, the making of matches, women's beauty, men's dominance, *inheritance* in all its forms—became charged with new difficulty."[25]

Given the pervasiveness of the flirtatious erotics of "female choice" as a key thematic component in Victorian fictional narrative well before the appearance of *The Descent of Man,* it is more than a little surprising that Darwin's suggestions concerning the aesthetics of female choosing should have proven so inimical to the thinking of his contemporaries.[26] The narratives of Victorian authors, published either before, contemporaneous with, or subsequent to the appearance of *The Descent of Man,* have as an animating fictional donnée what proved to be, not only for Victorian readers but for several subsequent generations of evolutionary theorists, the most recalcitrant feature of Darwin's argument in *The Descent of Man:* the proposition that female decision-making is an all-controlling element in relations between the sexes. Darwin's accent on delay was itself a staple of Victorian fictional form. Yeazell notes that like all necessarily circumspect Victorian fictionalists on matters of sex, the author of *The Descent* favored an incremental report of events leading to carnal acts, as opposed to a direct representation of those acts.

Throughout their work, both Eliot and Hardy made the subject of female choice the very engine of their fictions. George Eliot sought to integrate elements of flirting into her narratives of frustrated desire. Her gimlet-eyed taxonomy of Rosamond Vincy was as fierce a critique of a

prevailing model of female behavior as was Wollstonecraft's attack on
Rousseau's submissive coquettish woman. Still, Eliot repeatedly depicts
"aimless eros" as a momentary harmony, a carnal idyll existing outside
narrowly conceived arrangements between the sexes. In her portrait of the
"large-headed, long-limbed" Stephen Guest, "graceful and odiferous" owing to his upbringing on the "largest oil-mill and the most expansive wharf
in St. Ogg's," Eliot implied that an initial, jointly shared refusal to succumb to desire might soften the courting male, "feminizing" him without—and this is of great importance, given the feckless Philip Wakem's
proximity—rendering him, like Philip, a too-pallid, unappealing suitor.[27]
Flirtation thus serves to dissipate those sharp boundaries of gender that
Eliot so powerfully stressed elsewhere in *The Mill on the Floss*. For Stephen
and Maggie, accidentally caught in a "duet in paradise," flirting serves to
mitigate the infractible divisions that courtship and marriage only intensify.[28] Yet, for Eliot, the "great temptation" signified by flirting can
also serve sanctioned marital narratives. In *Middlemarch*, the two-couple
double plot momentarily intersects as Rosamond coquets with Will Ladislaw in the shadowy privacy of her home. Rosamond's brash toying is a climax of disclosure that facilitates a too-long-deferred choice, one Dorothea
initially refuses.

   With *Under the Greenwood Tree* (composed in 1871, the year of the publication of *The Descent of Man*, and published in 1872), Hardy was able to
render female coquetry as a tantalizing enterprise in a rustic setting, a female "treachery" that ultimately lacks the force to disturb male interests.
At most, Fancy's temporary acceptance of an offer of marriage from
Arthur Maybold, an act of which Fancy's fiancé Dick remains ignorant,
suggests hidden layers of feminine character that males, portrayed in *Under the Greenwood Tree* as bumptiously simple and single-minded, lack.
Yet only three years later, Hardy's perspective changed markedly. In *Far
from the Madding Crowd*, the novelist diagrammed sexual selection as a
rural tragedy of male rivalry turned explosive. In the figure of Bathsheba
Everdene, who owns her own farm and lords her beauty over three men,
Hardy could hardly have imagined a more dominating, capricious "Darwinian" female. Yet, in what suggests a respectful turn on Darwin's theorizing, it is not the prettiest male suitor, Sergeant Troy, who ultimately
thrives, nor is it the materially well-off Farmer Boldwood, but the unflashy
yet devoted shepherd Gabriel Oak, whose "virility" lies in his disinclination to play at rivalry. Hardy dramatized Darwin's point that not only masculine beauty but male vigor counted in the sexual sweepstakes of court-

ing. Later in his career as novelist, Hardy represents coy feminine choice as a never-ceasing display of feminine will that can only divide men from women, culminating in the tragedies of paralyzed decision in *Tess of the D'Urbervilles* and *Jude the Obscure* (1896). After the light pastoral brio of *Under the Greenwood Tree,* Hardy can never escape his increasingly pessimistic conclusion that flirtation functions in a harsh and sometimes deadly dynamic of erotic separation.

Darwin's impact on Victorian fictive practice went well beyond his influence on Hardy and Eliot. The connection between the implied "aestheticism" of Sergeant Troy or the dandiacal Stephen Guest and the dynamics of "purposeless" desire took on greater resonance at the fin de siècle. Even as the New Woman threatened socially proscribed paths, forced or electing to opt out of marriage, popular "theorists of love" such as the writer Grant Allen, emboldened by Darwinian ideas, insisted on the seamless connection between aestheticist practice and sexual courtship among humans. With the appearance of Gilbert and Sullivan's *Patience* (1881) and *The Mikado* (1885), one witnesses a satiric response to the premises of *The Descent of Man* and to the general cultural anxiety surrounding flirtation. Max Beerbohm's *Zuleika Dobson* adds another comic note, building an entire narrative on the premise that a commitment-averse femme fatale can devastate the male ruling class at Oxford and Cambridge. These works mock the cultural concerns over which the Victorian novel had brooded for nearly a century and with which Darwin had remained preoccupied until his death in 1882. The dandies of *Patience,* with their "languid love for lilies," like the self-preening males of *The Descent of Man,* always risk turning courtship into mere spectacle. Similarly, in the madcap kingdom of *The Mikado,* flirting has been declared a capital offense even as ostentatiously feathered samurai—like Darwin's exotically plumed male birds—are compelled to flirt with the widest array of females (and vice versa). As the sportive scientific writings of Grant Allen and the satiric burlesque of Gilbert and Sullivan together suggest, the anxieties generated by "coquetting" in works of high literary art are the stuff of irreverent mirth when transported to the realm of popular culture.

THE DESCENT OF MAN AND THE PROTRACTION OF FEMALE CHOICE

it is very amusing to see these little creatures . . . coquetting together. . . . The female pretends to run away and the male runs after her with

> a queer appearance of anger, gets in front and stands facing her again;
> then she turns coyly round, but he, quicker and more active, scuttles
> round too, and seems to whip her with his antennae; then for a bit they
> stand face to face, play with their antennae, and seem to be all in all to
> one another.
>
> —Sir J. Lubbock, as quoted in *The Descent of Man* (1871)

According to *The Descent of Man,* sexual selection, much like natural selection, was a frequently fierce struggle that involved competition for the
limited resources necessary for the sustaining of life. Not simply a minor
subcategory of natural selection, sexual selection acted as a prime mechanism for the perpetuation of a species. Nonetheless, there was a significant
difference in the implications of *The Origin of Species* and *The Descent of
Man,* however intricately intertwined their scientific theses. The arguments posited in *The Origin of Species* might or might not be interpreted
as harboring implications for humans, for the book's "evidence" for evolutionary change could be seen only after a careful examination of modifications occurring over exceedingly long periods of time. This was much
less the case with the theory of sexual selection, however, which sought to
elucidate the observed courting habits of creatures in the natural world in
a way that easily could be (and was) viewed as paralleling Victorian relations between the sexes.

It was the entwined questions of *female dominance* and *male beauty* that
rendered Darwin's propositions so problematic for his contemporaries.
For Darwin had not merely emphasized the role of female choice; he had
also suggested that in the heightened sexual contest of courtship, female
judgment would determine the fates of particular men. Maintaining that
all of the distinctions between the sexes originated in an attempt to attract
the opposite sex, Darwin had outlined two basic forms of sexual selection,
called "male competition" and "female choice." Referring specifically to
the example of antlered deer, Darwin claimed that males primp and compete aggressively for females in the breakneck process of procreation. *The
Descent* suggested too that sexual selection lay at the very origins of observable phenomena and that the degree of female choice surpassed all
expectations.

> With respect to . . . sexual selection (which with the lower animals is much
> the most common), namely, when the females are the selectors, and accept
> only those males which excite or charm them most, we have reason to believe
> that it formerly acted on the progenitors of man. Man in all probability owes

his beard, and perhaps some other characteristics, to inheritance from an ancient progenitor who gained in this manner his ornaments. But this form of selection may have occasionally acted during later times; for in utterly barbarous tribes the women have more power in choosing, rejecting and tempting their lovers, or of afterwards changing their husbands, than might have been expected.[29]

The shift from a discussion of "lower animals" to "utterly barbarous tribes" leaves no doubt that Darwin wished to make the case for sexual selection among humans by an argument *de animalibus.* That the degree of power held by these "barbarous" women in choosing a mate, rejecting husbands, and selecting new ones "surpassed all expectations" provided a rebuke, on anthropological grounds, to assumptions prepotent in Victorian society regarding the universality of male dominance in heterosexual courtship. Striking too is the sense in this passage that female decision-making in sexual selection does not end with an initial choice but is a power held in reserve *after* marriage.

As Stephen Jay Gould comments, sexual selection posits repeated scenarios in which "males strut and preen, display and bellow, and females choose to mate with the individuals that impress them the most. Peacocks, in other words, do not evolve their showy tails for direct victory in battle over other males, but to win a beauty contest run by females."[30] Male charm and attractiveness (as displayed before the standard-determining female) were thus explained by Darwin as defining elements in the evolutionary process:

> As the illustrious Hunter long ago observed, [the female] generally "requires to 'be courted'"; she is coy, and may often be seen endeavoring for a long time to escape from the male. Every one who has attended to the habits of animals will be able to call to mind instances of this kind. Judging from various facts, hereafter to be given, and from the results which may fairly be attributed to sexual selection, the female, though comparatively passive, generally exerts some choice and accepts one male in preference to others. Or she may accept, as appearances would sometimes lead us to believe, not the male which is most attractive to her, but the one which is the least distasteful. The exertion of some choice on the part of the female seems almost as general a law as the eagerness of the male.[31]

The Descent of Man conceived of female behavior as fundamentally coquettish, perpetually delaying a procedure that the male, single-mindedly fixed on one erotic plot, speeds to a conclusion.

Repeatedly in *The Descent,* Darwin insisted that males possessed stronger erotic passions than females. In one of those familiar fictions that the Victorians bequeathed even to a post-Freudian twentieth century, Darwin repeatedly depicted females as seeking to repel an aggressive male. And although Darwin's much-repeated proposition that female coyness stemmed from a basic inequity in sexual interest was hardly scandalous to those nineteenth-century readers accustomed to images of female sexual passivity and purity, the evolutionist's key ancillary contention—that males might need to render themselves ornately bedazzling (not just tastefully attractive) for a female chooser—did undermine a potent strain of prevailing Victorian *doxa*. While Darwin's depiction of a coyly calculating female unburdened by an appreciable libido seemed to mimic Manichean Victorian notions of a demonic vixen wedded to a virtuous maiden, the portrait of the male encouraged by *The Descent* was far more startling. The most successful males, according to Darwin, were not necessarily the "vigorous" or "best armed" but rather the "most attractive." And although Darwin did acknowledge that with sexual selection factors such as physical prowess were important, he explained that "females are most excited by, or prefer pairing with, the most ornamented males, or those which are the best songsters, or play the best antics."[32]

Even as *The Descent* was carefully evasive as to the implications of sexual selection for his contemporaries, Darwin gave a historical cast to his theory of sexual selection by affirming that males had succeeded in assuming a social and erotic superiority that once (precisely when, Darwin left unclear) had been denied to them in nature. But if this feminocentric moment in the history of sexual relations, in which females required that males vie for their attention, had a past, there was little comfort to Darwin's readers in the intimation that male dominance had come about only because an earlier, natural order had been inverted by the effects of "civilization." As Beer points out, "Darwin's reversal of the common order in making man the selector drew attention to the social constituents in human descent as opposed to other species." Darwin, according to Beer, "intensified and unsettled long-used themes and turned them into new problems."[33] Most alarmingly for his contemporary audience, Darwin intimated that the male's need to please a potentially fickle female could disrupt natural selection—as certain males devoted excessive energy to the frenetic game of sexual selection: "The development . . . of certain structures—of the horns, for instance, in certain stags—has been carried to a wonderful extreme; and in some instances to an extreme, which, as far as the general conditions of life are concerned, must be slightly injurious to the male."[34]

Such remarks were consistent with Darwin's observation that certain birds, exhausted by the demands of sexual selection, simply drop out of the courtship process. The evident implication was that the deferring female, unable or unwilling to arrive at a decision, inaugurates an extravagantly rigorous competition among males that may reduce the capacities of survival of individual males, if not an entire species populations. Thus, female indecisiveness—determined not by desire or sexual need but by a female "aesthetic" of choice—could be prolonged unendingly as males, in a contrapuntal reaction, preen and offer themselves unceasingly. By implication, then, Darwin's theorizing concerning sexual selection could be read as raising certain kinds of female flirtation to the level of a superdetermining dimension in the evolution of a given species. It was a process that in conventional Victorian terms feminized the male as it situated the female as the activist in erotic relations.

For Darwin, the moment in which the female of a species reached a resolution concerning a potential mate's suitability was decisive in determining which males would succeed or fail in sexual negotiations. From one perspective, then, sexual selection, like the ferocious conflicts cited on nearly every page of *The Origin of Species,* was a life-and-death struggle. As Gertrude Himmelfarb has pointed out, the variations employed for sexual selection "had the effect of favoring individuals not in the struggle for existence but in the struggle for females. Yet death was still, ultimately, the penalty for failure."[35] More accurately, death is the penalty for failure in terms of the evolution for *populations;* for individuals, however, the disadvantage is that certain individuals in a given species are denied the opportunity to reproduce. In the final analysis, however, certain populations with useless or "unpopular" traits simply would die out. Not only was the exercising of female choice of incalculable importance in the species continuance, but the failure of that choice—or its possible protraction—held potentially disastrous consequences.

Those objecting to Darwin's ideas continually ignored the historical component of Darwin's thesis, in which the female chooser had been consigned to the past. Instead, such critics chose to register the claims of *The Descent* as hinting at a world lying just below the surface of civilization in which female caprice could cause trouble for males in the erotic realm. While the notion of male competition struck most of Darwin's

Victorian audience as entirely acceptable, the proposal that in the natural world the female might enjoy a substantial (if temporary) reign of power was unthinkable. In insisting that nature required males to preen before a female chooser, Darwin struck many of his critics as positioning men in a role that by late-Victorian standards was disturbingly and effeminately dandiacal.

The larger part of those who denied the validity of the theory of sexual selection saw in it the vexing possibility of unchecked, escalating female power over male fate utterly dependent on "feminine" taste. "Shall we assume that . . . those females whose taste has soared a little higher than those of the average (a variation of their sort having appeared) select males to correspond, and thus the two continue heaping up the ornaments on one side and the appreciation on the other?" asked the evolutionary theorist T. H. Morgan in his *Evolution and Adaptation* (1903), conjuring up a female of ever-infinite aesthetic discriminations. "No doubt an interesting fiction could be built up along these lines, but would anyone believe it, and if he did, could he prove it?"[36] As Gould remarks, sexual selection theory has witnessed an antagonistic reception among the majority of evolutionary scientists until only twenty years ago primarily for two reasons: first, while male competition among various species struck most of Darwin's readership as, in Gould's words, "doin' what comes naturally," female choice required an additional mental step that seemed too close to cognitive abilities supposedly unique to humans. Notes Gould: "Females must survey a field and make a judgment based on some aesthetic criterion of beauty in sight or sound. Most biologists weren't willing to grant such capacity to animals." Furthermore, Gould argues, most evolutionary biologists were exceedingly reluctant to "place females in the driver's seat of evolutionary change" as is required by the reasoning behind Darwin's theory of sexual selection.[37] In fact, Darwin's argument did harbor a troublesome gap, for the author of *The Descent* did not so much explain the origins of female choice as simply point to its prevalence in nature.

For those of Darwin's contemporaries polemically opposed to social advances for women, Darwin's assertions as outlined in *The Origin of Species* had proved of salutary value, as was demonstrated by many of their responses to Darwin's theories. In *The Evolution of Sex* (1889), Patrick Geddes and J. Arthur Thomson soberly observed that "What was decided among the prehistoric Protozoa cannot be annulled by Act of Parliament."[38] Writing in the decades after the publication of *The Descent of Man,* however, Herbert Spencer, once a supporter of the abolition of legal restrictions that kept women tied to the domestic sphere, registered the fear that women might act as a dominant political force, just as in *The Descent* females functioned as a self-interested group. Women, he maintained with evident pessimism, "would increase the ability of public agencies to override individual rights in the pursuit of what were thought beneficent ends." Spencer, whose 1854 essay "Physical Beauty" celebrated the connection between what he considered women's superior physical attributes and what he took to be their innate qualities of goodness, altruism, and maternal generosity, was undoubtedly alarmed to see Darwin turn such propositions on their head. For the author of *The Descent of Man,* the world pivoted on the entwined issues of *male* beauty and a female "choosing" consciousness.[39] What fed male anxieties in the wake of Darwin's "discoveries," however, also gave new impetus to feminist ambitions.

VICTORIAN FEMINISM, FEMALE CONSCIOUSNESS, AND THE DESCENT OF MAN

> She stopped the horses, and Baker, a very completely-got-up-groom of some forty years of age, who sat behind, got down and put the impetuous Dandy "in the bar," thereby changing the rein, so that the curb was brought to bear on him. "They're called Dandy and Flirt," continued Lady Glencora, speaking to Alice. "Ain't they a beautiful match?"
> —Anthony Trollope, *Can You Forgive Her?* (1866)

While Darwin's speculations concerning female choice remained controversial in the scientific community until only recently, feminist thinkers, almost alone among those writing on *The Descent of Man,* welcomed the evolutionist's depiction of female supremacy in sexual courtship. If Darwin could reject feminist principles out of hand (dismissing, for instance, J. S. Mill's arguments for women's emancipation in *The Subjection of Women* as "unscientific"[40]), there was material in Darwinian evolutionary theory for Victorian feminist theory. In a relatively overlooked chapter in the history of the reception of Darwinian thought, writers associated with the suffragette movement regarded the scenario posited by *The Descent of Man* as a compelling model for more egalitarian social arrangements between the sexes.

In *The Evolution of Women* (1894), for example, Eliza Gamble remarked that the "female is the primary unit of creation, and that the male functions are simply supplemental or complementary." Although she found fault with much of Darwin's thinking, Gamble saw the scientist as having "proved by seemingly well established facts that the female organization is freer from imperfections than the male, and that it is less liable to derangements."[41] Several years later, in her landmark feminist study exploring the seemingly intractable economic causes for the diminished place of women in society, *Women and Economics: A Study of the Economic Relation between Men and Women As a Factor in Social Evolution* (1898), Charlotte Perkins (later Charlotte Perkins Gilman) discerned in the Darwinian plot of sexual selection a recognition of the female's once-powerful position in the natural kingdom. It was not nature that consigned women to secondary status, according to Perkins, but rather the "inordinate greed of our industrial world" that had adulterated nature's laws and that had displaced females from their rightful place as choosers. In Perkins's view, history was a dispiriting, downward narrative for the female, in which the brutalizing rites and primitive tournaments of the Middle Ages stood as a civilized exemplum in comparison to the dehumanized conditions of women in the nineteenth century. In the Middle Ages, Perkins argued, men, fully accepting their proper roles as objects of female approval, "fought under the cry 'Fight on, brave knights! Fair eyes are looking on you!'"[42]

For the utopian-socialist Perkins, such a relatively elementary cultural practice represented a "healthier process" than the modern-day marital marketplace, with its crass reduction of the individual to his or her monetary value. "Competition among males, with selection by the female of the superior male, is the process of sexual selection, and works to racial improvement," Perkins wrote approvingly of Darwin's thesis concerning sexual selection. "So far as the human male competes freely with his peers in higher and higher activities," she wrote, "and the female chooses the winner, so far we are directly benefitted. But there is a radical distinction between sex-competition and marriage by purchase. In the first the male succeeds by virtue of what he can do; in the second, by virtue of what he can get."[43] Thus Perkins nostalgically tried to evoke a once-dominant era of female selecting that previously had triumphed over "market values," a sort of lost Atlantis in the relations between men and women. This fantasy of female ascendance was shared by progressive-minded late-Victorian sexologists. Havelock Ellis, for example, held high hopes that a recognition of female power in sexual selection eventually would mean that women would "choose" to benefit the race. "The changing status of women," wrote the noted sexologist, "in bestowing economic independence, will certainly restore to sexual selection its due weight in human development."[44] On the other hand, the likely if inadvertent double entendre in Darwin's title—"descent" as genealogy but also as a fall in stature—may not have been lost on those who grasped Darwin's augmenting of the female role.

Sexual selection, then, was precisely the "intelligent direction" of nature that the Victorian writer John Herschel had found disturbingly absent in *The Origin of Species,* whose philosophical system Herschel mocked as positing a "law of higgledy piggledy." If Darwin, through his stress on random forces, typically "seemed to risk turning the world into an accident" (as George Levine notes), then the choosing, flirting female believes that at the social level, accidents in nature can be corrected through the clever exercising of her erotic power.[45] Nonetheless, for Darwin's contemporaries the most troubling problem fostered by *The Descent* was its suggestion that a well-developed aesthetic—and a female one at that—operated throughout nature. This was a point about which *The Descent* was often contradictory and with which Darwin remained preoccupied all through the last decade of his life. "The taste for the beautiful, at least as far as female beauty is concerned, is not of a special nature in the human mind," he had observed in *The Descent,* adding cautiously that "Obviously no animal would be capable of admiring such scenes as the heavens at night, a beautiful landscape, or refined music" and that "such high tastes, depending as they do on culture and complex associations, are not enjoyed by barbarians or by uneducated persons."[46]

To those who contested his attribution of an aesthetic sense to animals, Darwin replied by explaining that the aesthetic choice exercised by animals differed in kind from that employed by humans: "When an intense colour, or two tints in harmony, or a recurrent and symmetrical figure pleases the eye, or a single sweet note pleases the ear, I call this a sense of beauty," he wrote John Morley shortly after the publication of *The Descent:*

> and with this meaning I have spoken (though I now see in not a sufficiently guarded manner) of a taste for the beautiful being the same in mankind (for all savages admire bits of bright cloth, beads, plumes, etc.) and in the lower animals. If the blue and yellow plumage of a macaw pleases the eye of this

bird, I should say that it had a sense of beauty, although its taste was bad according to our standard.[47]

Such comments raised more questions than they settled, however, since Darwin's distinction between a supposedly crudely developed animal aesthetic sense and a more refined human aesthetic rested on a somewhat dubious single standard of the beautiful—and one that increasingly was imperiled with Pater's articulation, beginning in the 1870s, of an aesthetic determined not by a universal criteria but by personal "impressions." (Thus, it theoretically would take, in Paternian terms, only a single individual's declaration of aesthetic pleasure in the blue and yellow plumage of a macaw for Darwin's differentiation between human and animal aesthetic senses to collapse.) Nor did *The Descent*'s repeated reliance on analogies gleaned not simply from human courtship practices but from supposedly "elevated" achievements in the arts help to dispel a sense that Darwin had located a "human" aesthetic dimension in beasts. At one juncture in his argument, for instance, Darwin insisted that the ball-and-socket effect brought about by natural selection at first seemed as incredible as the likelihood that "one of Raphael's Madonnas should have been formed by the selection of chance forms of daubs of paint."[48] The evolutionist's self-critical gesture, hazarding that he should have been more "guarded" in his elucidation of an animal aesthetic, suggests, furthermore, that the ambivalence of his remarks on this problem was less a matter of indecision than the cagey exercising of professional tact.

Likewise, on the even more problematic matter of female motivation, Darwin remained intriguingly contradictory, as in this passage from the 1874 revised edition of *The Descent of Man*:

What then are we to conclude from these facts and considerations? Does the male parade his charms with so much pomp and rivalry for no purpose? Are we not justified in believing that the female exerts a choice, and that she receives the addresses of the male who pleases her most? It is not probable that she consciously deliberates; but she is most attracted by the most beautiful, or melodious, or gallant males. Nor need it be supposed that the female studies each stripe or spot of color; that the pea hen, for instance, admires each detail in the gorgeous train of the peacock—she is probably struck only by the general effect. Nevertheless, after hearing how carefully the male Argus pheasant displays his elegant primary wing-feathers and erects his ocellated plumes in the right position for their full effect; or again, how the male goldfinch alternately displays his gold-bespangled wings, we ought not to feel too sure that the female does not attend to each detail of beauty. We can judge, as already remarked, of choice being exerted, only from analogy, and the mental powers of birds do not differ fundamentally from ours.[49]

Darwin struggles to resist the temptation to infer that human faculties can be attributed to animals, yet his own evident astonishment at the multiplicity of ornamentation in the service of animal courtship persuades him that such a conclusion may be necessary. The evolutionist's uncertainty on this point is palpable. For difficult as it was for Darwin to imagine powers of aesthetic judgment in beasts, the sheer variety of male allurements argues for precisely such highly developed powers, particularly in the "choosing" female. His hesitation in considering this problem of motivation in the female, meanwhile, invited a possible psychological view of the female chooser as involuntarily, unwittingly directed in the elaborate rituals of sexual selection.

At another point in *The Descent,* Darwin maintained that the female was superdiscriminating in her attention to male allurements. After deploying a remarkable artillery of evidence in support of his theory of sexual selection, Darwin rhetorically asked his readers if he had not in fact presented a strong case for sexual selection. Through his frequent reliance on explicit or implicit analogies to human psychology and customs, he clearly indicated that his findings held implications for humans. "We can judge . . . of choice being exerted, only from the analogy of our own minds," he argued at one point, ". . . and the mental powers of birds, if reason be excluded, do not differ fundamentally from ours. . . . If this be admitted, there is not much difficulty in understanding how male birds have gradually acquired their ornamental characters."[50] Animals were as unpredictably fickle, as slavishly susceptible to trends in clothes, as the Victorian lady of means or the increasingly visible dandy: "It would even appear that mere novelty, or change for the sake of change, has sometimes acted like a charm on female birds, in the same manner as changes of fashion with us."[51]

In a last defensive gesture at explaining the precepts outlined in *The Descent,* delivered in 1882 before the London Zoological Society a few months before his death, Darwin backed down from his view of the role of intensified "female consciousness" in sexual selection. "It would . . . be more accurate to speak of females as being excited or attracted in an especial degree by the appearance, voice and conduct of certain males, rather than deliberately selecting them."[52] The quandary presented by the idea that animals could exercise aesthetic choice depended on the question of whether the female animal was consciously or unconsciously motivated in her judgments. By continually hedging on this fundamental issue, Darwin appeared to be advocating an extraordinary notion: that aesthetic choices were not related to the "complex associations" of culture but to unconscious processes outside mankind's acculturating province. If the female seemed to lack a full-fledged libido, she nonetheless harbored a highly evolved aesthetic drive in comparison to which the male had substantially diminished capacities. Darwin appeared to be robbing females of sexual impulses, but their consolation prize was that he granted them a fantastic repertoire of taste-determining capabilities. The male found himself reduced to an "animal nature," but the female looked more like a Victorian citizen of consummate deportment and taste—endlessly restrained, patient, and keenly discerning.

Why did the notion that the female might coyly, painstakingly judge men—that flirtatious delay in exercising a consciously deployed aesthetic choice was to be considered the female's proper domain in nature—continue to trouble Darwin? Beyond grasping the danger of anthropomorphizing an aesthetic faculty in nonhuman females, Darwin seemed concerned about the potential for unendingly elaborate acts of taste-making on the part of the female. In an addendum to *The Descent of Man* that appeared in *Nature,* entitled "Sexual Selection in Relation to Monkeys" (1876), Darwin retreated from the terms of his initial argument regarding female choice, drawing a distinction between excitement or attraction and a faculty of judgment, yet he unwittingly managed to affirm his depiction of conscious aesthetic discernment. Writing of the brightly colored hinder halves of monkeys, the evolutionist wrote:

> It has been objected that this form of selection, as far as the ornaments of males are concerned, implies that all females within the same district must possess and exercise exactly the same taste. It should, however, be observed in the first place, that although the range of variation of a species may be very large, it is by no mean indefinite. . . . Therefore the females of natural species cannot have an unlimited scope for their taste. In the second place, I presume that no supporter of the principle of sexual selection believes that the females select particular points of beauty in the males; they are merely excited or attracted in a greater degree by one male than by another, and this seems often to depend, especially with birds, on brilliant colouring. Even man, excepting perhaps an artist, does not analyze the slight differences in the features of the woman whom he may admire, on which her beauty depends.[53]

Darwin's anxiety is palpable, as he ends by inadvertently affirming links between the female and what he elsewhere posits as the highest species of man, that of the "artist."

The minimizing of female desire in *The Descent of Man* nonetheless could allow females a more successful role in assuming the upper hand with regard to another law essential to Darwinian thought, the rules of chance. Chance, of course, plays a major part in Darwin's theory of natural selection. For the amorous game-player, coquetry is a means of both multiplying choice and controlling chance in a programmatic strategy for insuring that the universe obeys human directives. The successful flirt seeks to place herself *above* desire, in effect intensifying Darwin's conception of female eros as slight but also, not least important, turning Darwin's theory against itself: if female desire pales in comparison to masculine eros, the strategy of the coquette intimated that it also freed the female to save herself by placing herself in a position of far-seeing control. "Chance" may have played a part in the marriage of Becky Sharp to the financially reckless Rawdon Crawley, but Becky believes (and in many ways the whole thrust of *Vanity Fair* cynically comes to affirm) that she can rectify the unfortunate fiscal condition that chance has assigned her through an astute display of interest in Lord Steyne and later, Jos Sedley. A flirt with a heightened sense of professionalism such as Becky continually must calculate into her strategy an understanding of society as composed of random, shifting forces. Ultimately, however, she cannot believe that the social realm is monolithically *dominated* by them in a strict Darwinian sense or else her carefully calibrated strategic maneuverings are pointless.

From an economic standpoint, in her faith that her own powers of erotic persuasion will triumph over the naïve Amelia Sedley, Becky Sharp is not only the Victorian flirt as capitalist entrepreneur, she is, in a prescient apprehension of *The Descent of Man* and its social ramifications, one of nineteenth-century fiction's fiercest social Darwinists; in an uncertain, unstable, and competitive economic market, where a spouse's money may evaporate overnight, the survival of the fittest depends on the careful multiplication of potential lovers who may come to serve as husbands, or at the very least, future providers of income. At the same time, the flirting female might tease her male suitors out of sheer mischief, quite independently of financial burden. The eponymous heroine of Shaw's *Candida* (1895) is no femme fatale, yet she impulsively introduces a rival into her financially serene marriage to the Reverend James Mavor Morell, threatening her husband's well-burnished confidence. That Candida's lover is a poet echoes a long Victorian tradition in which aesthete-charmers wooed conflicted heroines, yet Shaw's New Woman views all men as hopelessly self-preening. "You vain thing!" Candida tauntingly tells her husband. "Are you so sure of your irresistible attractions?" The bereaved Morell can only reply with worn-put pieties: "Candida: you are shocking me. I never thought of my attractions. I thought of your goodness, of your purity."[54]

The multiplicity of scenarios revolving around female choice and male preening fostered in Victorian fiction—both before and after the appearance of *The Descent*—militates against the insistence on the part of critics such as Yeazell and Jahn that sexual selection encompassed a univocal, happily negotiated courtship chronicle. With an ungovernable power that startled the evolutionist himself, Darwin's speculations exfoliated into innumerable story lines, none of them comprising a monolithic narrative. One "unnatural" plot that intersected with and drew inspiration from Darwin's postulations was late-Victorian aestheticism, seemingly divorced from scientific concerns yet the logical next phase in the history of Darwinian sexual selection.

QUEER DARWIN: SEXUAL SELECTION AND VICTORIAN AESTHETICISM

> Ethics, like natural selection, makes existence possible. Aesthetics, like sexual selection, makes life lovely and wonderful, fill it with new forms, and give it progress, and variety and change.
> — Oscar Wilde, "The Critic as Artist" (1890)

In *The Mikado,* the concerns of aestheticism and unfulfilled eros come to a spectacular head.[55] The impact of Darwin's thinking, in which chance and female choice are of all-determining importance in species survival, is continually spoofed. Gilbert and Sullivan luxuriate in registering the courtship processes by which humans must dazzle one another:

> Braid the raven hair—
> Weave the supple tress—
> Deck the maiden fair,
> In her loveliness—
> Paint the pretty face—
> Dye the coral lip—
> Emphasize the grace
> Of her ladyship!

> Art and nature, thus allied,
> Go to make a pretty bride.[56]

The ban on flirtation comes down to the censoring of specific acts, from the difficult to perceive to the laughably impossible to detect:

> This stern decree, you'll understand,
> Caused great dismay throughout the land!
>   For young and old
>   And shy and bold
>   Were equally affected.
> The youth who winked a roving eye,
> Or breathed a non-connubial sigh,
> Was thereupon condemned to die—
>   He usually objected.[57]

That Katisha should insist what a Mikado should enforce—namely, that arbitrary commitments are written in stone—becomes equally absurd. Exotically plumed male birds—like exotically dressed samurai—*should* flirt with the widest array of females in a new, Darwinian world. Meanwhile, the music of *The Mikado* has its own lilting, titillating scheme. For while flirtations are banned in Titipu, Sullivan's score teases us with romantic constructions that Gilbert's verbal text only dissipates. Koko's song about the little tom-tit is really perfect for Katisha and also for the listener who can warble the music yet who must become deaf to the belief in a one-to-one "fidelity" the words articulate.

If Gilbert and Sullivan turned the anxieties generated by aestheticism and unfulfilled eros into popular satire, the more scientifically minded continued to register their distress with Darwin's "insights." It was not simply the "choosing" female whom Darwin had portrayed as crucially directing nature in *The Descent of Man*. Darwin's study lent a fresh sense of urgency to the importance of the strategy-conscious male who carefully preened himself. As I have been arguing, it was around the question of male self-fashioning that the most strident objections to Darwin's ideas arose in the years after the publication of *The Origin of Species*. In his study *Darwinism* (1889), an otherwise sympathetic self-described "exposition" of Darwin's ideas, Wallace pointedly eschewed the theory of sexual selection. In a leap to human relations that Darwin repeatedly had left only tacit, Wallace catalogued male self-primping through the ages but asserted that while women admire their "sweethearts" for their "ornaments," they do not marry their mates on account of them.

> A young man, when courting, brushes or curls his hair, and has his mous-
> tache, beard or whiskers in perfect order, and no doubt his sweetheart ad-
> mires them; but this does not prove that she marries him on account of these
> ornaments, still less that hair, beard, whiskers, and moustache were devel-
> oped by the continued preferences of the female sex. So, a girl likes to see her
> lover well and fashionably dressed, and he always dresses as well as he can
> when he visits her; but we cannot conclude from this the whole series of male
> costumes, from the brilliantly coloured, puffed and slashed doublet and hose
> of the Elizabethan period, through the gorgeous coats, long waistcoats and
> pigtails of the early Georgian era, down to the funereal dress-suit of the pres-
> ent day, are the direct result of female preference.[58]

Nowhere did Wallace provide a foundation for the pervasiveness of the
empirically verifiable male self-preening he colorfully identified except,
presumably, in "culture." Wallace's lush, detailed cataloguing of male self-
fashioning over the centuries arguably comprised empirical evidence for
the prevalence in history of a phenomenon without an evident cause, in
comparison to which the austere Victorian male dress suit was itself, presumably, an historical aberration. Indeed, in Darwinian terms, the austerity of the period's male attire might signal male unavailability and nonre-
production. In short, Victorian male self-display hinted at the refusal of
men to take a role in courting, rendering the typical Englishman far more
"sexless" than his polyamorous female counterpart, with her restless stirring up of masculine insecurities.

It remains curious that the implied links between human and animal
behavior as expanded upon in *The Descent* became such a heated issue for
Darwin's critics. After all, in *The Origin of Species,* Darwin repeatedly had
analogized in the direction of human behavior in making his points about
the nonhuman world. As John R. Durant notes, sexual selection "was simply the most overtly voluntaristic interpretation of a fundamentally anthropomorphic analogy between nature and human artifice."[59] The most
obvious explanation of the massively hostile response to *The Descent* is
that this time it was male self-preening that was the focus of Darwin's
key analogy. The late-Victorian cultural backlash against aestheticism encompassed an agitated response to the aesthetes' excessive investment in
dressing up. (Thus, the Victorian critic Robert Buchanan denounced the
French writer Théophile Gautier as "that hairdresser's dummy of a stylist,
with a complexion of hectic pink and waxen white, his well-oiled wig, and
his incommunicable scent of the barber's shop."[60])

The beliefs and aspirations of the Aestheticist Movement were given a
striking scientific foundation with the dissemination of Darwin's theories

of sexual selection. Before the publication of Darwin's *Descent of Man,* writers seeking to legitimize iconoclastic forms of eroticism sought sustenance in Enlightenment philosophy, with its valorization of a completely independent sovereign subjectivity associated with Greek art and culture. Although from a strictly philosophical perspective the premises of aestheticism did not necessarily harbor intimations of homosexual desire, Victorian aesthetes searching for a philosophical basis in German thought for a homoerotically inflected aestheticism garnered support from Kantian theories. Kant's central claim concerning works of art—that they are disinterested, "pure," and that they bespeak a second nature through human agency—carried a covert carnal undercurrent for sexual dissidents. If "second nature" were conceived of in erotic terms, the concept might imply the doubling that was such a crucial component of Victorian homosexual identity. Kant's view of art as "purposiveness without purpose," moreover, might be adapted to the view that procreative sexuality was inessential to a substantive existence. Kierkegaard's negative diagnosis of "aesthetic man" in *Either/Or* (1864) contrasted the man of aesthetic commitments with ethical man because of the former's absorption in a series of moods to which he completely surrenders himself. In a rebuttal of Paterian aesthetics several years before Pater himself articulated them, Kierkegaard criticized aesthetic man because of his refusal to assume a single, coherent personality. Without ever alluding to homosexual eros, Kierkegaardian ideas gave a certain ideological framework for a life devoted to "amoral" impulses. The schism between moral austerity and an aesthetically based detachment from convention identified by Kierkegaard was one that homosexually inclined writers frequently chose as the very subject of their treatment of aestheticist enterprises—Wilde in *The Picture of Dorian Gray,* most notably. With Darwin's principle of sexual selection, however, moral and aesthetic categories had a far more productive relationship. Ventriloquizing through his character Gilbert in "The Critic as Artist," Wilde insisted, *pace* Kant, that ethics and aesthetics worked in tandem, much as Darwin had seen natural selection as functioning in consort with sexual selection. "Ethics, like natural selection, made existence possible," as Wilde declared, but it was sexual selection that rendered that existence more than possible. Transforming the functional into the "lovely and wonderful," sexual selection suggested that Nature, like Wilde's ideal critic, rendered aesthetic judgments independent of some limited, "human" morality.

The protoaestheticist dimension in Darwinian thought is palpably apparent in the journals recounting Darwin's 1831–36 voyage aboard the

Beagle, first published in 1839, which tell of his visits to South America and Australia. The affable twenty-two-year-old naturalist who embarked on these travels is a receptive, easily distracted connoisseur of natural mutations, less a scientist with a unified scientific theory than an aimless dandy equipped with an enormous capacity for taking aesthetic pleasure in natural observation. Writing of chirping Hyla frogs in Rio de Janeiro, Darwin comments that "Nature, in these climes, chooses her vocalists from more humble performers than in Europe. . . . When several [frogs] were together they sung in harmony on different notes. Various cicadae and crickets, at the same time, kept up a ceaseless shrill cry, but which, softened by the distance, was not unpleasant. Every evening after dark this great concert commenced; and often have I sat listening it, until my attention has been drawn away by some curious passing insect." [61] Primitive nature functions splendidly as aesthetic distraction for this European exile, rivaling Europe in its "selection" of singers. In the journals of the *Beagle,* moreover, Darwin reveals himself to be a young explorer of proto-decadent impulses, who locates in dead glowworms (who in life emitted the "most brilliant flashes when irritated") "luminous property nearly twenty four hours after" their death. When the "insect was decapitated," Darwin observes with an almost boyish absorption in his specimens, "the rings remained uninterruptedly bright, but not so brilliant as before." [62] Not unlike the hero of Joris-Karl Huysmans's influential novel of decadent sensibility *A Rebours* (1884), who watches a tortoise inlaid with jewels slowly die and then assume a tantalizing afterlife as a favorite totem, Darwin reveals the aesthete's naïve heartlessness, aesthetic man's taste for beautiful dead curiosities.

It was, however, Darwin's theorizing in *The Descent of Man* concerning courtship that most powerfully transformed German philosophical abstractions concerning the aesthetic realm into recognizable erotic plots in which intrigues, rivalry, and breakneck conflict ruled. [63] A crucial figure in the accommodation of aestheticist precepts to Darwinian science was the popular Victorian writer Grant Allen, who over the years had provided upbeat journalistic glosses on Darwin's more controversial formulations. [64] Allen wrote rhapsodically throughout the 1880s of the evolutionist's speculations on sexual selection, although he later fell under the more reactionary influence of Herbert Spencer. Gillian Beer claims that Allen's suggestion in 1882 that "beautiful" should be the "healthy, the normal, the strong, the perfect" tacitly endorses eugenics. Allen's beliefs more properly may be understood as part of the history of aestheticism. [65] In his light

"A thing of beauty is a joy for ever."
Oscar Wilde.

THE BRITISH FUNGUS AND THE *WILD* AMERICAN SUNFLOWERS.

"The British Fungus and the Wild American Sunflowers" (caricature of Oscar Wilde), Thomas Nast, *Harper's Weekly,* January 21, 1882

"The Aesthetic Monkey," wood engraving (artist unknown), *Harper's Weekly*, January 28, 1882

essays and more serious exploratory works such as *The Colour-Sense* (1892), Allen brought a social positivist's perspective to Darwin's evolutionary theories, helping to promote ideas that even when well received by Darwin's adherents had usually been read as confirming intractable, grim truths in nature.

With a proto-Wildean epigrammatic directness, Allen questioned Victorian pieties by insisting on the primacy of naturally occurring beauty over clammy moral verities. "We know that sometimes we meet people possessing every virtue and grace under heaven," he asserted. "And yet for some unknown reason we could no more fall in love with them than we could fall in love with the [T]en [C]ommandments."[66] Commented Allen: "Moralists have always borne a special grudge to pretty faces," and then quoted Spencer to the effect that "the saying that beauty is but skin deep is itself but a skin-deep saying." Allen expressed the entire issue with a bracing succinctness: "To be beautiful is to be efficient."[67] On personal terms with both Darwin and Wilde, Grant provided the most explicitly expounded philosophical links between the claims of sexual selection theory and Oxford-based aestheticism. In 1891 he wrote a fan letter to Wilde praising the playwright's "Soul of Man under Socialism" (1891) as a "noble and beautiful" essay. "I would have written every line of it myself," exulted Allen, "if only I knew how."[68]

Whereas many of Darwin's contemporary readers had understood him as effectively lowering man in the hierarchy of nature, Allen regarded the theory of sexual selection as having humanized nature. Man took flirting to greater heights of refinement. "For the very butterflies are coy, and must be wooed and won," Allen remarked, adding that it is "only in the human race itself that selection descends into such minute, such subtle, such indefinable discriminations."[69] In a chapter on "The Theory of Courtship" in *Charles Darwin* (1893), Allen was giddily explicit regarding the implications of sexual selection where Darwin himself had been nervously ambiguous:

> [Darwin] collects from every quarter and from all sources whatever available evidence can be obtained as to the courtship and rivalry of birds and butterflies, of deer and antelopes, of fish and lizards. He shows by numerous examples and quotations how even flies coquet together in their pretty rhythmical aerial dances; how wasps battle eagerly with one another to secure possession of their unconcerned mates; how cicada strive to win their "voiceless brides" with stridulating music; how sphinx-moths endeavor to allure their partners with the musky odour of their penciled wings, and how

emperors and orange-tips display their gorgeous spots and bands in the broad sunshine before the admiring and attentive eyes of their observant dames.[70]

Allen's sappy immersion in nature's flirting phenomena—as well as his eagerness to erase the boundaries between beasts and humans—shades into the alarmism of Herbert Spencer on the diminished state of relations between the sexes. In "The Decline of Marriage" (an 1894 essay published in the *Westminster Gazette*), Allen fretted that sexual selection had ceased to have its familiar dynamism owing to a new type of male, the bachelor of cloistered, homosocial affiliations. "Young men of a certain type don't marry, because—they are less of young men than formerly. Wild animals in confinement seldom propagate their kind."[71]

The connections between aestheticism and sexual selection remained latent not only in the premises underpinning *The Descent of Man* but throughout much of Darwin's other scientific work. The force and originality of *The Descent* consisted in its sustained depiction of a natural kingdom that competed with the human realm in physical variety, ever-mutating complexity, and, not least important, beauty. Even as Darwin portrayed the natural universe as overrun by "inhuman laws," a key feature of both *The Origin of Species* and *The Descent of Man* was the appreciation of nature as a panoramic, unceasing parade of eye-pleasing specimens. From the very beginning of his scientific vocation, Darwin represented an awed gentleman-aesthete encountering the swarming spectrum of natural phenomenon, his prose Paterian in its continual elaborations and refinement of its author's shifting series of "impressions." In an unstated, reciprocal move, the philosophical ethos of *l'art pour l'art* as explored in Pater's and Wilde's decadent aesthetics confirmed Darwinian maxims. All experience could be aestheticized, and additionally, decadent aesthetics, in seeking to render the "aberrant" beautiful, tacitly sought to erase the distinction between "unnatural" and "natural," much as Darwin rendered such distinctions meaningless.

The links between Darwinian thought and decadent aesthetics did not remain a recondite aspect of the intellectual histories of these two cultural movements. There was, as well, a popular contemporary recognition of the connections between the arguments of *The Descent* and a nascent aestheticist movement. In 1882, the year of Darwin's death, Oscar Wilde was traveling through America on his celebrated tour on behalf of the still-controversial cult of aestheticism. Then the target of international satire

(Wilde had recently been parodied successfully in Gilbert and Sullivan's *Patience*), the playwright made an oblique appearance on the cover of the *Harper's Weekly* of January 28, 1882. Entitled "The Aesthetic Monkey," this cartoon depicted a disturbingly humanlike simian, elegantly dressed in a suit, his hands cupped below his chin, as he stared at a large sunflower, the traditional emblem of the aestheticist movement. A caricature in the previous issue of *Harper's Weekly* had portrayed Wilde, his head in the shape of a mushroom, gazing at a group of sunflowers. The caption read: "The British Fungus and the *Wild* American Sunflowers." If the references to Charles Darwin were not satisfactorily explicit, the wallpaper behind the aesthete-monkey, depicting peacocks, would have made the point. American readers of *Harper's* cognizant of aestheticist claims on their country's cultural life might have grasped that the peacock wallpaper itself evoked an earlier aestheticist incarnation of Darwin's ideas. In 1873 the painter James MacNeil Whistler, arguably the American artist who had been most thoroughly won over to the claims of the Aestheticist Movement, invented a peacock scheme for Aubrey House (today located in the Freer Gallery of Art at the Smithsonian Museum in Washington, D.C.) in which extravagantly long, gold-tinted peacock feathers are painted so that they seem to be draped from ceiling to floor. Entitled "Harmony in Blue and Gold: The Peacock Room," the celebrated painting evokes a harmonious distillation of Darwinian tenets and *l'art pour l'art* posturings, the successful appropriation of the aesthetics of courting as explicated in *The Descent* to "pragmatic" interior design. It was the unsettling cover of *Harper's* magazine, however, that hinted at the "perverse" implications of Darwinian belief, suggesting that sexual selection could culminate in an arrested plot of courtship. In Beard's drawing, the captivated monkey gazes adoringly at a sunflower while lost in an aesthete's contemplative fugue. The process of sexual selection has resulted not in the smooth continuation of the species, but rather in a dreamy cessation of the operations of Darwinian courtship. In *The Descent of Man* and in the work of the evolutionist's aestheticist heirs, one finds an altogether curious phenomenon: a naturalized theory of the "unnatural."

George Eliot and Thomas Hardy

Flirtation, Female Choice, and the Revision of Darwinian Belief

THE MILL ON THE FLOSS AND THE TAMING
OF THE DANDY-AESTHETE

"Choose!"
— Tom Tulliver to Maggie, in George Eliot's *The Mill on the Floss* (1860)

The two major Victorian novelists who consciously acknowledge and assimilate Darwinian structures of thought throughout their writing, George Eliot and Thomas Hardy, had long been absorbed by the latent, prickly subtextual predicament raised by *The Descent of Man:* what might occur if the female grew to relish too greatly the initial stages of sexual selection, protracting choice and thus perversely honoring, but also disturbing, the "rules" of nature? Given that Eliot (as Sally Shuttleworth has illustrated) was a supporter of Darwin's *The Origin of Species* but resistant to the equation of "evolution" with human progress, it is likely that the novelist found *The Descent of Man* more intellectually appealing.[1] For the later work evoked a natural universe responsive to deliberate directives and commands, to the "intelligent direction" that Herschel had alleged was missing from *The Origin*. However, while critics have explored the links between Darwin's *The Origin of Species* and the fictions of Eliot and Hardy, little attention has been paid to how these novelists confronted sexual selection theory.[2] That both Hardy and Eliot are drawn to "rustic" settings in much of their work suggests a fictional illustration of Darwin's claim in *The Descent* that the phenomenon of sexual selection occurred in "utterly barbarous tribes."[3] At an even deeper level, Eliot's work, beginning with *The Mill on the Floss* and culminating in *Daniel Deronda*, suggests a thoughtful accommodation of the basic terms of sexual selection. The most perspicacious heroines, Eliot's fiction attests, recognize the necessity of flirting as well as its distinction from love. "She had a fine sensibility," notes the narrator of *Felix Holt, The Radical* (1866) of Esther, "to the line at which flirtation must cease; and she was now pale, and shaken with feelings she had not yet defined for herself." [4] For Hardy, on the other hand, "female choice" meant the hazards of female indecision. With the exception of *Under the Greenwood Tree,* in which a woman's coquettish ways are seamlessly part of a pastoral comedy of manners, Hardy's fiction soberly registered the implication of *The Descent* as grim evidence of a "tragic" natural design. For the author of *Far from the Madding Crowd* and *Jude the Obscure,* the fickle female unwittingly engineers saturnine scenarios of male subjugation.

In the wake of Darwin's "discoveries," a different set of emphases takes on importance in the novels of Eliot and Hardy. Heredity, the choice of mate, species survival, physical appearance, all assume urgency with the publication of *The Origin of Species* and *The Descent of Man.* "Was she beautiful or not beautiful?"—the opening sentence of *Daniel Deronda*—is not only a narrator's appeal to an arbitrary matter of taste. It is the start of a line of Darwinian inquiry. Jane Austen's Emma and Knightley blithely discuss the relative merits of Harriet Smith, "blue-eyed" with "regular features," but there is the assurance that the girl (as Knightley coolly puts it) "will marry somebody or other." [5] In *The Mill on the Floss,* Mr. Tulliver is as improvident in his choice of a mate as Elizabeth Bennet's father is in Austen's *Pride and Prejudice,* but whereas in Austen the key oppositions are playfulness and regulation, feeling versus reason, in Eliot's novel the polar oppositions become reducible to Darwinian notions of communal survival versus individual independence, the interests of a "species" as opposed to those of a single "creature." In *Middlemarch* and *Daniel Deronda,* the reader knows that a poorly chosen marriage may shade not into a comic mismatch (Mr. and Mrs. Bennet) but a tormenting death-in-life. In both Eliot and Hardy, the world depends on life-or-death choices as to an appropriate mate.

Comedy resolves most of the parental discord and sibling friction in *Pride and Prejudice,* but in *The Mill on the Floss* and *Tess of the D'Urbervilles* the heroines cling to the limited emotional haven that is home because the outer world offers no transcendent meaning. For Maggie, familial and communal bonds allow for permanence and survival but also bitterness, despair, and suffocated longings. Eliot depicts Maggie's Edenic state of childhood as fading, as memories replace actualities. "I can't set out on a fresh life," Maggie tells Stephen Guest in the face of what the novel represents as her only chance of emancipation, "I shall feel as if there were nothing firm beneath my feet."[6] In *Far from the Madding Crowd*, published three years after *The Descent of Man*, Bathsheba Everdene's irresolution as to an ideal mate culminates in Sergeant Troy's death at the hands of Bathsheba's scorned suitor, Farmer Boldwood, who himself becomes a lunatic. Darwin's scientific "revelations" did not simply raise new questions about arrangements between the sexes. Beyond toppling an Austenian universe, Darwin forced novelists such as Eliot and Hardy, both of whom had begun their literary vocations with idealized depictions of pastoral communities. Both writers were required to consider the probability that the community might impose a binding, brutal law, as nature dictated sexual arrangements.

Eliot's concern with the representation of extended female choice might be said to have begun with *The Mill on the Floss*, where she raises the question in the context of a preening male's "coxcombry" epitomized by Stephen Guest's comic vanity. Stephen is a prototype for a series of heroes in Eliot's subsequent fiction who begin as men of precious affectations and later take on more assertive, masculine contours. Ladislaw, with his "abundant and curly" locks, "girls' complexion," and penchant for stretching out full length on rugs, and Daniel Deronda, uncomfortable with the role of neo-Byronic bachelor to which Hugh Mallinger consigns him, are both men whom Eliot carves into more manly specimens.[7] Ladislaw's and Deronda's early incarnations as "aesthetic" figures are, however, essential to the appeal of these men for Dorothea and Gwendolen.

In the much-disputed scenes between Maggie Tulliver and Stephen in the sections entitled "The Great Temptation" and "The Final Rescue," Eliot allowed her heroine to succumb to the lighthearted Stephen's flamboyant charms. My focus on the last section of *The Mill on the Floss* might seem to slight the greater scope of the work, but as Nancy Miller has maintained, the last two chapters of Eliot's work ("The Great Temptation" and "The Final Rescue"), in which the novelist charts Maggie's erotic destiny, contain "a plot of their own."[8] For the reader fairly defeated by the increasingly oppressive provincial atmosphere evoked in Eliot's second major novel, the comparatively "worldly" Stephen's accidental entrance into the narrative may seem less a dissonant intrusion than a welcome idyll. Like her rapturous childhood days with Tom, Maggie's fuguelike escape with Stephen takes place in an atemporal, pastoral realm of the senses. Viewed in the light of Darwinian sexual selection, the familiar antipodal thematics of the Maggie-Stephen friendship—an uncontrolled surrender to carnal dictates versus the demands of a rational, organic community—collapse. For Darwin, the exercising of female choice is inherently communal, as nature serves a teleological social program.[9]

Yet of all the amorous relations explored by Eliot in her fiction, none has generated such an extraordinarily hostile set of responses among critics as the charged near-affair between Maggie and Stephen. Indeed, the verdict that Stephen is a feckless coxcomb and that Maggie's spree with him a troublingly enigmatic component of her character forms a rare consensus in criticism of the novelist's fiction over the last hundred years. (In its power to induce discomfort in devotees of Eliot's work, it is rivaled only perhaps by the catastrophic flood that concludes *The Mill on the Floss*.) On the novel's initial publication, even reviewers who responded favorably to the novel questioned the "naturalness" of Maggie's responses to Stephen, whom they viewed as an inappropriately effete potential suitor. In perhaps the first extended disparagement of this aspect of *The Mill on the Floss*, Edward Bulwer-Lytton (himself a much-lampooned exponent of dandyism early in his career) penned a private letter to Eliot's publisher, John Blackwood, in which he insisted on the "error of the whole position towards Stephen": "It may be quite natural that she should take that liking to him, but it is a position at variance with all that had before been Heroic about her. The *indulgence* of such a sentiment for the affianced of a friend under whose roof she was, was a treachery and a meanness according to the Ethics of Art."[10] In a letter to Blackwood, Eliot defended her choice by insisting that she had only sought to provide the "truthful presentation of a character essentially noble but liable to error—error that is anguish to its own nobleness," adding that the "ethics of art" evinced by Bulwer-Lytton's remarks was "too narrow, and must be widened to correspond with a widening psychology." With an astute stress on the crucial part she felt Stephen played in her novel, Eliot insisted to Blackwood that her heroine's "position towards Stephen . . . is too vital a part of my whole conception and purpose for me to be converted to the condemnation of it."[11]

Bulwer-Lytton's identification of the Maggie-Stephen interlude as the outstanding flaw of *The Mill on the Floss* was echoed in subsequent reviews of Eliot's novel. The critic in the *Guardian* objected to the "picture of passion stealing like a frightful and evil poison" over the young Maggie, while the notice in the *Times* found in the relationship between Eliot's heroine and Stephen "only a detailed unlikely picture of animal feelings" comparable to the "coarseness of Joseph Andrews."[12] That soon after her adventure Maggie recuperated what the *Times* termed her "moral balance" was little comfort to the majority of Eliot's Victorian critics, for whom Maggie's lapse cast into doubt the whole question of the heroine's character. An appalled Swinburne, a writer one might have imagined would have delighted in the ostentatious Stephen, wondered "that a woman of Maggie Tulliver's kind can be moved to any sense but that of bitter disgust and sickening disdain by a thing—I will not write, a man." [13] Swinburne's comments (he went on to call Stephen "revolting," "shameful," and "vile") indicate that Maggie's suitor struck Victorian readers as not only repellant and effete but unmanly as well. In fact, Swinburne's point was reiterated in what is perhaps the most well-known condemnation of the effect Stephen exercises over Maggie, Leslie Stephen's remark that "George Eliot did not herself understand what a mere hair-dresser's block she was describing in Mr. Guest," a figure the critic called, in an evocation of Darwinian terms, "a very poor animal." Reading the passages detailing Maggie's interest in Guest, the critic claimed to wish to exhort the author of *The Mill on the Floss* to "save this charming Maggie from this irrelevant and discordant degradation." [14]

Such views persisted into the twentieth century even among critics such as F. R. Leavis who sought to revive Eliot's literary reputation. In *The Great Tradition* (1948), Leavis characterized the Maggie-Stephen relation as "universally recognized as a sad lapse on Eliot's part," an early instance of an "immaturity" that Leavis claimed Eliot "never leaves safely behind." Exclaimed Leavis: "Renunciation is a main theme in [Maggie's] history and in her daily meditations; but when temptation takes the form of Mr. Stephen Guest! It is incredible, or insufferable in so far as we have to accept it." Leavis noted with undisguised dismay that "it is quite plain that George Eliot shares to the full the sense of Stephen's irresistibleness—the vibration establishes it beyond a doubt." [15] Tony Tanner, in his study of adultery and its formal consequences in Continental fiction, *Adultery and the Novel* (1979), goes so far as to discuss *The Mill on the Floss* in terms of Maggie and Stephen's "adulterous" yearnings for each other, although neither character is married (Maggie is informally committed to Philip, while Stephen is engaged to Maggie's cousin Lucy). [16]

Other contemporary commentators have been no less skeptical of those sections of *The Mill on the Floss* relating to Stephen Guest than their Victorian predecessors, although their reservations have been aesthetic rather than moralistic. U. C. Knoepflmacher calls Stephen "insipid," and regards his appearance, like the flood that concludes the novel, as "extraneous and accidental." [17] George Levine claims that "With Stephen Maggie falls into oblivion"—a comment that fails to convey just how sweetly carnal Eliot elects to depict the quality of that oblivion. [18] More recently, Gillian Beer has interpreted the Maggie-Stephen interlude as a moment in the text when Eliot suspends what has been until then a successfully sustained negative appraisal of the conditions in which Maggie is forced to live. "The level of desire explored at the end of the book is *ahistorical,* and ceases to be focused as a criticism of a social order," argues Beer. "Up to that point, when it seemed that Maggie must endure attrition, misunderstanding, the drudging work of being a governess, the mode of the novel had been that of social critique: a recognition of the grinding power of social mores which are capable of being *changed.*" In this view, Maggie's idyll with Stephen contains less logic, in narrative terms, than the flooding river which kills off the heroine, given that the flood, unlike the "unnatural" episode with Stephen, is a part of those natural conditions which have determined the particular economic order of St. Ogg's. [19] Referring to feminist scholars such as Jenny Calder who lament Eliot's refusal to reward her heroine's longings, Nancy Miller claims that such critics mistakenly "would have Maggie live George Eliot's life." Miller insists that the "plots of women's literature are not about 'life' and solutions in any therapeutic sense, nor should they be." [20]

Eliot's depiction of Maggie's attraction to Stephen Guest affords an opportunity to explore the novelist's intensely equivocal attitude toward a strand of Victorian dandyism taking form in the aftermath of Byron's influential example, as an incipient aestheticist ethos was making substantial inroads into middle-class English culture. Eliot's initial response to the aestheticism promulgated by the reigning figure of the "New Hellenism," Walter Pater, was quite harsh. She judged the Oxford scholar's *Studies in the History of the Renaissance* (1873) as "quite poisonous in its false principles and criticism and false conception of life." (On another occasion, she informed Richard Jebb that it was a "comfort and a strength" to hear of his distaste for Pater's book.) [21] Still, Eliot's fictional conception of foppish display as suggested by her depiction of Guest (as well as by her characterizations of Ladislaw and the youthful Daniel Deronda) indicates a far more ambivalent perspective on dandiacal deportment. Eliot seems determined to suggest the early manifestations of aesthetic sensitivity in the youthful suitors as a way of softening their aggressive masculinity. Yet, aware of the potential for preciousness in "aesthete personalities," she never allows such qualities to get out of hand and makes a point of dissipating them. Stephen abandons smooth badinage with Maggie and becomes an assertive suitor. Ladislaw, introduced to the reader as he is drawing in Casaubon's garden, becomes a reform-minded newspaperman. A young gentleman of privilege, raised among the "falling rose petals" of the grounds of Hugh Mallinger's cloistered estate, the Cambridge-bound Daniel harbors a "grief within," which the narrator likens to "Byron's susceptibility about his deformed foot."[22] Gradually Eliot's hero sheds his foppish baggage, as he assumes a daunting political mission in the Middle East. Dandiacal proclivities, stirred by the cool breezes of privilege, must give way to the claims of a virile maturity.

Those readers left uncomfortable by Stephen's role in *The Mill on the Floss* seldom note that Eliot treats this character satirically, not harshly, and that once he is firmly rejected by Maggie he evokes a sympathetic chord in the reader far beyond that generated by Tom's narrow-minded fraternal devotion or by Philip's masochistic infatuation. Nor do critics of Stephen's position in the novel note another suggestive feature of Eliot's portrayal: Stephen is represented as a subtly *evolving* figure. The Stephen Guest who boasts to Philip that he knows he is "universally pleasing" becomes a man who is won over by Maggie—and then devastated by her rejection—in the course of a chapter and a half.[23] Once again he can be contrasted suggestively with Tom and Philip as a figure who grows in his relations with Maggie. No mere caricature of a popinjay, Stephen is swiftly transformed (owing to the overpowering erotic influence of Maggie) from a dandiacal figure of glib opinions into a man of assertively heterosexual impulses. Eliot grasped the problematic attractions for Maggie of a figure such as Stephen, but she did not stop at satire. The segments of *The Mill on the Floss* involving Stephen disclose a novelist registering but also containing the discordant energies of dandyism.

There is more than a little of Frank Churchill of Austen's *Emma* (1816) in Stephen Guest. Churchill is a possible source for Eliot's conception of Stephen, given the several qualities he shares with Austen's character. Frank, like Stephen, is associated with excessive attention to the management of hair. (Stephen, of course, is introduced to the reader as he is about to clip Lucy's blond locks.) Not only is Frank "seized" by a "sudden freak" at breakfast requiring that he travel sixteen miles to London for a haircut, he is so taken with what he calls Jane Fairfax's "outré" curls that in chap-

ter 26 of the novel he stuns Emma by abandoning her at a waltz in order
to ask Jane about them. Stephen and Frank, each well-heeled, display a
talent for music—Frank because he dances splendidly and Stephen because he is immediately introduced to the reader as he serenades Lucy and
Maggie with his singing. The affinities between Stephen and Frank, however, tend to bring into high relief the differences in Austen's and Eliot's
conceptions of the perils of a misguided "courtship."

In Austen's novel, where tragedy has no place, the failure of Frank to
assume the role of the heroine's suitor is merely a part of a "natural" design; Frank is intended for another woman. As we shall see, in *The Mill on
the Floss,* Maggie's renunciation of Stephen means that happiness itself
"seemed to slip away and fade and vanish, leaving only the dying sound of
a deep thrilling voice that said, 'Gone—forever gone.'" [24] Insofar as both
Maggie and Stephen believe themselves to be engaged informally to others, their near-affair has the quality of an insurgent force within Eliot's
semipastoral narrative. Nonetheless, it forms part of a larger, cohesive pattern. For Maggie, the full exercising of female choice depends on a male
whose "feminine" attributes lend him special charisma. Knoepflmacher
claims that Maggie follows Stephen because "she confuses sexual impulse
with rational choice." [25] But Eliot seems far less certain as to whether her
heroine is "rational" or misguided in ultimately rejecting Stephen. While
critics have discussed Maggie's choice as perversely wrong-headed, arguably it signifies a doubly meaningful *departure* from a desire depicted
as unnatural. The prolonging of Maggie's (incestuous) adolescent tie with
Tom is a greater threat to Maggie's independence, just as her "pure" bond
with Philip increasingly seems more a perverse sacrifice to duty than a
freely elected seizing of opportunity. (Stephen himself, at the moment
Maggie informs him that she believes herself engaged to Philip, tells her
that her choice is "unnatural" as well as a "perverted notion of right." [26])
In a proto-Darwinian scheme where the laws of sexual selection dominate,
the division between a self-preserving reason and all-engrossing passion
becomes a distinction without a difference. The narrator of *The Mill on the
Floss* pointedly insists that Maggie is without feminine craftiness, "so entirely without those pretty airs of coquetry which have the traditional reputation of driving gentlemen to despair, that she won some feminine pity
for being so ineffective in spite of her beauty." [27] Yet even without coy manners, the mature Maggie has retained the rebelliousness of spirit that
marked her girlhood, now expressed through her dalliance with Stephen.

(As has often been noted, his very surname suggests the necessarily momentary place he will take in her affections.)

Eliot's sense of a "new psychology" informing her heroine's actions was an engagement with Darwinian precepts decades before the evolutionist himself would articulate them. The novel is replete with allusions to natural phenomena that Darwin would make the very subject of his scientific enterprise. (Maggie at one moment sits with Stephen and senses "only the sense of a presence like that of a closely-hovering broad-winged bird.") More importantly, Maggie's attraction to Stephen arises out of an expanding responsiveness to his role as self-preening aesthete-dandy. The smooth Stephen—with his polished repertoire of fashionable attire, including a "diamond ring, attar of roses and air of nonchalant leisure," knowingly adopts the air of Beau Brummell with just a hint of Wildean self-posturing.[28] At times, Stephen's self-presentation borders on the willfully androgynous; shortly after he is introduced to Maggie, he is described as having "sauntered to the piano humming in falsetto." At other moments his constant primping operates independently of any instinct to woo the opposite sex:

> Stephen was paying [Maggie] the utmost attention on this public occasion; jealously buying up the articles he had seen under her fingers in the process making, and gaily helping her to cajole the male customers into the purchase of the most effeminate futilities. He chose to lay aside his hat and wear a scarlet fez of her embroidering; but by superficial observers this was necessarily liable to be interpreted less as a compliment to Lucy than as a mark of coxcombry. "Guest is a great coxcomb," young Torry observed; "but then he is a privileged person in St. Ogg's—he carries all before him: if another fellow did such things, everybody would say he made a fool of himself."[29]

It would be a stretch to see Stephen as signifying a foppish stance of specifically homoerotic import, yet neither is Stephen's self-preening merely for the benefit of Maggie. Witness his teasing of his "rival" Philip:

> [W]alking up to Philip, he sat down behind him, and put his hand on his shoulder.
>
> "Are you studying for a portrait, Phil," he said, "or for a sketch of that oriel window? By George! It makes a capital bit from this dark corner, with the curtain just marking it off."
>
> "I have been studying expression," said Philip, curtly.
>
> "What! Miss Tulliver's? It's rather of the savage-moody order to-day, I think—something of the fallen princess serving behind a counter. Her

cousin sent me to her with a civil offer to get her some refreshment, but I have been snubbed, as usual. There's a natural antipathy between us, I suppose: I have seldom the honor to please her."

"What a hypocrite you are!" said Philip, flushing angrily.

"What! because experience must have told me that I'm universally pleasing? I must admit the law, but there's some disturbing force here."

"I am going," said Philip, rising abruptly.[30]

Stephen's playful taunting of Philip, a gesture Eliot renders as sheer droll vanity, invites Philip's acknowledgment of his "pleasing" good looks. Disguised as a jauntily homosocial appreciation of Maggie as a fetchingly fickle woman, it induces a feminine "blush" in his companion. But if Stephen conquers Philip in his rivalry for Maggie's affection, it is a Pyrrhic victory; rejected by the taciturn Maggie, the two men come to share an inadvertent, inescapable bond: the sullen homosociality of jointly rejected men.

Maggie's already-frustrated relations with Philip collide with her unfolding plot of flirtation with Stephen, but her attraction to a new suitor also rescues her from what Eliot has increasingly depicted as a sterile tie. Maggie's attraction to Stephen is not simply a minor complication of plot or a youthful peccadillo; like her impulsive decision as a girl to escape from home in order to live with a tribe of gypsies, Maggie's awareness of Guest as a "great temptation" arises from a suppressed but deep rebellious spirit. In an encounter that occurs in an oddly suspended present tense, Eliot takes pains to evoke Maggie's choice of Stephen not as a lapse into unconscious carnality but as a "courageously" orchestrated decision to flirt:

But this must end some time—perhaps it ended very soon, and only *seemed* long, as a minute's dream does. Stephen at last sat upright sideways in his chair, leaning one hand and arm over the back and looking at Maggie. What should he say?

"We shall have a splendid sunset, I think; shan't you go out and see it?"

"I don't know," said Maggie. Then, courageously raising her eyes and looking out the window, "If I'm not playing cribbage with my uncle."

A pause: during which Minny is stroked again, but has sufficient insight not to be grateful for it—to growl rather.

"Do you like sitting alone?"

A rather arch look came over Maggie's face, and, just glancing at Stephen, she said, "Would it be quite civil to say 'yes'?"

"It *was* rather a dangerous question for an intruder to ask," said Stephen, delighted with that glance, and getting determined to stay for another.[31]

A simple gesture, Maggie's raising of her eyes toward a window, assumes the weight of a boldly asserted ethical action. Eliot subtends the temporal scheme through a repeated stress on pauses and hesitations that evoke not so much the passage of time as time itself—time as trembling opportunity—in what are some of the most tremulously tender moments in all of Eliot's fiction. The narrator of *The Mill on the Floss* repeatedly needles the reader with the exhortation that the scene drawn for us, with such slow, painstaking attention to both gesture and timing, may immediately disappear from view, as if Eliot were declaring, "It is *that* precious." The animal kingdom—here represented by a growling but adorably anthropomorphized cat equipped with human "insight"—offers the flirting human world, and the "kittenish" Maggie in particular, its tacit, vocal consent. That Stephen would speak the name of his romantic "rival" at such a moment suggests as coquettish a retreat on his part as Maggie's glance out a window or her hint that she may prefer to sit alone.

Note too that when Eliot wishes to introduce an element of playful affectation into Maggie's behavior, it is indirectly conveyed through a cautious reference to the *appearance* of coyness in her behavior; a "rather arch look" comes over Maggie's face, but archness itself is not imputed to her. (In a corresponding touch, designed to eroticize Maggie while protecting her from the charge of coyness, the narrator notes that "if Maggie had been the queen of coquettes she could hardly have invented a means of giving greater piquancy to her beauty in Stephen's eyes."[32]) Repeatedly, we stand in parallel proximity to Stephen as we are forced to decipher Maggie's facial cues. As pleasingly dreamlike as this encounter with Stephen is for Maggie, several lines later their interaction is described by Eliot as an "oppressive spell" abruptly dissipated by Stephen's mention of Philip's name. Nevertheless, these playful, seemingly minor interludes swell into major chords.

It is through the public rituals of dance that Maggie finds herself lured toward Stephen. Although dance is sometimes a stylized metaphor for the ceremonies of courtship, what it evokes more successfully in metaphorical terms are the shifting rites of flirtation.[33] Typically in dance, any "commitment" lasts only the duration of a sequence of instances in a musical score. (In certain dances such as the minuet, one must constantly change partners.) Maggie and Stephen are not simply another couple who use dance as a way of teasing each other into passion. The narrator notes that Stephen's "glance and tone of subdued tenderness" bring the "breath of poetry with them into a room that is half-stifling with glaring gas and hard flirtation." [34] As Maggie and Stephen draw together during their waltz, one may locate the necessarily contradictory nature of their "affair," for the two find themselves close even as the dance keeps them at an eroticized distance:

> The possibility that he too should dance with Maggie, and have her hand in his so long, was beginning to possess him like a thirst. But even now their hands were meeting in the dance—were meeting still to the very end of it, though they were far off each other.
>
> Stephen hardly knew what happened, or in what automatic way he got through the duties of politeness in the interval, until he was free and saw Maggie seated alone again, at the farther end of the room. He made his way towards her round the couples that were forming for the waltz, and when Maggie became conscious that she was the person he sought, she felt, in spite of all the thoughts that had gone before, a glowing gladness at heart. Her eyes and cheeks were still brightened with her childlike enthusiasm in the dance; her whole frame was set to joy and tenderness; even the coming pain could not seem bitter—she was ready to welcome it as part of life, for life at this moment seemed a keen vibrating consciousness poised above pleasure or pain. [35]

Just as Maggie's feelings of tenderness toward her new friend are most pronounced in the social context of a dance, her disgust with him emerges when she is left alone with him in the boat. Maggie's behavior thus highlights a key aspect of Darwin's scheme as it will come to be articulated in *The Descent:* desire is profoundly constituted through social rituals. It is never merely a private experience between lovers. At the very moment when Maggie decisively rejects Stephen with the prim retort, "I would rather die than fall into temptation," Eliot undercuts her heroine's words by underscoring the "animal" nature that Maggie is denying: "Her breath was on his face—his lips were near hers—but there was a great dread dwelling in his love for her. Her lips and eyelids quivered; she opened her eyes full on his for an instant, like a lovely wild animal timid and struggling under caresses, and then turned sharp round towards home again." [36] Nature is not an unsavory, primitive wildness; it is, notably, exalted "lovely wild" nature. Knoepflmacher warns of the mistake of wishing a "Lawrentian" fate for Maggie given her attraction to Stephen in such scenes. Critics might be forgiven, however, for exactly such conclusions, especially given Eliot's depiction of Maggie as reflecting "delicious opposites" in her responses to Stephen, a condition in which Eliot's heroine reaches her apotheosis as a character of moral nuances and aesthetic interest.[37] Maggie's sense of life at its most intensely satisfying is entwined with her consciousness of the passing of these moments, conveyed in language that is often intensely proto-Lawrentian. Her consciousness of her attraction to Stephen constitutes, most importantly, a sense of life as non-productive *process* that receives no acknowledgment from the St. Ogg's community. Eliot goes further, rebuking her readers for failing to grasp how the procedures of desire are as paramount as desire's effects: "We judge others according to results; how else?—not knowing the processes by which results are arrived at."[38] Eliot's rhetorically heavy commentary is, of course, a boast of the powers of the realist novelist herself, without whom readers would remain blind to crucial "processes" whereby the self is formed.

In a tacit affirmation of the erotic sublimity that adheres to temporary flirtatious pleasure, Eliot's narrator announces that "The hovering thought that they must and would renounce each other made this moment of mute confession more intense in its rapture." Neither Maggie nor Stephen ever fully comes to terms with the conflicted nature of their attraction, the source of whose contradictions seems to lie not in Stephen, although initially his capriciousness is a fine match for hers. "He wished he had never seen this Maggie Tulliver, to be thrown into a fever by her in this way," thinks Stephen after he and Maggie have gone for a stroll. "He would master himself in the future. He would make himself disagreeable to her—quarrel with her perhaps. Quarrel with her? Was it possible to quarrel with a creature who had such eyes—defying and deprecating, contradicting and clinging, imperious and beseeching—full of delicious opposites?"[39] When Stephen seeks to leave this bewildering realm of flirtation in order, we are told, to become a man of "passionate pleading," he has, for Maggie, committed a betrayal. Significantly, Maggie's resolute rejection occurs the instant after Eliot's narrator assumes the viewpoint of a dumbstruck Stephen. The narrator luxuriates over Maggie with the doting eye of a connoisseur, inviting the reader to consider her body—most specifically, her arm—as an isolated piece of art. It is a coldly appreciative view of Maggie that Stephen himself will shatter through an act of impulsive physicality:

> Stephen was mute; he was incapable of putting a sentence together, and Maggie bent her arm a little upward towards the large half-opened rose that had attracted her. Who has not felt the beauty of a woman's arm?—the unspeakable suggestions of tenderness that lie in the dimpled elbow, and all the

varied gently-lessening curves down to the delicate wrist, with its tiniest, almost imperceptible nicks in the firm softness. A woman's arm touched the
soul of a great sculptor two thousand years ago, so that he wrought an image
of it for the Parthenon which moves us still as it clasps lovingly the time-
worn marbles of a headless trunk. Maggie's was such an arm as that—and
it had the warm tints of life.

    A mad impulse seized on Stephen; he darted towards the arm, and show-
ered kisses on it, clasping the wrist. . . .

    "How dare you?"—she spoke in a deeply shaken, half-smothered voice.
"What right have I given you to insult me?"[40]

Maggie's sharp reprimand is as much directed at the narrator and the
reader as toward the impulsive Stephen.

The novelist who would come to consider Pater's aesthetic philosophy
with such scorn could hardly have been more Paterian in her heightened
attention to the Hellenic components of Maggie's weirdly disembodied
arm. In this synechdochal eroticization, observing, attentive consciousness *is* subjective aestheticism. Indeed, it arrives as a culmination of the
narrator's purely aestheticizing eye. Stephen's move to snatch Maggie's
arm—signaling, for her, the abrupt destruction of their relationship—
rescues Eliot from the charge that her doting narrator had rendered
Maggie a piece of statuary. Through his unthinkingly rash act, Stephen
rescues a narrative that here hovers on fetishistic "aestheticization." Eliot's
"taming" of the showy Stephen (in a chapter entitled "The Spell Seems
Broken") is a process whereby Stephen is rendered more sexually assertive,
more manly in conventional Victorian terms, and (in an irony crucial to
the effectiveness of these scenes) less likely to hold Maggie's interest.

Stephen's transformation into an assertive lover inspires Maggie's renunciation of him, because having generated her independent impulses,
he assumes the excessively possessive role of the other males who seek to
control her fate. Maggie's choice of Stephen as a near-lover gains added
meaning because it is a freely elected decision. It is not only that Maggie's
contradictory actions—first to accept, then to reject this suitor—are subversive gestures against the constricted St. Ogg's community. Maggie's relation with Stephen, because it has been badly timed, cannot be absorbed
into the limited expectations of St. Ogg's. To be sure, the Maggie Tulliver
whose alliance with Stephen heralds the relations of the sexually awakened, unrestrained, Nietzschean women of Lawrence's fiction disappears
from Eliot's text, retreating, finally, into a faceless gallery of self-denying
Victorian heroines. In *The Mill on the Floss,* male "coxcombry" is at once

an enhancement of romantic passion and a threat to the proprieties of courtship. "Aesthetic" man liberates the Victorian heroine into a momentary experience of carnal freedom. Yet, having introduced into her novel an aesthete-dandy to touch the wellsprings of her heroine's spirit, Eliot nevertheless needed to contain the energies released by Stephen's magnetic "coxcombry." The "taming" of Stephen Guest is a process in which this upstart dandy is converted into a familiar fictional type. If he is briefly a playful descendant of Frank Churchill, arriving, like Austen's Frank, late in the narrative, he is later a touching but more conventional figure: the misguided, cast-off Romeo. In succumbing so completely to Maggie, Stephen, like pitiable Philip Wakem, loses his tensile, masculine strength.

It is a conspicuously cruel irony of *The Mill on the Floss* that after Maggie returns from her "elopement" with Stephen, she is rejected by both her brother and the St. Ogg's community as if she indeed *had* consummated her relationship with Stephen. "She had not, then, eloped in order to be married to Mr. Stephen Guest," Eliot's narrator dryly informs us. "At all events, Mr. Stephen Guest had not married her—which came to the same thing, so far as culpability was concerned."[41] Indeed, Maggie becomes the "fallen princess" jauntily evoked in Stephen's conversation with Philip. Yet the flooding waters that give Maggie mythic status are less a punitive natural force acting as a moral agent than unpredictable nature retrospectively offering assent to a seemingly irrational desire. Put another way, the forces of nature that kill off Maggie and Tom are as destructive to community as is Maggie's decision to momentarily elope with Stephen. An attempt to decipher the larger meaning of a natural catastrophe such as the flood is as misguided as an effort to explain the unstoppable forces that draw together Maggie and Stephen. And like the all-determining flood, which Eliot tells us "had left no visible trace on the face of the earth" except invisible "scars" and "marks" (visible, presumably, only to the novelist and reader), Maggie's dalliance with Stephen is an overwhelming event that leaves only textual traces.

Henry James, who made the termination by natural disaster of the Maggie-Stephen flirtation plot the focus of his 1866 review of *The Mill on the Floss,* claimed that the novel's ending "shocks the reader most painfully." Alone among contemporary critics, James wanted *more* of Stephen Guest, less as a convincing solution to what he called Maggie's "difficulties" than as an enhancement of the novel's aesthetic appeal. With a hint of the "decadent" James of the later years (and whose *The Golden*

Bowl featured another heroine named Maggie who seemed to accept her husband's adulterous affair), James speculated wistfully that "one thing is certain: a *dénouement* by which Maggie should have called Stephen back would have been extremely interesting."[42]

LEARNING FROM BEASTS: THE FLIRTATION PLOT IN *MIDDLEMARCH* AND *DANIEL DERONDA*

In *Middlemarch* and *Daniel Deronda* the distinctions between romantic desire and "purposeless" coquetry are continually asserted, disturbed, and evaded. Despite Rosamond Vincy's morally repellent manipulation of other men, it is exactly her repertoire of feminine wiles, adulterous in spirit if not in law, that must be adopted by Dorothea if she is to save herself from what Eliot intimates could be a desolate spinsterhood. Gwendolen Harleth, who knows feminine wiles all too well, must confront the consequences of ill-conceived choice if she is to save herself from another kind of death-in-life, a marriage to a crafty sadist. Within the more global compass of *Daniel Deronda,* the need to keep a flirtation sustained forces the narrative into more far-fetched turns in plot when Gwendolen inadvertently meets Deronda among the British upper classes sojourning in Genoa. In Eliot's last, despairing novel, where the sweepstakes of sexual selection have been cued to a heightened pitch, Gwendolen's vain choice of husband to guarantee her "survival" mirrors the dilemma of her friend the future Jewish leader Deronda, for whom the survival of an entire people becomes a messianic mission.

Rosamond's increasingly vital function in *Middlemarch* is related to the recuperation of her character on behalf of the erotic "education" of the morally exemplary heroine whose story is at the heart of *Middlemarch.* Rosamond's role reaches a climax in chapter 77 of Eliot's novel when, in an abrupt breakdown of narrative time, her coquettish kneeling before Ladislaw, traumatically registered (or perhaps only misconstrued) by Dorothea at last forces a crisis and then a resolution of the too-long-deferred courtship between Dorothea and Ladislaw. In *Middlemarch,* even the flirtatious Rosamond, immersed in artifice, finds a salutary function in nature's drama of courting well before she is "officially" reformed in the narrative when she expresses her contrition to Dorothea near the novel's conclusion.

In what might be termed a feminist reconstitution of the terms of

Darwinian sexual selection as well as an unsentimental recognition of the
morally neutral effects Darwin's theory fosters, Eliot accentuates the role
of the female as controlling the rituals of courtship. The section of *Middlemarch* entitled "Waiting for Death" presents Lydgate's attraction to Rosamond as a gradual procedure. Lydgate, cautious before Rosamond's artifices, does not fall immediately in love; only when Rosamond's artifice
seems to give way to a natural moment does she stir Lydgate:

> After sitting two long moments while he moved his whip and could say noth-
> ing, Lydgate rose to go, and Rosamond, made nervous by her struggle be-
> tween mortification and the wish not to betray it, dropped her chain as if
> startled, and rose, too, mechanically. Lydgate instantaneously stooped to pick
> up the chain. When he rose he was very near to a lovely little face set on a fair
> long neck which he had been used to see turning about under the most per-
> fect management of self-contented grace. But as he raised his eyes he now
> saw a certain helpless quivering which touched him quite newly, and made
> him look at Rosamond with a questioning flash. At this moment she was
> as natural as she had ever been when she was five years old: she felt that her
> tears had risen, and it was no use to try to do anything else than let them
> stay like water on a blue flower or let them fall over her cheeks, even as they
> would.
>   That moment of naturalness was the crystallizing feather-touch: it shook
> flirtation into love. Remember that the ambitious man who was looking at
> those Forget-me-nots under the water was very warm-hearted and rash. He
> did not know where the chain went; an idea had thrilled through the recesses
> within him which had a miraculous effect in raising the power of passionate
> love lying buried there in no sealed sepulchre, but under the lightest, easily
> pierced mould.[43]

Despite Lydgate's surrender to a Rosamond whom he believes has revealed
herself through tears as a Wordsworthian child of nature, Rosamond still
plays at coquetry, only with a new gambit: she drops her jewelry "as if"
startled. Acting naturally for Rosamond is itself an affectation, although
Eliot's description in this passage tends to erase the distinction. It is the
male, significantly, who is represented by Eliot as unsuspectingly caught in
a process of steadily more nuanced female coquetry. "This play at being
in love was agreeable, and did interfere with graver pursuits," Eliot's narrator notes of Rosamond and Lydgate's growing affection. "Flirtation, after all, was not a singeing process."[44] With her genius for depicting the
incremental stages in an inexorable procedure, Eliot emphasizes a naturalized operation whereby Lydgate is selected (and simultaneously transformed) into the role of a devoted, appreciating husband: "In fact, they

flirted; and Lydgate was secure in the belief that they did nothing else."[45] The female chooses a male who, sweet-natured but deluded, must imagine himself the chooser.

Eliot's evocatively "scientific" image of a "pierced mold"—flirtation's metamorphosis into an apparently naturalized process of lovemaking—is also a stage in a process whereby the individual is conjoined to the greater community. For Eliot, this is the rightful location for passion if it is to be allowed to take a place in the larger scheme of society. With the inevitability of a physical law, the Middlemarch community subtly acts on Rosamond and Lydgate so that each of the deliberately paced stages in the "sexual selection" of their courtship may ensue. "It was not more possible to find social isolation in that town than elsewhere," notes Eliot's narrator, "and two people flirting could by no means escape from 'the various entanglements, weights, blows, clashings and motions, by which things severally go on.'"[46] The narrator of *Middlemarch* stresses the community's function in ensuring that coquetry is domesticated and prevented from having perilous consequences.

Rosamond exercises dominion over other males long after her own husband has failed to advance her entwined economic and social ambitions. If in Eliot's scheme society exacts a price on the individual in the form of a moral accounting, it also inculcates deception given the necessity of adoption of artifice in sexual relations. Rosamond's awareness of the value in protracting her carnal power begins as a girlhood consciousness of a French royal past in which females reigned supreme. What she intuitively grasps is that the aristocracy may be vanishing but its social ethos endures even in the provincial setting of Middlemarch. Her appreciation of the privileges of sexual selection is compelling enough to suggest, if not Eliot's approval, at least a recognition of Rosamond's daydreaming as largely an actuality:

> Rosamond felt herself beginning to know a great deal of the world, especially in discovering—what when she was in her unmarried girlhood had been inconceivable to her except as a dim tragedy in bygone costumes—that women, even after marriage, might make conquests and enslave men. At that time young ladies in the country, even when educated at Mrs. Lemon's, read little French literature later than Racine, and public prints had not cast their present magnificent illumination over the scandals of life. Still, vanity, with a woman's whole mind and day to work in, can construct abundantly on slight hints, especially on such a hint as the possibility of indefinite conquests. How delightful to make captives from the throne of marriage with a husband as

crown-prince by your side—himself in fact a subject—while the captives
look up forever hopeless, losing their rest probably, and if their appetite too,
so much the better![47]

This arresting image of the married female's commanding power over an
array of gradually enfeebled, faint-hearted males, dependent on metaphors of military prowess, constitutes the exaggerated consummation of
the female's role in nature as it will be articulated in *The Descent of Man*.[48]
What Darwin had provided for but refrained from taking to its logical culmination—that the female might so savor the power that "nature" had
granted her that she would return to the sources of her privilege—is the
basis on which George Eliot confers power on Rosamond. "She con-
structed a little romance which was to vary the flatness of her life: Will
Ladislaw was always to be a bachelor and live near her, always to be at her
command, and have an understood but never fully expressed passion for
her, which would be sending out lambent flames every now and then in
interesting scenes." Yet Rosamond's daydream of a delimited, enduring
flirtation with Ladislaw must ultimately give way to Dorothea's own
choice. Even as Eliot depicts Rosamond and Ladislaw's encounter in the
terms of a sordid tryst, the larger thrust of *Middlemarch* demands that
Dorothea too must discover the advantage of keeping in mind—*during*
marriage—other men as potential suitors. The personal crisis that follows
Dorothea's union to Casaubon signifies not merely the heroine's faulty
judgment—although it is this, too—but the necessity of extending judgment in order to maintain admirers in reserve. Eliot's high-minded heroine does select a second suitor once Casaubon has died, but he has already
been positioned in her path in several earlier scenes in order to stress the
providential naturalness of their bond. Like the species of birds described
in *The Descent of Man* who, exhausted by the games of courtship, drop out
of the process of sexual selection, Casaubon registers his recognition of his
defeat before a younger, more vigorous rival and expires.

Casaubon's muffled rage before his youthful rival stems from the older
man's recognition that there are no manageable "happy endings" in nature, only unceasing process, new "phenomena," along with unpredictable if cyclically occurring matings. Dorothea repeatedly is placed in implausible situations so that she will encounter the man who eventually will
become her second husband. Such cannily deployed devices in plot even
permit (or especially permit) Eliot's married heroines the occasion to realize their need to flirt. Such flirtations, as much a part of the heroine's

"education" as the far more explicitly pronounced matter of her moral development, must be camouflaged through encounters that appear exquisitely accidental. Eliot, as much as Darwin, depicts the messy heterogeneity of nature as yielding to a literary artist's aesthetic requirements. This is accomplished through a series of perfectly timed positionings of Ladislaw in Dorothea's path, as when Dorothea encounters Ladislaw in the Vatican at the very moment when the breakdown of her marriage is becoming apparent to her. The surging rapport between Dorothea and Ladislaw that was inaugurated and made pure in the prelapsarian Edenic setting of Casaubon's garden is sanctified this time by its reemergence in an exalted religious setting. Ladislaw's initial reaction to Dorothea is one of exultant attraction—"But what a voice!" he thinks to himself. Dorothea's potential romantic interest in her upstart secret suitor is only implied in a brief synopsis the narrator offers indicating what Dorothea observes in his features: "The cousin was so close now, that, when he lifted his hat, Dorothea could see a pair of grey eyes rather near together, a delicate, irregular nose with a little ripple in it, and hair falling backward: but there was a mouth and chin of a more prominent, threatening aspect than belonged to the type of the grandmother's miniature."[49] As this passage suggests, the unfolding plot of flirtation has a syntactic girding in sentences that tease the reader with expectations that are hinted at but not fulfilled. From the initial, bold eroticization of Ladislaw's mouth and chin, the narrator retreats to a comfier evocation of Ladislaw's grandmother, all perceived through Dorothea's eyes at the very moment in the novel when the blunder of her marriage to Casaubon has registered with the reader, if not with her.

This sink-or-swim need to revive and naturalize a partly hidden, parallel erotic plot, one that has been carefully consigned to the wings in the narrative after Dorothea has encountered Ladislaw in Casaubon's garden, also is conveyed through a number of astonishingly vivid metaphors of animal life that evoke Darwin's rhetorical collapse of the "human" and "animal" spheres. After her husband's death, Dorothea is paralyzed while awaiting a first move from her old admirer. "The longing was to see Will Ladislaw," the narrator indicates soon after Dorothea's unexpected widowhood:

> [S]he was helpless; her hands had been tied from making up to him for any unfairness in his lot. But her soul thirsted to see him. How could it be otherwise? If a princess in the days of enchantment had seen a four-footed creature from among those which live in herds come to her once and again with a

human gaze which rested upon her with choice and beseeching, what would
she think of in her journeying, what would she look for when the herds
passed her? Surely for the gaze which had found her, and which she would
know again.[50]

Dorothea's brooding daydream of salvation from her death-in-life is expressed here as a lustrous cross-species communication. We witness the
silent anthropomorphic "understanding" of human suffering by a four-
legged beast, through which the heroine must discover her future path.
That heroine is an unawakened sleeping beauty, who fantasizes that an admirer will be obliged to choose a female, given that "her hands were tied."
In the end Dorothea must work toward a deeper appreciation of the need
to act as choosing female after Casaubon's death, just as the fairy-tale
princess from the "days of enchantment" must decide to answer the beseeching gaze of the animal who stirs her to consciousness. The beast gen-
tly reminds a woman of her true "descent"—that is, the animalistic origins of her human nature. The narrator's rhetorical question ("How could
it be otherwise?") is a characteristic gesture on Eliot's part wherein impulses the author wishes to designate as elevated are naturalized. The
male—even a suave, self-confidant suitor such as Ladislaw—is a mutely
conscious observer, a silent but sentient animal. It is the female who must
awaken herself to the urgency of choice. Ladislaw forever places himself in
situations where he will encounter Dorothea (in Casaubon's garden and
later at the Vatican), but it is Dorothea who must convert these circum-
stances into opportunities.[51]

   Dorothea's decision finally is forced by a shock-producing encounter,
when, hearing "a voice speaking in low tones which startled her with a
sense of dreaming in daylight," she witnesses the "terrible illumination of
a certainty which filled up all outlines": "Seated with his back towards her
on the sofa which stood against the wall on a line with the door which she
entered she saw Will Ladislaw: close by him and turned towards him with
a flushed tearfulness which gave a new brilliancy to her face sat Rosamond,
her bonnet hanging back, while Will leaning towards her clasped both her
upraised hands in his and spoke with low-toned fervour."[52] Eliot's own
narrative "omniscience" works in tandem with Dorothea's; we disturb a
strangely ambiguous scene, perhaps the early stage of a physical embrace
or an awkward enactment of Rosamond's vision of sustaining a sexually
charged, never-to-be-consummated relation with Ladislaw. (That Rosamond's tears in this scene cannot be relied on as evidence of sincerity already is clear from her "artificial" courtship with Lydgate.)

In their never-to-be-resolved quality of abstruseness, generating what might be termed a radical instability of meaning in the text, these scenes echo those between Thackeray's Becky Sharp and Lord Steyne. Flirtatious scenarios allow for a multiplicity of interpretations that may be exploited by participants when they are accused of sexual indiscretions. Ladislaw's reaction to Dorothea's entrance and abrupt departure, for example—angrily insisting that Rosamond defend the encounter witnessed by Dorothea—is depicted in such overwrought terms that the reader may be forgiven for thinking Ladislaw is guilty of what Dorothea chooses not to imagine. Because of the hallucinatory quality of this scene, Dorothea can accept Rosamond's explanation of what transpired; the scene of flirtation allows for a loophole in the moral judgment that omniscience usually affords.[53] In *Middlemarch,* coquetry not only mitigates the rifts keeping apart the sexes, it dissipates the divide separating the "useless" coquette and the commendable heroine. The eagle-eyed narrative perspective Eliot favors in the scene between Rosamond and Ladislaw, in its aggressive seeking of "evidence" supposedly typical of Eliot's artistry, is hardly an omniscience that the novelist uniformly endorses.

In a similarly enigmatic scenario in *Daniel Deronda,* Deronda privately confers with Gwendolen in her home but is reduced to silence, unable to comfort the obviously distraught woman who seems to seek both his moral guidance and his physical assurance. Deronda's paralysis before Gwendolen, moreover, is delineated in carnally compelling terms: "He felt himself holding a crowd of words imprisoned within his lips, as if letting them escape would be a violation of awe before the mysteries of our human lot." Syntactically, Eliot seems to establish a sexually taut encounter only to dissipate the erotic implications of the pair's private interlude, as Deronda and Gwendolen's dilemma becomes generalized into all of humankind's. After this syntactic evasion, Grandcourt's return supplies an additional "out" for a novelist unable to resolve her misgivings over a romantic consummation for Gwendolen and Deronda. What Eliot has wrought between her future Zionist leader, too high-minded to draw a woman into adultery, and Gwendolen, imprisoned by a sadistic husband but yearning for deliverance, defies prevailing categories. "'Don't flirt with her too much, Dan,'" admonishes Hugh Mallinger, "meaning to be agreeably playful," Eliot notes, for he is worried that Deronda will make Grandcourt "savage." Grandcourt himself thinks that "there was some 'confounded nonsense' between [Gwendolen and Deronda]: he did not imagine it exactly as flirtation, and his imagination in other branches was

rather restricted; but it was nonsense that evidently kept up a kind of sim-
mering in her mind—an inward action that might become disagreeably
outward." Not so much exploiting the scenario of flirtation as finding an
authorial deliverance from fully exploring this scene, Eliot engineers
Grandcourt's abrupt return for a staging of Darwinian principles. Grandcourt's "surprise" return to his own home generates the tension of an un-
masked adultery. The scene makes great sense when seen in the light of
Darwin's continued stress on male rivalry for female approval: "But
Grandcourt took no notice; he was satisfied to have let her know that she
had not deceived him, and to keep a silence which was formidable with
omniscience."[54] The all-seeing Grandcourt's "omniscience" is part of his
all-encompassing sadism, and Eliot is here calibrating how it robs Gwendolen of the smallest opportunity for freedom.[55]

Even as she is trapped by her husband, the male "rivals" vie for female
favor. In the presence of Deronda, Grandcourt moves with cunning and
assurance: "Without any show of surprise, Grandcourt nodded to Deronda, gave a second look at Gwendolen, passed on, and seated himself
easily at a little distance, crossing his legs, taking out his handkerchief and
trifling with it elegantly."[56] Eliot complicates Darwinian "choice" without
ever violating the basic spirit of Darwinian precepts. Faced with a con-
tender for his wife's attention in his own home, even the coolly malevolent
Grandcourt attends to appearances. And as in the climactic disclosure at
Rosamond's drawing room, Grandcourt's discovery of his wife's intense
friendship with Daniel takes on a vitally important function in the narrative. Gwendolen is summarily taken on a yachting trip by Grandcourt
and into yet another, this time far more ethically cloudy, spectacle: her
passive allowance of her husband's death by drowning. Having "chosen"
badly in marriage (the title of the chapter detailing Gwendolen courtship
is entitled "Gwendolen Gets Her Choice"), Gwendolen finds liberation
through a brutal split-second decision that borders on manslaughter.

As Eliot implies, sexual selection harbors within it the potential for a
morbid exercising of erotic will, as much for Grandcourt as for the death-
dealing Gwendolen.[57] In another nod to Darwinian belief as it is articulated in *The Origin of Species,* the novel depicts Daniel as caught in a
struggle of choice that will determine the survival of his people. His rivalry
with Grandcourt is an instinctive defense of his own "species"—the Jewish "race"—against a representative of yet another species, the property-
controlling English, Matthew Arnold's now-desiccated "barbarians." As

Deronda assumes a grander role as a missionary to the Middle East, it is Grandcourt whose elegant manners become an impediment to the survival of his "people." The captain of a gleaming yacht who himself cannot swim, he is a mockery of virility and assurance. His death is the cancellation by nature of an error in "choice" in the interests of a more elevated survival.

THOMAS HARDY'S COMEDIES AND TRAGEDIES OF FICKLENESS

> Bathsheba was no schemer for marriage, nor was she deliberately a trifler with the affections of men, and a censor's experience on seeing an actual flirt after observing her would have been a feeling of surprise that Bathsheba could be so different from such a one, and yet so like what a flirt is supposed to be.
> —Thomas Hardy, *Far from the Madding Crowd* (1874)

Thomas Hardy's novels—and some of his poetic work—are permeated by a nearly obsessive preoccupation with the effects of female choice, in which heroines find themselves in romantic cul-de-sacs encompassing two and sometimes more lovers. Beginning with *Under the Greenwood Tree,* Hardy's entire fictional oeuvre comprises an extensive exploration of the concerns that would find their culmination as scientific principle in *The Descent of Man.* In *Under the Greenwood Tree,* the young schoolmistress Fancy Day succumbs to the protracted attentions of Dick Dewy, yet as their marriage plans proceed Dick realizes his wife has a distressingly roving eye. In *A Pair of Blue Eyes* (1873), Elfride Swancourt, engaged to the handsome architect Stephen Fitzmaurice Smith, ends up abandoning him for another man when her father disapproves. But the results of her choice destroy her engagement when her fiancé discovers her previous affair. The capricious Bathsheba Everdene of *Far from the Madding Crowd* (1874), passionate but fickle in her judgments, at once embodies an archetypal flirt and flies free of the type, generating "surprise" in a censorious observer who has become jaded by the mannered spontaneities of an overused literary phylum. Unlike Hardy's other heroines, Bathsheba has the advantage of considerable economic independence as the overseer of her own farm. Toying with three suitors simultaneously—she sends one of them a note insisting "Marry Me" and then instantly retracts it—

Bathsheba indulges in her Darwinian privileges. Yet Hardy implies that by choosing the handsome Sergeant Troy, who knows nothing of rustic life, she skips a key aspect of sexual selection: men must be "vigorous" as well as "attractive." (Hence the arrogant Troy's misguided decision to dance late until the night while Bathsheba's farm is threatened by a storm.) Troy and Boldwood are both brushed aside to make way for the simple but stalwart Gabriel Oak, whose commonsense virility manifests itself in his keen attention to Bathsheba's farm during that same storm.

By the time we confront Sue Bridehead of *Jude the Obscure,* Hardy has grafted hazardous female coquetry onto the figure of the New Woman, where she represents indecision not so much as erotic overreaching as an unconsciously driven paralysis in judgment. In *The Well-Beloved* (1892, revised 1897), Avice Caro is courted by her social superior Pierston, all the while married to her cousin Isaac. In two later incarnations of the same affair, Pierston courts and loses a second Avice, who is secretly married, and then fails to capture a third Avice, a governess. In differing ways, all of these works depict female coquetry as throwing the rules of sexual selection into disarray through the prolonging of the moment of choice that Darwin discerned as simply a key stage in the process of courtship. Hardy continually implies that the flirtatious female may, if she chooses, interrupt evolutionary "progress," as the novelist explores the forms of disaster that proceeds from the overdetermined logic of sexual selection. Hardy's fiction is populated by women both consciously and unconsciously given over to reckless coy behavior. In fact, Hardy is preoccupied with suggesting that the very division between unconscious and conscious flirting is a distinction without a difference. "Nature," whose laws prevail over human initiatives, itself erases the disparity between "primitive" impulse and deliberate human design. Thus the sweet-natured Fanny Robin of *Far from the Madding Crowd,* single-mindedly committed to her fiancé Francis Troy, infuriates him when she accidentally shows up at the wrong church on her wedding day, causing the chagrined sergeant angrily to leave her.

Although Hardy's fictional extrapolation of Darwinian concepts has been a mainstay of criticism of the novelist's work, such correlations more often have been evoked than fully illustrated.[58] And while Hardy is commonly supposed to have reflected Darwinian concepts with bleakly unquestioning piety, the novelist offers a pastoral interpretation of the precepts "objectively" rendered throughout *The Descent of Man.* What remained so unresolved in the pages of *The Descent*—the question of whether the female was consciously aware of her aesthetic and erotic judgments, and whether such judgments could be as exacting as those determining analogous human behavior—is again and again enacted in Hardy's novels. In their moments of flirtatious desire—now consciously experimental, now mutely involuntary—many of Hardy's heroines (Sue Bridehead is the prime example) seem poised between two eras in the literary representation of women of "advanced" consciousness.

With *Under the Greenwood Tree,* the first of his Wessex novels, Hardy does not simply register the precepts of sexual selection. Rather, he luxuriates in its richly comic possibilities. With this uncharacteristically blithe Hardy work (Leslie Stephen admired the novel as a "prose idyll"), we witness a strand in Hardy's artistry that never saw full fruition, one that imagines Darwinian laws as vitally innocent "rustic" truths.[59] My focus here is on *Under the Greenwood Tree* partly because in this rare pastoral comedy, wry and serene, Hardy had yet to succumb to the passionate negativism of his more familiar philosophical axioms. In this novel, chronic female indecision has yet to become pathological. If Eliot humanizes Darwinian ideas in *The Mill on the Floss* by depicting sexual selection as opening up deeper recesses of female and male feeling and consciousness, in *Under the Greenwood Tree* Hardy pastoralizes those ideas. He renders sexual selection as neither a meaningless aristocratic game nor as risk-taking social mischief, but as a salutary feature of daily, folk ritual.

There is very little in the way of plot in this extraordinarily breezy work, the first line of which immediately evokes Darwin's most recognized work: "To dwellers in a wood almost every species of tree has its voice as well as its feature."[60] Set in the town of Mellstock in the early part of the nineteenth century, *Under the Greenwood Tree* concerns a young man's infatuation with a woman he gradually realizes is an inveterate coquette. Hardy exploits the humor of a situation that he never permits to darken into tragedy, in which a young country boy recognizes that his beloved "far from being the simple girl who never had a sweetheart before, as she had solemnly assured him time after time, she was, if not a flirt, a woman who had no end of admirers: a girl most certainly too anxious about her frocks; a girl whose feelings, though warm, were not deep; a girl who cared a great deal too much how she appeared in the eyes of other men."[61]

Dick Dewy's courtship of Fancy is primarily an attempt at freeing her from several suitors, the vicar Shiner and the wealthy farmer Arthur Maybold. Like Eliot in her evocation of Maggie's temptation of Stephen, Hardy is absorbed in the excitement of flirting, the possibility of rendering in bodily terms what, in a description of romantic courtship, might have taken on an excessively abstract significance:

> Good-luck attended Dick's love-passes during the meal. He sat next to Fancy, and had the thrilling pleasure of using permanently a glass which had been taken by Fancy in mistake; of letting the outer edge of the sole of his boot touch the lower verge of her skirt; and to add to these delights the cat, which had lain unobserved in her lap for several minutes, crept across into his own, touching him with fur that had touched her hand a moment before. . . . He also, from time to time, sipped sweet sly glances at her profile; noticing the set of her head, the curve of her throat, and other artistic properties of the lively goddess, who all the while kept up a rather free, not to say too free, conversation with Mr. Shiner sitting opposite.[62]

The cat as consenting go-between is not the only element in Hardy's novel that evokes the earlier *The Mill on the Floss*. Dick's rival here, like that the rival of Philip Wakem, is the local fop, the ostentatious Mr. Shiner, a "pretty man with brass studs, and a copper ring, and a tin watch chain."[63] Unlike Maggie Tulliver, Fancy Day does not express intermittent acts of nonconformity, for Fancy's impulse to toy with many men is harmonized with her entire free-spirited, occasionally prim personality. She is no Rosamond Vincy, but, rather, a cheerful Everylass, a "simple" member of Wessex society. (She is a schoolteacher and the chief organist at Mellstock Church School.) Her eyes are "softened by a frequent thoughtfulness" and contain a "certain coquettishness; which in its turn was never so decided as to banish honesty."[64]

As in chapter 9 of "The Maiden" section of *Tess of the D'Urbervilles* (1891), in which Tess first meets Angel Clare at a local outside ball where she has declined to participate, it is through the rituals of dance that Hardy's characters locate the symbolic distillation of flirtatious desires. The frantic dance sequence, although situated in a rural locale, replicates an urban frenzy of flirtatious promiscuities. In *Under the Greenwood Tree*, coquetry does not stem solely from an uncomplicated erotic satisfaction. In one of the most remarkable scenes in Hardy's fiction, the tranter Dick Dewy, smitten with Fancy Day, finds himself in a macabre country dance called "six-hands round," the scene of a spooky carnivalesque:

> It was the time of night when a guest may write his name in the dust upon the tables and chairs, and a bluish mist pervades the atmosphere, becoming a

distinct halo round the candles; when people's nostrils, wrinkles, and crevices in general seem to be getting gradually plastered up; when the very fiddlers as well as the dancers get red in the face, the dancers having advanced further still towards incandescence, and entered the cadaverous phase; the fiddlers no longer sit down, but kick back their chairs and saw madly at the strings, with legs firmly spread and eyes closed, regardless of the visible world. Again and again did Dick share his beloved's hand with another man, and wheel round; then, more delightfully, promenade in a circle with her all to himself, his arm holding her waist more firmly each time, and his elbow getting further and further behind her back, till the distance reached was rather noticeable; and, most blissful, swinging to places shoulder to shoulder, her breath curling around his neck like a summer zephyr that had strayed from its proper date. Threading the couples one by one they reached the bottom, when there arose in Dick's mind a minor misery lest the tune should end before they could work their way to the top again, and have anew the same exciting run down through. Dick's feelings on actually reaching the top in spite of his doubts were supplemented by a mortal fear that the fiddling might even stop at this supreme moment; which prompted him to convey a stealthy whisper to the far-gone musicians to the effect that they were not to leave off till he and his partner had reached the bottom of the dance once more, which remark was replied to by the nearest of those convulsed and quivering men by a private nod to the anxious young man between two semiquavers of the tune, and a simultaneous "All right, ay, ay," without opening the eyes. Fancy was now held so closely that Dick and she were practically one person. The room became to Dick like a picture in a dream; all that he could remember of it afterwards being the look of the fiddlers going to sleep as humming-tops sleep, by increasing their motion and hum, together with the figures of grandfather James and old Simon Crumpler sitting by the chimney-corner, talking and nodding in dumb-show, and beating the air to their emphatic sentences like people near a threshing machine.

The dance ended. "Piph-h-h-h!" said tranter Dewy, blowing out his breath in the very finest stream of vapour that a man's lips could form. "A regular tightener, that one, sonnies!" He wiped his forehead, and went to the cider and ale mugs on the table.

"Well," said Mrs. Penny, flopping into a chair, "My heart haven't been in such a thumping state of uproar since I used to sit up on old Midsummer-eves to see who my husband was going to be." [65]

The fever produced by the accelerated dance, set at a witching hour when humans are transformed into purely sensual figures, is a primitive rite of furious synergistic intensity. Despite the eerily ritualized, even mechanized quality of the dance, Darwinian precepts are enacted as a pleasurable game of Pagan carnality. As in the scenarios of courtship detailed throughout *The Descent*, eros is not a private encounter but a communally based ceremony. Hardy gives sexual selection a sweeping, lyrical impetus and incandescent fluidity. Like Maggie and Stephen in the boating scene, Dick and Fancy here reach a level of intimacy denied them at other points in the novel.

After Dick and Fancy have married, Dick's efforts at living in temporal sync with Fancy are frustrated by her slowing down of time:

> "How long will you be putting on your bonnet, Fancy?" Dick inquired at the foot of the staircase. Being now a man of business and married, he was strong on the importance of time, and doubled the emphasis of his words in conversing, and added vigour to his nods.
>
> "Only a minute."
>
> "How long is that?"
>
> "Well, dear, five."
>
> "Ah, sonnies!" said the tranter, as Dick retired, "'tis a talent of the female race that low numbers should stand for high, more especially in matters of waiting, matters of age, and matters of money." [66]

Although *Under the Greenwood Tree* is largely informed by the perspective of the fretful Dick, the novel concludes with a view of Fancy's inner thoughts as she is beckoned by an anthropomorphized bird:

> "Fancy," he said, "why we are so happy is because there is such full confidence between us. Ever since the time you confessed to that little flirtation with Shiner by the river (which was really no flirtation at all), I have thought how artless and good you must be to tell me o' such a trifling thing, and to be so frightened about it as you were. It has won me to tell you my every deed and word since then. We'll have no secrets from each other, darling, will we ever?—no secret at all."
>
> "None from today," said Fancy. "Hark! what's that?"
>
> From a neighbouring thicket was suddenly heard to issue in a loud, musical, and liquid voice—
>
> "Tippiwit! swe-e-et! ki-ki-ki. Come hither, come hither, come hither!"
>
> "O, 'tis the nightingale," murmured she, and thought of a secret she would never tell. [67]

This final image of sphinxlike Fancy, self-secluded with a private knowledge of having "betrayed" her husband and now "wooed" again, projects an image of a secret female realm beyond male understanding.

Hardy came to accept the rules of sexual selection and to warn of the perils in veering from nature's scheme. Thus, in the Trantridge dance sequence in *Tess of the D'Urbervilles* (the town's name echoes the name of Dick, the son of a tranter), the changing of partners signifies a widely accepted fealty before the edicts of a natural order. "Changing partners simply meant that a satisfactory choice had not yet been arrived at by one or other of the pair, and by this time every couple had been matched." Females remain in charge of a social ritual that seems to have no consequences since all the partners are already matched or will be guaranteed, although there is the occasional mishap, as when couples topple over one another as the fiddle-playing becomes more accelerated: "'You shall catch it for this, my gentleman, when you get home!' burst in female accents from the human heap—those of the unhappy partner of the man whose clumsiness had caused the mishap; she happened also to be his recently married wife—in which assortment there was nothing unusual at Trantridge, as long as any affection remained between wedded couples; and, indeed it was not uncustomary in their later lives, to avoid making odd lots of the single people between whom there might be a warm understanding." [68]

If flirtation is a maddening process for the love-bestirred, duped Dick, for the married revelers of *Under the Greenwood Tree* and *Far from the Madding Crowd,* it is a constant, lovely diversion from the everyday grind of actual wedlock. In chapter 36 of *Far from the Madding Crowd* (entitled "Wealth in Jeopardy: The Revel"), the dance sequence that immediately precedes the storm is a key instance in a process of sexual selection. Troy's indulgent dancing, a feature of what Hardy calls his "romanticism" and enacted to the tune of "The Soldier's Joy," is presented "in juxtaposition" (Hardy's words) to Gabriel's awareness of hazardous natural forces.[69] The erratic Bathsheba delays in her choice of a mate—and then chooses badly—but nature corrects that misguided decision. In Hardy's melancholy meditation on the processes of sexual selection, Boldwood's murderous action is, like Gwendolen's allowance of Grandcourt's drowning, an act that is sanctioned by nature. What counts as a crime in the community is given silent assent by nature herself, which punishes Troy's excessive devotion to self-preening just as it reprimands Bathsheba's dallying.

The negative logic of *Tess of the D'Urbervilles* also affirms the sovereignty of sexual selection through the public rituals of dance. The exquisite Tess, although she "does not abhor dancing," declines to participate in the "passionate" dance of partners. Instead, she "reluctantly" joins Alec D'Urberville, who has been waiting nearby, and thus accepts her fate. In the retrospective shadow cast by Stonehenge, however, the reader is made aware of the grim consequences for Tess's social retreat. Had she been a shrewd coquette, or at least shrewdly coquettish, and thus intent on making chance work in her favor (instead of a fragile naif convinced that a single romantic plot would sustain her in perpetuity), Tess would have flirted with *all* of the young men at the Trantridge dance. She would have then gained greater control over her fate. Like the homely Katisha of Gilbert and Sullivan's *The Mikado* or poor Boldwood of *Far from the Madding Crowd*, Tess is fixed on a single erotic plot when she should have recognized the advantage sexual selection allowed for the multiplication of opportunities. Stated another way, Tess's tragedy consists in her surrendering herself too greatly to the dictates of chance.

In *Jude the Obscure*, it is the tragic logic of protracted female choice rather than the tragedy of missed opportunities that makes the novel's design. Evolutionary progress is stymied by the eruption of unconscious flirtatious desire. Sue Bridehead's role as a New Woman ensures she will be foiled by her inability to decide between suitors. Still, Sue struggles to comprehend the meaning of her tragedy. Standing in antithetical relation to Arabella (the novel's conventional coquette, whose conniving comprises a desperate mimicry of Brontë's rakish Ginevra Fanshawe or Austen's roguish Isabel Thorpe), Sue signals flirting as an unconscious inability to surrender power. In the final pages of Hardy's novel, she delivers a poignantly befuddled self-defense in which she emphasizes her condition as woman stalled in an act of indecision.

> "At first I did not love you, Jude; that I own. When I first knew you I merely wanted you to love me. I did not exactly flirt with you; but that inborn craving which undermines some women's morals almost more than unbridled passion—the craving to attract and captivate, regardless of the injury it may do the man—was in me; and when I found I had caught you, I was frightened. And then—I don't know how it was—I couldn't bear to let you go— possibly to Arabella again—and so I got to love you, Jude. But you see, however fondly it ended, it began in the selfish and cruel wish to make your heart ache for me without letting mine ache for you."
>
> "And now you add to your cruelty by leaving me!"
>
> "Ah—yes! The further I flounder, the more harm I do!" [70]

Equated with a "craving" that is both "inborn" and morally destructive, Sue's flirtations have the quality of an overwhelming unconscious force— indeed, flirtation has become stronger in its destructive power than "unbridled passion." Moreover, Sue's sequence of qualifications—"I did not exactly flirt with you," "I don't know how it was," "I couldn't bear to let you go—possibly to Arabella again"—discredits her as both unreliable and inconsistent. Her timorous self-defense only serves as another confirmation that she is a flirt who wavers uncertainly between options, as much a tragic heroine as a pre-Freudian clinical "female case."

In the deterioration of Sue Bridehead, we witness the degeneration of female "choice" into callous indecision. Of her several heartless acts of trifling with Jude, perhaps the cruelest is her insistence on taking him through a mock marriage ceremony in a church the day before her wedding with Phillotson. In its somnambulant brutality, Sue's flirting with Jude in this scene of mock marriage resembles the sleep-walking mock "burial" of Tess by Angel Clare after Tess has confessed to Angel her past with Alec. Her guilt over her coquetries is intertwined with her confusion as to the sources of her actions. Whereas Becky Sharp's utterly public persona offers a self that is "inwardly resolved" (as Simmel claims for the coquette), Sue signals the flirt in an incognizant state of psychic uncertainty and even chaos: coquetry as psychopathology. Her "true" sexual nature, coupled with her status as female aesthete, links her to another principal figure of turn-of-the-century cultural anxiety, the bachelor dandy who, like Sue, represents civilization in a regressive mode and whose self-conflict over his sexual nature places him into a state of devolution. In *The Well-Beloved,* female irresolution is projected onto a male artist, the sculptor Jocelyn Pierston, who yearns for an ideal lover/muse as he raises suspicions that he is a disgraceful philanderer.

The coquette's emergence as a figure of unnatural, dangerous potency in late-Victorian and fin-de-siècle fiction drew considerable strength from the implications of Darwinian evolutionary thinking even as Darwin's Victorian and late-Victorian readers often interpreted his work differently, that is, as offering a kind of model of the normative. The coquette becomes a more insidious figure, epitomizing not simply sexual immorality but an unconstituted self, simultaneously society's "aberration" and nature's castoff. Hardy's Sue Bridehead and Fancy Day are women whose status as flirts is conflated with their roles as creatures with perilously heightened powers of aesthetic and, in turn, erotic "appreciation." The free-thinking Sue's purchase of "taboo" Hellenic sculptures, Fancy's preference for an alluring hat that her fiancé Dick judges "too coquettish and flirty for a young woman," mark these women as inordinately invested in their Darwinian roles as female aesthetes and taste-dictating choosers. These women reflect a central preoccupation in Hardy's fiction: the power of a recondite scheme embedded in nature, a secret pattern encompassing a semi-available superfecundity of activity. This half-hidden design finds a perfect metaphor in the games of coquetry, which, having an anarchic power and "producing" nothing, nevertheless leave behind traces. For Hardy, however, the comic potential in the half-hidden rites of Darwinian courtship is eclipsed by an inexorable tragic calculus.

❧ 4 ❧

Deadly Deferrals

Henry James, Edith Wharton,
Gustave Flaubert, and the Exhaustion
of Flirtatious Desire

JAMES'S "INNOCENT AMERICAN FLIRT": DAISY MILLER
AND THE PERILS OF THE UNCONSCIOUS LIFE

By the end of the nineteenth century, in works as different in tone, style, and subject matter as James's *Daisy Miller,* Hardy's *Jude the Obscure,* and Bram Stoker's *Dracula,* novelists increasingly represent the female flirt as a social menace, her strategies not only perniciously insincere, a threat to customary methods of unraveling identity, but unnatural as well. The coquette looms large as an individual whose connotations of danger—an admixture of theatricality and power—coupled with her status as a connoisseur of male beauty, shape her as an insurgent who wreaks havoc with nature's courtship plot and its aim of species procreation. Simultaneously, the plot of flirtation takes on intensified significance as a disreputable avenue of erotic pursuit as writers increasingly figure it a plot "against nature." As suggested earlier, by the end of the century the cultural weight adhering to flirtation in the high Victorian novel had become insupportable, to the point that it was left to the comic duo of Gilbert and Sullivan to puncture the received wisdom of flirting as a fate-determining activity. With the writing of Henry James and Edith Wharton, however, the novel continued to require the figure of the coquette in order to refine the aesthetic aims of realist fiction. In James, that refinement took the form of a rebuke of European social manners that also saw flirting as a means of expressing a modernist conception of experience as necessarily subjective. The "innocent American flirt" Daisy Miller, supremely unreadable in the swirl of overly sophisticated "readers," is the paradigmatic modernist cipher. With Wharton, the "innocent enough adventure" of flirtation became in *The Age of Innocence* a morbid investment in pointless desire that had devolved into a moribund set of European literary conventions.[1] Even as she devised a trademark ambivalent bachelor, in *The House of Mirth* her naturalist sympathies led her to stress flirtation as a zero-sum game.

This chapter departs from what largely has been an account of European fiction in order to explore how James and Wharton, because they are the two major modern American writers most energetically engaged with the tradition of the European novel, dramatize the differences between European and American notions of flirting as they complicate how flirtation determines plot and character. With the figures of Daisy Miller and Lily Bart, the tragicomic dimension of the professional flirt Becky Sharp's behavior is shorn of much of its comic resonance. The image of Becky as a survivor in the final pages of *Vanity Fair* fairly oozes with ironies, yet in tenaciously overcoming financial ruin and social opprobrium, she demonstrates the value of flirty artifice over heartfelt sincerity. For James and Wharton, however, coquetry is a life-and-death conflict and as such remains centrally caught up in the very enterprise of fiction.

The issue of unconscious motivation that was so often only tacit in Victorian fiction, whether in Steerforth's admiration for David Copperfield's physique or Sue Bridehead's vacillation between two suitors, is the commanding matter of public debate in *Daisy Miller*. In what proved to be James's most controversial venture into fiction, the heroine captivates others in large part because she perplexes, undermining the conventions of European coquetry that have been shaped by centuries of drawing-room practice. Winterbourne and the American exiles of the Swiss resort of Vevey must come to terms with whether Daisy *knows* what she is doing. By supplying Daisy with a family fortune (her father, we are told by her brother Randolph at the outset, is in "big business" in Schenectady, New York), James frees his Daisy of the burdens of flirting professionally, as Thackeray could not with Becky and as Wharton later refused to do with Lily Bart. In James's novella, the Puritan preoccupation with virtue gives way to a new understanding that motivations may be "innocent" in being outside of consciousness. But if James demonstrates a pre-Freudian preoccupation with unconscious motivation—and goes so far as to link unconscious flirting with a death wish—his representative American flirt refuses to surrender herself to analysis. His heroine dies an enigma, a martyr to a school of realism that James himself now found exhausted. "The art of fiction has, in fact, become a finer art in our day than it was with Dickens and Thackeray," observed William Dean Howells in an 1882 article in the *Century Magazine* in which Howells called James the "chief exemplar of a new school" of the novel, "largely influenced by French fiction in form." Asked Howells: "Will the reader be content to accept a novel which is an analytic study rather than a story. . . ?"[2] James's turn toward the more nuanced, opaque style of his late phase is presaged in the circuitous analytic commentary attending to the heroine of *Daisy Miller*. This new attitude toward fictional characters comes to fruition in *The Wings of the Dove* (1902) and *The Ambassadors* and reaches its apotheosis in the stunning opacities of *The Golden Bowl*.

Wharton also revises the figure of the coquette in *The House of Mirth,* where a bitter naturalist scheme trumps Thackeray's love-hate relation to the figure of the virtuoso flirt. At the same time, Wharton projects characteristics usually defined as feminine onto male coquette-figures such as Lawrence Selden and Newland Archer. In *The Age of Innocence,* she expands on this rebuke of European fiction, this time through a protofeminist revision of Flaubert's *Sentimental Education* that views the nineteenth-century European novel as morbidly and relentlessly mired in scenarios of unrequited desire. Although Wharton claimed to be disappointed by her friend James's increasing experimentalism in the modernist mode, in *The Age of Innocence* she herself discovers the terms for a rebellion against the European novel of realism. In doing so, she not only distances herself from its investment in unconsummated desires, drawing out its connection to Puritan self-denial, she offers an implied rebuke to James himself, who had hailed Flaubert as the "novelist's novelist" and *Sentimental Education* itself as "that indefinable last word of restrained evocation and cold execution."[3]

"He's the handsomest man in the world," Daisy Miller exclaims to her friend Winterbourne of her suitor Giovanelli, but then coquettishly adds, "Except for Mr. Winterbourne!" Well before she acquires Giovanelli as a companion, Daisy revels in her self-appointed role as the judge of a private male beauty contest. Whereas Sue Bridehead frantically acts out her neurotic confusions, self-punitively aware that she is caught between the ideals of Hellenic culture and Christian values, Daisy Miller is an evident "innocent," who serenely flaunts public decorum without herself seeming self-conflicted. Her death is a martyrdom of American innocence on the pyre of European attitudes, although (in a characteristic Jamesian irony) these values are expressed not by Europeans but are assumed unquestioningly by transplanted Americans. The sources of her flirting are well hidden, so completely missing from view that she is, for all around her, a walking enigma. Much of the drama of James's novella centers on the attempts by others, chiefly Winterbourne, to decipher Daisy and to read her socially opaque, provocative, and, we are instructed, American behavior.

> Poor Winterbourne was amused and perplexed—above all he was charmed. He had never yet heard a young girl express herself in just this fashion; never at least save in cases where to say such things was to have at the same time some rather complicated consciousness about them. . . . Never indeed since he had grown old enough to appreciate things had he encountered a young compatriot of so "strong" a type as this. Certainly she was very charming, but how extraordinarily communicative and how tremendously easy! Was she simply a pretty girl from New York State—were they all like that, the pretty girls who had had a good deal of gentlemen's society? Or was she also a designing, an audacious, in short an expert young person? Yes, his instinct for such a question had ceased to serve him, and his reason could but mislead. Miss Daisy Miller looked extremely innocent. Some people had told him that after all American girls *were* exceedingly innocent, and others had told him that after all they weren't. He must on the whole take Miss Daisy Miller for a flirt—a pretty American flirt. He had never as yet had relations with representatives of that class. He had known here in Europe two or three women— persons older than Miss Daisy Miller and provided, for respectability's sake, with husbands—who were great coquettes; dangerous terrible women with whom one's light commerce might indeed take a serious turn. But this charming apparition wasn't a coquette in that sense; she was very unsophisticated; she was only a pretty American flirt. Winterbourne was almost grateful for having found the formula that applied to Miss Daisy Miller.[4]

Daisy's apparent "innocence" points to the inefficacy of stock ethical categories. Her flirting is itself synonymous with the female unconscious, libidinal predilections that are observable only in a limited degree but ultimately absent. In the account above, a perspectival head-shaking dominates the narration. That Daisy, in this obsessively backtracking description, is repeatedly described as unsophisticated and youthful hints that she is still somehow a child. Just as Freud had designated the child—and particularly the female child—as the locus of perverse feeling, so too does Winterbourne come to see Daisy as a child unaware of her own perverse unconscious.[5]

In appearing so completely unaware of the social peril of her flirting with Giovanelli, Daisy is an altogether new type of flirtatious female. Taking flirtation out of the domain of the salon and into the public arena, she is a female relative of the figure Walter Benjamin regarded as a representative cosmopolitan type: the street-ambling flâneur, whom Benjamin saw as a man "who demanded elbow room and was unwilling to forgo the life of a gentleman of leisure," much as the flirt is a woman unwilling to surrender her privileges of choosing among different men.[6] Even as her scandalous behavior is dependent on public procedures, the flâneuse becomes a deeper psychic enigma. We are told immediately that Daisy is not a "typical" American flirt; she is introduced to the reader and to Winterbourne as embodying, rather, a bewildering prototype, what Winterbourne terms an "innocent American flirt." Indeed, the "new coquette" Daisy is neither fully aware of her coquetries nor economically motivated in her serene deployment of them. Still, although Daisy the coquettish flâneuse, like the Benjaminian flâneur, dreams of an aristocratic detachment, in carrying the amusements of flirtation into the public realm she embarrasses her own socially uneasy (if financially secure) class, anchored as it is in well-defined notions of propriety.

By continuing to insist on Daisy's sincerity in the face of her obvious coquettishness, Winterbourne proposes that she is inspired by unconscious motivations. Indeed, there is no deception in Daisy's behavior, only a serenely impenitent (because it is "innocent") sexual exuberance. Thus Daisy Miller represents a crisis in the ability of others to understand women as a "species." Winterbourne finds himself in repeated paroxysms of confusion as to how to decipher her behavior. Forced to rely on a virtually phrenological criterion for understanding Daisy, he keeps returning to complicate once-resolved questions. On one occasion he wonders, for example, if "it very possible that Master Randolph's sister was a coquette; he was sure she had a spirit of her own; but in her bright, sweet, superficial little visage there was no mockery, no irony."[7] In her resistance to the deciphering strategies of others, Daisy transforms the basis on which female flirtation is understood. No longer suggesting the increasingly useless distinctions designating sincere versus insincere behavior, Daisy intimates that flirtatious desire may arise from an unknowable psychic source.[8]

EDITH WHARTON: REWRITING THE VICTORIANS

"Sincerity," in many minds, is chiefly associated with speaking the truth; but architectural sincerity is simply obedience to certain visual requirements.
—Edith Wharton, *The Decoration of Houses* (1897)

The thematics of flirtation occupy a paramount role in Edith Wharton's fiction, where as a disruption of a naturalized courtship plot, coquetry serves to link the homosexual male, the marriage-postponing bachelor, and the alluring woman of coquettish devices.[9] Wharton's *The House of Mirth* and *The Age of Innocence* provide especially rich occasions for an exploration of plots of coquetry. Like Hardy, Wharton's writing reveals a career-long preoccupation with the new terms established by sexual selection theory. And much like the author of *Jude the Obscure*, Wharton's pessimism grew considerably as she registered Darwinian "laws" of erotic relations, foremost in *The House of Mirth*, where flirtation is profoundly overdetermined by Lily Bart's need to find a suitable husband before her inheritance evaporates. It is Lily's ill-defined friendship with Lawrence Selden, the lawyer of modest means whom she initially rejects as a suitor, that assumes a too-heavy emotional value in Wharton's novel. In *The Age of Innocence*, the postponement of desire is critiqued as it is conflated with a specific literary genre—the nineteenth-century novel itself. Beyond this ambivalence, much of Wharton's originality lies in her projection of traits commonly associated with the female flirt onto indecisive, marriage-postponing bachelors, who themselves emerge as Darwinian "choosers."

Depicted as an expression of the self's deepest and—in social terms— most illegitimate eros, flirtation in Wharton's fiction confounds the paradigm of the homosocial that in the last decade has proven so influential in the field of gay studies and queer theory. For unlike the homosocially structured affinities between men, male-male flirtatious desire, as depicted in *The Reef* (1912), and heterosexual flirtation, as enacted in *The Age of Innocence*, undermine the proper functioning of legitimized heterosexual relations. Simultaneously a protracted erotic promise, a "perversion" of a Darwinian natural order, and a self-negotiated search for an authentic self, coquetry is a means by which Wharton's characters negotiate the distance between illegitimate desire and an acceptable social identity. As Alexandra Johnson has written, Wharton's fiction typically registers "the *frisson* of possibility of the unfulfilled self." [10]

Throughout her literary career, Wharton continually strove to resolve her outlook on the figure of the indecisive male; indeed, her novelistic oeuvre constitutes an extended study of the type. Beginning with *The House of Mirth, Madame de Treymes* (1907) and *Ethan Frome* (1911), capped by *The Reef* and *The Age of Innocence,* culminating in *The Children* (1928) and *Hudson River Bracketed* (1929), Wharton's novels evince an enduring, even obsessive, absorption in vacillating bachelors and husbands tempted by forbidden romantic relations. A focus on Wharton's attraction to this subject highlights thematic patterns that might be otherwise enigmatic. Both *The Reef* and *The Children,* for example, represent male ambivalence as an excruciating choice between proper upper-class women (Anna Leath, Rose Sellars) and socially inferior, inappropriate females (the lowborn Sophy Viner, the adolescent Judith Wheater). Set in the Europe of the self-exiled American rich, both novels suggest that a Darwinian order as well as a cohesive set of social conventions have been inverted; Darrow's romantic involvement with Sophy, his fiancée's future stepdaughter-in-law, has suggestions of incest, while the brood of offspring in the satirical *The Children,* casually jettisoned by their sybaritic, divorced parents, bespeak a world in which procreative acts have been severed from rites of courtship. With the move from the brooding triangular narrative of *The Reef* to the near-antic comic scheme of *The Children,* however, Wharton shifted toward a more serenely philosophical resolution of her view of male emotional uncertainty.[11]

For Wharton, the mutable self encouraged by coquetry holds the potential for deeply paradoxical results. In *The Custom of the Country* (1913), flirtation is the nouveau riche heroine Undine Spragg's Machiavellian strategy for advancement through the higher tiers of New York and Paris. Similarly, Lily Bart relies on a complex repertoire of flirtatious techniques as she vies for a suitable husband in New York's brutal marriage market. Yet she maintains a tenderly flirtatious *amitié amoureuse* with Lawrence Selden, which he describes in almost pastoral terms as a shared, elevated "special republic of the spirit." In *The Age of Innocence,* the protracted flirtation between Archer and Ellen defines itself as a sequestered realm beyond what Archer characterizes as a "hackneyed vocabulary" of conventional romantic love.[12] These lovers' unconsummated affair culminates in a stark image of an emotionally paralyzed, subjugated Newland, "held fast by habit, memories," unable to visit Ellen Olenska as he sits outside her Paris home.[13] As with Flaubert's disillusioned Frédéric, coquetry has reached the limit where unconsummated love has exhausted and even debased its transcendent possibilities. In both *The House of Mirth* and *The Age of Innocence,* flirtatious desire holds heightened resonance precisely because it lacks purpose in terms of the socially sanctioned rituals of courtship, even as such flirtations, in relying on sheer appearance, seem to exaggerate and mimic those rituals.

Wharton's shifting attitude toward sexual vacillation in her male protagonists was bifurcated according to genre. When she chose to address homoerotic relations between men directly, she did so through a reliance on the myth of Persephone in the vehicle of the ghost story, in which a married man is beckoned to a forbidden subterranean realm [as in the tales "Afterward" (1909) and "Pomegranate Seed" (1931)] or, in tales such as "A Bottle of Perrier" (1926), "The Eyes" (1910) and "The Triumph of the Night" (1914), by linking homosexual carnality with the vampirish influence of a decadent older man over a younger male, as Carol J. Singley has argued.[14] In her novels, however, Wharton expressed "perverse" male desire through depictions of men steeped in indecision on matters of the heart, a hesitancy often expressed as coquettishness, a trait traditionally gendered as feminine and thus, by implication, effeminately denaturalized. The underground-bound husbands of the gothic tales and the irresolute males of the novelist's fiction stand in oppositional relation to social convention and to the marriage plot fostered in nineteenth-century literary narrative. More specifically, such figures avoid the preordained "courtship plot" that Darwin, whom Wharton considered one of her most substantial intellectual influences, posited as operating in nature.[15] The various ambivalent men of Wharton's fictional universe share a reluctance to play a part in a preordained Darwinian scheme of "sexual selection" in which, as Darwin maintained in *The Descent of Man,* females choose their mates for the siring of offspring. In expressing male erotic ambivalence as coquettish desire rather than through a dynamic of sexual repression and release, Wharton's bachelors are linked to such risk-taking females as Lily Bart and Ellen Olenska, women whose deepest emotional bonds consist of erotically charged but deliberately delimited romantic relations with "unsuitable" men.

The House of Mirth concludes with Lily Bart's grisly and in all likelihood self-willed death, and although the novel itself is bitter in its denunciation of its New York social milieu, there are revealing cracks in Wharton's harsh deterministic scheme. For while exposing the costs, both economic and spiritual, of protracted flirtation as a form of sexual self-marketing, in her portrait of Lily Bart's near-pastoral coquetries with Lawrence Selden, Wharton rehabilitated flirtation as a realm of freedom. At pivotal moments in *The House of Mirth,* Wharton allowed flirting to encompass what Simmel described as the "most mysterious and tragic relation of life in its ultimate ecstasy and most glittering attraction."[16] Such scenes, in which Lawrence and Lily conduct their peculiarly inconclusive, erotically inflected friendship, function in contrapuntal tempo with those scenes with the married Gus Trenor, who, initially coquetting with Lily through seemingly benevolent investments on her behalf, lecherously hopes to take advantage of her stubborn refusal to accept his sexual advances. (Like Selden, Lily has an ambivalent relation to the everyday indecencies of "decent" society.) The contrasting scenes involving Selden and Trenor reveal the dual, seemingly contradictory status of flirtation in *The House of Mirth:* it is an activity that simultaneously induces the self at its most artificial and most authentic.

With *The House of Mirth,* Wharton's first commercially successful venture into fiction, the novelist revised several works that had positioned the flirt as a touchstone of cultural crisis: Hannah Webster Foster's *The Coquette* (1797), one of the two best-selling novels of the eighteenth-century, as well as Thackeray's *Vanity Fair* and George Eliot's *Daniel Deronda.* The heroine of Foster's epistolary novel is Eliza Wharton (a name that suggests its likely appeal to the author of *The House of Mirth*), who is courted by two men—the Reverend Boyer, a bore eager to be her fiancé, and Major Sanford, a suave but insincere cad. (The pair anticipates Lily Bart's two admirers in *The House of Mirth,* the feckless Percy Gryce, the tiresome collector of Americana who pursues Lily with limp ardor, and the charmingly ambivalent Lawrence Selden.) She agrees to an engagement she does not want because "both nature and education had instilled in me an implicit obedience to the will and desires of my parents." After her fiancé's death, Elizabeth submits to Sanford, only to find herself pregnant and abandoned. She dies in childbirth (a scenario that Wharton may have reworked in the final pages of *The House of Mirth,* in which Lily Bart dies of a laudanum overdose, as one of her last thoughts concerns another woman's child). Foster had based her novel on the much-publicized case of the seduction and death of Elizabeth Whitman, a poet from Hartford, Connecticut. As Cathy N. Davidson notes, Foster's novel differed conspicuously from the numerous solemn tracts written about Whitman's case, which invariably saw her story as a cautionary tale implying that "virtuous choices will be rewarded with personal happiness." But in the realistic complexity of *The Coquette,* the equation between virtue and happiness

breaks down: "Where women lack the power to procure their own rewards, happiness, in marriage or affairs, depends largely on the luck of
the draw."[17]

With the evolutionary theories of Charles Darwin, the "realistic complexity" of the dilemma faced by Foster's protagonist took on new intensity and intricacy. Like George Eliot, who had welcomed the 1859
publication of the scientist's *The Origin of Species* as marking an "epoch"
in human consciousness, Wharton claimed to have absorbed whole-
heartedly Darwin's theories of evolutionary biology.[18] In a 1908 letter to
Charles Eliot Norton, she referred to the Victorian evolutionary theorist as
the greatest of her "formative" influences, along with the evolutionary social philosophers Herbert Spencer and W. E. H. Lecky.[19] In her autobiography, *A Backward Glance* (1934), Wharton recalled her early exposure to
the "wonder-world of nineteenth-century science," and discussed her
youthful enthusiasm for Spencer, the physicist John Tyndall, as well as the
biologists T. H. Huxley, Ernst Haeckel, and George John Romanes, men-
tioning in particular Alfred Russell Wallace's work on Darwin. She regret-
ted that it had become intellectually de rigueur to minimize the relevance
of what she described as the "great evolutionary movement," maintaining
that it was "hopeless to convey to a younger generation the first overwhelming sense of cosmic vastness which such 'magic casements' let into
our little geocentric universe."[20]

In revising both *Vanity Fair* and *Daniel Deronda,* Wharton incorpo-
rated into *The House of Mirth* her understanding of Darwin's theoretical
formulations as put forth in the evolutionist's *The Descent of Man* (a volume whose impact on Wharton's thinking may be gauged by her use of it
for the title of her third volume of fiction, a collection of stories). Wharton shared with naturalistic novelists such as Émile Zola and Theodore
Dreiser a solemn investment in Darwinian notions of social and economic
determinism. At a deeper level, however, it is Darwin's idea of "sexual selection" that most fully informs the narrative logic of *The House of Mirth.*
Even while offering a powerful neo-Victorian critique of flirtation as a social strategy in the service of sexual selection, Wharton presents both a
sober reassessment of Thackeray's semicomic treatment of Becky Sharp's
elaborate social transactions in *Vanity Fair* and a modification of the cautionary pathos driving George Eliot's portrait of Gwendolen Harleth in
Daniel Deronda. In addition, Wharton renovated the fin-de-siècle conception of the flirt as malevolent femme fatale, an engineer of her own and oth-

ers' destruction. (In Bram Stoker's *Dracula,* for example, the self-described flirt Lucy Westenra lacks the virginal strength necessary to ward off Dracula's repeated attacks and is gruesomely killed twice, then decapitated.)

Wharton's response to evolutionary precepts was not only philosophical but it also determined her literary aesthetics. It was Wharton's profound identification with Darwin's ideas that led her to critique both Victorian and modern novelists as blind to a truer, "scientific" plot of nature. In a polemical 1934 essay on "Tendencies in Modern Fiction," published in *The Saturday Review of Literature,* which offered a sharp reprimand to a new generation of writers on behalf of a more rigorous aesthetic, Wharton provided an assessment of modernist writing that indirectly revealed her unshaken convictions in a Darwinian ordering of the world. Her opening words acknowledged a universe jolted by historical ruptures but then asserted that a greater pattern prevailed:

> The moral and intellectual destruction caused by the war, and by its far-reaching consequences, was shattering to traditional culture; and so far as the new novelists may be said to have any theory of their art, it seems to be that every new creation can issue only from the annihilation of what preceded it. But the natural processes go on in spite of theorizing, and the accumulated leaf-mould of tradition is essential to the nurture of new growths of art, whether or not those who cultivate them are aware of it. All the past seems to show that when a whole generation misses the fecundating soil stored for it by its predecessors its first growth will be spindling and its roots meagre. So one waited; one hoped; one watched tenderly over every shoot that seemed to have sap in it.[21]

In characterizing her belief in a set of natural processes, Wharton adopts the voice of the scientific empiricist who believes that whatever the rifts in history or (modern) fashion, a greater order ultimately will reassert itself in literary art. The low esteem in which she held modernist texts was matched by her belief that Victorian novelists such as Thackeray and George Eliot had been hampered by a blindness to an unyielding pattern of nature. Wharton referred in her 1914 essay "The Criticism of Fiction" to "plot, that complicated and arbitrary combination of incidents that, in the English novel of the nineteenth century, replaced the absent logic of life." The "whole machinery of the passions," wrote Wharton of Victorian fiction, "is put into motion for causes that a modern school-girl would smile at." She directed readers "beyond the Channel" to the work of Balzac, Flaubert, Stendhal, and Tolstoy, bemoaning the inability of their

English counterparts such as Dickens, Charlotte Brontë, and Meredith to "keep in touch with the solid earth of reality."[22]

Wharton's conception of how Victorian plots might be "rectified" along stringent naturalistic lines may be glimpsed in the way in which in *The House of Mirth* she revised a key incident in *Vanity Fair*. Her revisionary gesture involves the scene in the final chapter of Thackeray's novel in which Becky reveals to Amelia that George Osborne had indeed flirted with her. Becky shows Amelia the letter that George had slipped into her bouquet on the night of the ball before he departed for Waterloo, the unambiguous evidence of what Dobbin calls a "desperate flirtation": "'Look there, you fool,' Becky said, still with provoking good humour, and taking a little paper out of her belt, she opened it and flung it into Emmy's lap. 'You know his hand-writing. He wrote that to me—wanted me to run away with him—gave it me under your nose, the day before he was shot—and served him right!' Becky repeated."[23] In *The House of Mirth*, Lily Bart comes into possession of letters that substantiate Bertha Dorset's affair with Lawrence Selden, documents that could allow Lily (as Simon Rosedale tells her) a secure reentry into society as Rosedale's wife.

In the case of *Vanity Fair*, Becky's willingness to implicate herself in order to free Amelia from a morbid absorption in her dead husband suggests that the nonheroine of *Vanity Fair* is capable of a genuinely magnanimous gesture. Her act of cruel exposure liberates Amelia into a satisfying marriage. In *The House of Mirth*, Lily's ethically exemplary behavior is saturated in paradoxical meaning. Lily's refusal to use the Dorset letters provides her with a moral elevation analogous to Becky's, suggesting at one level that Wharton's novel is not entirely beholden to naturalist philosophical principles, and at another that morally elevated behavior means little in New York's ritualized power hierarchy. As Lee Clark Mitchell argues, "Refraining . . . from a simply self-serving act, she defines the possibility of moral integrity by renouncing her desperate desires as naturalist characters are unable to do."[24] Still, moral calibrations aside, its social effects are precisely the opposite of those resulting from Becky's decision in *Vanity Fair*. In *The House of Mirth*, a Darwinian law keeps reasserting itself, rendering moral logic meaningless. While both Becky's and Lily's actions are moments of ethical enhancement, there is an all-important difference: Becky's disclosure has markedly positive ramifications, both in terms of its larger results and within Thackeray's narrative as a way of generating the plot of marriage. Lily's nondisclosure, meanwhile, enhances Lily's personal character but dooms her to a downward spiral so characteristic of the plot of naturalism. Wharton's modifications of such scenes in Thackeray's novel preserve the possibilities for the exercising of individual free will, but she presents such possibilities as a (Darwinian) choice between a superdetermining physical survival and a worthless moral high ground.

In discussing what she understood as the novelist's proper task, Wharton continually borrowed from the era's evolutionary vocabulary, most noticeably in her persistent stress in her own literary criticism on the necessity of "selection." In her essay "The Criticism of Fiction" (1914), she asked, "Once selection is exercised, why limit its uses, why not push it to the last point of its exquisite powers of pattern-making, and let it extract from raw life the last drop of figurative beauty?" She added that since "design is inevitable, the best art must be that in which it is most organic, most inherent in the soul of the subject." Criticism itself had its basis in a predetermined design in nature, and she described it as "all-pervading as radium," insisting that "if every professional critic were exterminated tomorrow, the process would still be active wherever any attention to observe life offered itself to any human attention."[25] But it was the Darwinian proposition concerning nature's pattern of species courtship during sexual selection that most profoundly shaped Wharton's thinking, a ritual that she, in some ways more fundamentally than the evolutionist himself, elected to consider as a life-and-death struggle of individuals for social dominance.

THE HOUSE OF MIRTH AND THE REHABILITATION OF THE FLIRTING BACHELOR

Unlike the majority of recent critics of Wharton's work, I would argue that the representative "ambivalent male" of her novels is not a calculating playboy, a gothic bachelor, or an emotionally paralyzed Prufrock. The typical Wharton bachelor harbors a divided conscience, for he is erotically unresolved rather than sexually self-deluded, able to transform his ambivalence through acts of flirtatious desire. While erotic ambivalence is fear and uncertainty, it can also stand for sexual freedom, encompassing the privilege of remaining indecisive while keeping all erotic options open.

By employing such relatively neutral terms as "ambivalent" in characterizing Wharton's fictional male, used in tandem with equivalent expressions such as "wavering," "undecided," "ambivalent," "uncertain," and "equivocal," I am aiming to avoid the negative implications of such value-laden nomenclature as "immature," "unsatisfactory" and "neurotic" employed by many of Wharton's critics who have attended to Wharton's bachelor figures.[26] Such terms have their roots in a particular moment in the modern conceptualization of homosexual desire; throughout the late nineteenth and early twentieth century, male erotic "ambivalence" was linked to a distinctly feminized masculinity and, more specifically, to homosexual identity itself. The English writer Edward Carpenter, advocating a Whitmanesque acceptance of same-sex eros, elliptically designated the man of homosexual inclinations under the rubric of the "intermediate sex," amongst whose traits were "subtlety, evasiveness, timidity," as well as a "sensitive spirit" and "wavelike emotional temperament." [27]

Wharton's novels represent indecision on the male's part not only as sexual ambivalence, however, but as erotic independence, a radical "undecideability" of self expressed as flirtatious desire. Neither identifiably homosexual nor situated within an orthodox role of husbandly provider, figures such as Newland Archer, Lawrence Selden, George Darrow, Martin Boyne, and Vance Weston, in their relative freedom from societal restraints and their attraction to an off-limits demimonde, stand in *analogous* relation to the real-life homosexual bachelors who inhabited the novelist's social orbit, particularly in France during the same three decades in which the novelist resided there. Whereas the English bachelor (figured as morally and sexually degenerate in much fin-de-siècle literature) signifies a social outsider, Wharton's would-be heroes are simultaneously outsiders *and* insiders, men willing to flirt with the night side of erotic life in the form of femme fatales such as Countess Olenska, Lily Bart, and Sophy Viner yet bound to legitimizing convention. Flirting with the possibilities of calumnious social behavior yet never surrendering to scandal's perilous charms, Wharton's irresolute males are all equipped with part-time passes to an aesthete's demimonde that is depicted as disreputably European in kind. In addition to his own volumes by such decadent authors as John Addington Symonds, Vernon Lee, and Pater, it was "chiefly works of fiction" in Countess Olenska's home that "had whetted Archer's interest with such new names as those of Paul Bourget, Huysmans, and the Goncourt brothers," while the artistic milieu of the countess's Europe denotes "things . . . inconceivable in New York, and unsettling to think of." [28]

Wharton's novels indicate a uniquely responsive comprehension of how unstable the concept of masculine sexual identity had become by the beginning of the twentieth century. However troubled Wharton was by the "homosexual question" (as is especially evident in several of her supernatural tales), in giving literary embodiment to the wavering bache-lor in her novels she expressed a heightened appreciation of those indi-viduals who, through choice or temperament, found themselves outside sexual categories deemed conventional in a late-nineteenth-century Anglo-American context. In such works as *The House of Mirth, The Reef,* and *The Age of Innocence,* masculine indecisiveness, communicated through acts of erotic deferral, becomes a source of considerable anxiety but also alluring appeal for the heroine. Yearning to escape New York's inviolate social rules, women such as Ellen Olenska seek to complicate pre-scribed protocols and, in so doing, to free themselves from delimited so-cietal positions.

Flirtatious desire in Wharton's fiction is not simply an act of romantic deferral, a private system of communication between and across sexual lines, or a refusal to assume a predesignated capacity in a Darwinian scheme. Coquetry demonstrates an individual's relation to his or her own self, a way of keeping sexual identity at bay, of acknowledging the mutable nature of an individual's erotic self-definition. This is powerfully under-lined in *The House of Mirth* when Selden is accused by Lily Bart of cruelly playing the coquette, of "making experiments" with her. He responds with uncharacteristic and even poignant directness: "I am not making experi-ments. Or if I am, it is not on you but on myself. I don't know what effect they are going to have on me."[29] Supremely conscious of his own unre-solved feelings (which are neither repressed nor given full expression), Selden freely chooses the experiment of an artfully managed desire in his relations with Lily. Out of the experimental chrysalis of Paris at the begin-ning of the century, Wharton recast "perverse" male eros as masculine ambivalence and then, again, as the self-postponing, identity-forming dy-namic of male flirtation.

The danger inherent in protracted female sexual choice is a central theme of *The House of Mirth.* Whereas Lawrence Selden has settled into an untroubled bachelorhood, Lily Bart's agitated search for a husband is the paramount issue driving Wharton's novel. On the one hand, Lily Bart has a polished penchant for trickery as a means of surviving in the sexual marketplace. Described as "at once vigorous and exquisite," with a "talent for profiting by the unexpected," Lily "still had the art of blushing at the right time."[30] This last trait betrays a peculiar unnaturalness that, as Walter Benn Michaels has noted, converts "something like a reflex into something like a display of artifice."[31] Lily's tragedy stems from protracted timing, for not only has she waited too long to make her choice of a suitor, but her prolonged coquetry with Gus Trenor ultimately guarantees her downfall. Unlike the archetypal nineteenth-century heroines of infidelity such as Anna Karenina, Emma Bovary, or Edna Pontellier of Kate Chopin's *The Awakening* (1899), Lily is treated punitively not for actual adulterous transgressions but for having given the *appearance* of an adulterous relation with Gus Trenor. Lily's endless erotic deferrals with Trenor have, in terms of social perception, solidified into an actual affair. Like *Vanity Fair, The House of Mirth* delineates a society where an unfounded rumor holds the testimonial value of an incriminating document.

In Wharton's novel, the ambiguous language of public flirtation is ingeniously exploited by Lily's more cunning rival, Bertha Dorset. Understanding far better than Lily the social centrality of "mere" externals, Bertha orchestrates Lily's defeat through the creation of hearsay based on observable, open flirtations. The rumor that Bertha spreads, unfounded in fact, sets into motion a string of events—the blocking of Lily from New York's elite, Lily's disinheritance by her aunt, Selden's cowardly (because hypocritical) retreat from Lily when she most needs him—all of which accelerate the downfall of Wharton's heroine. It is important that Bertha be older than Lily and that like Madame Arnoux in Flaubert's *Sentimental Education,* she be married. For it is the married, more mature woman who can flirt without consequences, whereas Lily has confused the protractions of coquetry with the strategies entailed in husband-hunting.

Bertha recognizes that the survival of the fittest in tightly structured Old New York depends on the calculated guises in which actions veil themselves. Those guises are unrelated to actions in their own right. As in Eliot's *The Mill on the Floss,* the appearance of impropriety supplants any actual sexual transgression. Like Maggie, who decides to renounce Stephen Guest but nonetheless suffers pariahdom in the community of St. Ogg's, Lily might as well have indulged in an affair, given the effects of seeming to have had one. Only, by having the flooding river kill off her heroine, George Eliot was suggestively equivocal as to whether nature had acted as punitive force or as an accidental agent without larger social resonance. In the more intensified naturalistic scheme of *The House of Mirth,* however, "society" functions where nature would seem to have no identifiable presence. There is nothing especially ambiguous about Wharton's rendering of the causes of Lily's fall (although whether Lily's death is in actuality a suicide has been the subject of some critical debate.) It is one of the more salient ironies of *The House of Mirth* that Lily's position comes to resemble that of the arriviste Simon Rosedale, whose name, like Lily's, evokes a functionless, floral embellishment, echoing Wharton's original title for her novel *A Moment's Ornament*. Like Lily, Rosedale is a gambler, a free-floating entrepreneur who always risks becoming dispensable. Unlike her, he is, as the owner of property in the form of apartment houses and businesses, supremely able to deliver on his fiduciary promises.

Lily's hesitations regarding marriage early in the novel stem from something that closely resembles an identifiable female "aesthetic" sense on which Darwin had timorously predicated his theory of sexual selection. Although readers often assume that Lily Bart is primarily searching for a husband with substantial financial resources, in actuality Wharton represents her heroine as a woman governed by a treacherously unpractical aesthetic sense. That aesthetic sense becomes the chief obstacle to her economic ambitions. Again and again, Lily cannot relinquish her fondness for the beautiful in order to enforce a more frugal domestic economics. In the few paragraphs that Wharton devotes to Lily's upbringing, we learn that Lily's attachment to fresh flowers created conflict between her and the drably economical Mrs. Bart; Lily is already described as one who "knew very little the value of money."[32] Her break with an early admirer, the wealthy Dillworth, has ended, according to Lily, after his mother made Lily promise she "wouldn't do over the drawing room"—the "very thing," Selden drolly insists to Lily, for which Lily was marrying Dillworth. This gap between Lily's financial requirements and her overdeveloped faculty for appreciating beauty adds a necessary tensile strength to Wharton's narrative. (An opposition that is reproduced in the contrasts between Lily's suitors in *The House of Mirth*—between, say, the fashionably refined Selden, a man of mildly daring literary tastes, and the crass social climber Simon Rosedale, or between the boorish Gus Trenor and the affluent Percy Gryce, whose well-tended collection of "Americana" seems, for Lily, a sign of feeble pedantry.)

While flirtation is an economic necessity for Lily, allowing her to gain time in which to find a sufficiently wealthy husband, *The House of Mirth* strikingly offers no evidence that romantic love will follow the coquettish games of courtship. The connubial landscape haunting *The House of Mirth* is a desolate one, lacking even a single marriage anchored in desire. (It is as if the institution of marriage had reverted back to its historical status in the sixteenth century as a largely economic unit, useful primarily for the consolidation of capital.[33]) Bertha Dorset's adulterous pursuit of Selden, Gus Trenor's extramarital tracking of Lily, Rosedale's efforts at securing an attractive wife who will give him an anchor in high society, all these details insist on the complete debasement of romantic eros. From a strictly Darwinian perspective, the affluent, inbreeding husbands and wives of *The House of Mirth* have reached a level of financial adaptation that precludes genuine love. This is because romance has become an economic risk that endangers the steady functioning of class interests. All emotional bonds must be converted into marital "corporations"; romantic love, fully expressed, ominously raises the possibility of marrying outside one's caste.

The House of Mirth remains, its naturalistic affinities notwithstanding, an imperfect offshoot of American literary naturalism. The novel does not simply calibrate the spiritual costs of flirtation as an "unnatural" plot that can function in the service of monetary self-advancement. The most lyrical moments of *The House of Mirth,* which operate against the novel's bleak deterministic framework, take place in intimate, continually irresolute relations between Selden and Lily. The special flirtation between these two friends takes on added resonance precisely because it challenges the standard practice of coquetry in New York's marriage market. Although flirtation operates on a principle of protracted eroticism in the economic sphere, coquetry is in fact purposefully deployed there (and as such debased) in having an aim. It is a point about which Selden sportively attempts to remind Lily on several occasions. He and Lily can be amorously playful together, he implies, only because he remains an unserious suitor by her lights. This is made emphatic in their meeting in Selden's apartment at the beginning of the novel:

> She leaned forward with a shade of perplexity in her charming eyes. "I wish I knew—I wish I could make you out. Of course I know there are men who don't like me—one can tell that at a glance. And there are others who are afraid of me: they think I want to marry them." She smiled up at him frankly. "But I don't think you dislike me—and you can't possibly think I want to marry you."
>
> "No—I absolve you of that," he agreed.
>
> "Well, then——?"
>
> He had carried his cup to the fireplace, and stood leaning against the chimney-piece and looking down on her with an air of indolent amusement. The provocation in her eyes increased his amusement—he had not supposed she would waste her powder on such a small game; but perhaps she was only keeping her hand in; or perhaps a girl of her type had no conversation but of the personal kind. At any rate, she was amazingly pretty, and he had asked her to tea and must live up to his obligations.
>
> "Well, then," he said with a plunge, "perhaps *that's* the reason."
>
> "What?"

> "The fact that you don't want to marry me. Perhaps I don't regard it as
> such a strong inducement to go and see you." He felt a slight shiver down his
> spine as he ventured this, but her laugh reassured him.[34]

This delicate pas de deux, at once verbally and physically resonant, clashes
with the soul-destroying warfare of sexual selection among New York's
proprietary class, where Lily emerges as the principal loser. (The notion of
marital marketplace as a military battleground is nicely enforced by
Selden's image of gunpowder when he describes Lily's tactics in the passage
above.) Most importantly, in this scene there is a clear indication that the
flirtations between Lily and Selden are generated by an egalitarian dynamic, or at least a dynamic that does not give an emotional upper hand
to either of them. Moments after inquiring about Selden's reasons for not
visiting her, a question that suggests that Lily yearns for Selden's attentions, Lily pauses "to smile at him with a smile which seemed at once designed to admit him to her familiarity, and to remind him of the restrictions it imposed."[35]

In a sense, Wharton forcefully confirms Simmel's idealized conception
of coquetry by demonstrating how flirtation in *The House of Mirth* is cor-
rupted when it is transported to a money-dominated connubial "system."
With an almost Lawrentian accent on a nonverbal and asocial sublimity of
desire, Wharton situates Lily and Selden amid a pastoral setting, in the
"glitter of the American autumn," during "one of those moments when
neither seemed to speak deliberately, when an indwelling voice in each
called to the other across unsounded depths of feeling."

> She leaned on him for a moment, as with a drop of tired wings: he felt as
> though her heart were beating rather with the stress of a long flight than the
> thrill of new distances. Then, drawing back with a smile of warning—"I shall
> look hideous in dowdy clothes; but I can trim my own hats," she declared.
>   They stood silent for a while after this, smiling after each other like adven-
> turous children who have climbed to a forbidden height from which they dis-
> cover a new world. The actual world at their feet was veiling itself in dimness,
> and across the valley a clear moon rose in the denser blue.[36]

Wharton's narrator strikingly demonstrates that while the "forbidden"
plot of flirtation stands outside a preordained plot of sexual selection, it
nonetheless takes its place in a natural order. Lyrically inflected, the games
of flirting are also connected here with childhood states of consciousness.

Selden's insistence that Lily reside with him in a "special kingdom of
the spirit" (a region that she mocks as his "closed corporation") has generally been viewed by critics of *The House of Mirth* as Selden's self-serving

gambit that benefits only Selden, who cannot acknowledge Lily's precarious economic position. The commonplace understanding of Selden views him as the antihero of Wharton's novel, a self-satisfied dandy who selfishly neglects to "save" Lily from her fate. It is a critical perspective that neglects a crucial aspect of the novel: in a society in which marriage is a wholly degraded institution, an offer by Selden to betroth Lily would constitute a further debasement. In the context of the radical critique of wedlock offered by Wharton in *The House of Mirth,* Selden's idea of an affectionate, eroticized camaraderie between himself and Lily articulates a "special kingdom" above the spiritually bankrupt world in which Lily struggles to gain a foothold. Because of their inability to play the marriage game, Selden and Lily are the only characters in *The House of Mirth* who are allowed an enhancing inwardness of character. This "interior" aspect of both Selden and Lily is itself borne of their mutual pleasure in flirtatious desire, which in Wharton's novel depends on the cultivation of a secret, "genuine" self in tension with a thoroughly theatricalized public realm. This amplified, inner dimension of fictional character was seen by Georg Lukács as part of the European novel's "adventure of interiority," which Lukács saw as characteristic of the nineteenth-century novel as a genre, the "story of a soul that goes to find itself."[37] The flirtation between Lily and Selden contains precisely the spiritual magnitude of an adventure of the soul.

Since the publication of *The House of Mirth,* critics have viewed Selden as a tragically disappointing suitor, insufficiently masculine in his makeup, and even venal in his relations with Lily. Indeed, a long-standing critical consensus on *The House of Mirth* considers Selden as weightily implicated in Lily's death.[38] These critiques are unmindful of the irreducible opacity of Selden's character as well as his complex relation to power. His role in the novel is indeed that of detached spectator; yet Selden is portrayed not only as a remote observer of Lily's actions but of the proprietary class in which both of them remain insecure, dissatisfied members. Selden's uneasy relation to the reigning cenacles of Old New York is dramatized in one of the book's most remarkable scenes, the moment at Monte Carlo in which Selden observes his friends, who, not noticing that they comprise a group, pose themselves in an inadvertently stylized human diorama.

> It was mid-April, and one felt that the revelry had reached its climax and that the desultory groups in the square and gardens would soon dissolve and re-form in other scenes. Meanwhile the last moments of the performance

seemed to gain an added brightness from the hovering threat of the curtain. The quality of the air, the exuberance of the flowers, the blue intensity of the sea and sky, produced the effect of a closing *tableau,* when all the lights are turned on at once. The impression was presently heightened by the way in which a consciously conspicuous group of people advanced to the middle front, and stood before Selden with the air of the chief performers gathered together by the exigencies of the final effect. Their appearance confirmed the impression that the show had been staged regardless of the expense, and emphasized its resemblance to one of those "costume plays" in which the protagonists walk through the passions without displacing a drapery. The ladies stood in unrelated attitudes calculated to isolate their effects, and the men hung about them as irrelevantly as stage heroes whose tailors are named in the programme. It was Selden himself who unwittingly fused the group by arresting the attention of one of its members.[39]

Individual rites of vanity have evolved into atomized acts of self-theatricalization. Self-theatricalizing, meanwhile, has encouraged a severing of those tribal chords that might redeem the spiritual depletions Wharton so mordantly has taxonomized. Herein lies one component of Wharton's "modernity," if not her investment in the formal strategies of modernism: a kind of "mass consciousness" has even permeated the self-enclosed orbit of New York's leisure class. While Selden accidentally comes to link these disparate actors, in standing outside their unwittingly arranged performance he is himself represented as alien to them. Like the authorial voice of *The House of Mirth,* which dotes over the scenic charms of this stunning tableau ("The quality of the air, the exuberance of the flowers, the blue intensity of the sea and sky"), Selden remains, in the midst of viewing a disturbing scene of social artifice, very much the aesthete-connoisseur. Just as Lily's status as a coquette is interwoven with her aesthetic impulses, so too is Selden's role as an indecisive male entwined with his dandiacal position as a gentleman aesthete, the collector of first editions of La Bruyère, and the "gentleman lawyer" who scorns a direct engagement with the marketplace that Lily must confront.

The egalitarian matrix on which Lily and Selden's friendship rests becomes unequal in the latter half of the novel, as Lily's economic situation deteriorates along with her public reputation. (There is some evidence in the textual history of *The House of Mirth* that Wharton sought to rectify this imbalance.[40]) That Lily is barren when she dies, that her last thought is of Nettie Struther's child resting on her arm, that her suitor arrives too late to save her, all of these details enforce a sense of Lily as a female who has forsaken her proper role in a Darwinian procedure of sexual selection, the principal purpose of which is, of course, procreation. *The House of Mirth* is most characteristically "naturalistic" in these final, shattering images of Lily's dissolution. Still, a reading of *The House of Mirth* as an inverted Cinderella fable indebted to naturalist precepts, a desentimentalized allegory of a feckless Prince Charming, minimizes the degree to which Wharton is proposing a powerful critique of modern marriage and conventional conceptions of identity. Lawrence Selden may have arrived too late to save Lily with his "one word," yet earlier in the novel he continually reiterates how inappropriate he is as a conventional suitor. Although he might marry Lily, Selden insists, he is fundamentally unconstituted—an enigma, to her but above all to himself, as he notes in a passage cited earlier:

> "Do you want to marry me?" she asked.
>
> He broke into a laugh. "No, I don't want to—but perhaps I should if you did!"
>
> "That's what I told you—you're so sure of me that you can amuse yourself with experiments." She drew back the hand he had regained, and sat looking down on him sadly.
>
> "I am not against making experiments," he returned. "Or if I am, it is not on you but on myself. I don't know what effects they are going to have on me—but if marrying you is one of them, I will take the risk."
>
> She smiled faintly. "It would be a great risk, certainly—I have never concealed from you how great."
>
> "Ah, it is you who are the coward!" he exclaimed.[41]

This discussion of marriage itself follows a dynamic of coquettish play, as Selden initially claims not to want to marry. In the same breath, however, he insists that he "should" wish to do so if Lily herself wished to wed. Her remark that marriage would be a "risk," beyond the obvious implication that a union between the two of them might end unhappily, is also a recognition that there are no exemplary marriages in Wharton's novel, only functional ones. Selden's remarks here push his relations with Lily into a higher register. Selden here moves coquetry beyond the terms of "ideality" and of the inwardly resolved self in which Simmel discussed coquettish desire. For Wharton's wavering would-be suitor, the ideality of flirtation consists in the way in which it holds the self in a continual state of indeterminacy. Implicit in Selden's stance is a conviction that coquetry in its purest form offers the individual the chance to resist social codification, whether in the form of an unnatural plot or the role of "chooser."

The experimental possibilities for a continuous suspension of the self,

which Mikhail Bakhtin has termed the self's "unfinalizability," are vigor-
ously expressed through coquetry in *The House of Mirth.* Although we
tend to think of Bakhtin in terms of such literary categories as the "dialogic" and "heteroglossia," the concept of unfinalizability was an equally
fundamental component of the Russian critic's work, particularly in his
writing on Dostoevsky. As Bakhtin observed, Dostoevsky's characters

> all acutely sense their own unfinalizability, their capacity to outgrow, as it
> were, from within and to render *untrue* any externalization and finalizing
> definition of them. As long as a person is alive he lives by the fact that he is
> not yet finalized, that he has not yet uttered his ultimate word. . . . man is not
> a final and defined quantity upon which firm calculations can be made; man
> is free, and can therefore violate any regulating norms which might be thrust
> upon him. . . . A man never coincides with himself. One cannot apply to him
> the formula of identity A=A.[42]

Just as Bakhtin imagines speech utterances as intimately bound up with
their distinctive social context, for Wharton, it was impossible to imagine
the self independent of the social nexus in which it found its expression.
In her essay "The Great American Novel" (1927), Wharton asks what possible meaning "human nature" can have when it is "denuded" of "the web
of custom, manners, culture it has elaborately spun about itself." To do so,
she argues, is to leave one with merely "that hollow unreality, 'Man', and
invention of the eighteenth-century demagogues who were the first in-
ventors of standardization." Wharton went on to assert that "human nature" and "man" are simply intellectual abstractions, whereas actual men
are inextricably linked with the effects of climate, soil, laws, religion,
wealth—and, above all, leisure."[43] In *The House of Mirth,* Wharton demonstrates that it is not only romantic union that is forever postponed by
flirtatious desire, but identity itself as well.[44]

"BELATED ELOQUENCE": WHARTON'S *THE AGE OF
INNOCENCE,* FLAUBERT'S *SENTIMENTAL EDUCATION,* AND
THE FAILURE OF NINETEENTH-CENTURY REALISM

If *The House of Mirth* is a tragic recasting of *Vanity Fair,* Wharton's *The Age
of Innocence* is a revision of Flaubert's *Sentimental Education.* In the section of *The Writing of Fiction* entitled "Constructing a Novel" (1924),
Wharton had described the much-discussed ending of Flaubert's novel,
in which Madame Arnoux returns to see Frédéric Moreau after years of

separation, as a "poignant," decisive, "illuminating incident." That moment in Flaubert's text, according to Wharton, "need only send its ray backward; but it should send a long enough shaft to meet the light cast forward from the first page." Wharton considered such incidents to be the "magic casements of fiction, its vistas on infinity," and of which she claimed "nothing gives such immediate proof of the quality of his imagination—and therefore of the richness of his temperament" as the writer's choice of such episodes.[45] Nonetheless, in finding affinities between *Sentimental Education* and Tolstoy's *War and Peace*—they were, she observed, "two of the longest of modern novels"—she noted that the French novelist, unlike his Russian counterpart, had been "endowed with the rare instinct of scale." Flaubert, she wrote, "manages to establish the right relation between subject and length." Still, Wharton concluded that "there are moments when even [Flaubert's] most ardent admirers feel that *L'Education Sentimentale* is too long for its carrying power."[46]

Both *Sentimental Education* and *The Age of Innocence* are preoccupied with matters related to time either slowed down or accelerated. If *The House of Mirth* concerns the peril of time speeding up (Lily's rush to marry as she becomes too old for the marriage market), *The Age of Innocence* is absorbed with the dangers of time as it is protracted. Flaubert's hero is a virtuoso of delayed gratification, with the large part of *Sentimental Education* a protraction of his desire to see Madame Arnoux, the married, dark-eyed woman with whom he is enamored. Indeed, protraction of desire is the very culmination of desire in Flaubert's novel:

> He chose days for calling on her; when he reached the second floor, he stood outside her door, hesitating as to whether to ring the bell or not. Steps approached; the door opened, and at the words: "Madame is out," he would feel a sense of deliverance, as if a weight had been lifted from his heart.[47]

In *The Age of Innocence,* following this logic, accelerating the temporal works to defeat erotic longing. Newland Archer repeatedly urges his fiancée May Welland to accept an early wedding because, it becomes clear, he is determined to ward off romantic temptation with Ellen Olenska. Or is it because this will allow him an avenue of coquetry with a woman who, because she is still married and a distant relation, is off-limits as a potential wife?

Lily's fatal incapacity to dispense the erotic favors she has perhaps unwittingly proffered to Trenor has its corollary in Wharton's rendering of the male economic domain in *The Age of Innocence*. In the later work, the

greatest infraction committed by a character, and one that has catastrophic consequences for others, is Beaufort's inability to deliver on his
financial pledges. His ill-fated investment scheme (financial "coquetries"
in lieu of a never-realized windfall) unexpectedly supersedes the parallel
plot of Newland's flirtation with Ellen, a relation that although it remains
the locus of interest in the narrative, retrospectively becomes inconsequential in terms of the novel's larger events. As with Lily's association
with Selden, Archer's relationship with Ellen has transcendent private
meaning and for that very reason risks becoming meaningless. That their
unrealized romance may become "useless," that it cannot transform itself
into a betrothal, that it may dissolve into oblivion, haunts the forlorn
lovers of *The Age of Innocence,* for whom "unrequitedness" denotes an absence from an ultimate history. In one of the novel's more evocative scenes,
Ellen and Newland meet in the "queer wilderness of cast-iron and en-
caustic tiles" of the old Metropolitan Museum. The two search for seclu-
sion in a deserted room containing the "Cesnola antiquities," fragments
of vanished Ilium. Ellen wanders over to an exhibition case:

> "It seems cruel," she said, "that after a while nothing matters . . . any more
> than these little things, that used to be necessary and important to forgotten
> people, and now have to be guessed at under a magnifying glass and labeled:
> 'Use unknown.'"
> "Yes; but meanwhile——"
> "Ah, meanwhile——"[48]

It is in the realm of the "meanwhile," of course, that the couple must reside. "Use unknown," moreover, could well be utilitarian Old New York's
severest designation for its two prodigal offspring. In strict evolutionary
terms, Newland and Ellen's tie forms a vestigial component that society
considers useless in that it has little if any effect on the direction of human
affairs. The rapport between Archer and Ellen is an attempt to reach an
essence denied in the rest of New York's social realm. "In reality they all
lived in a kind of hieroglyphic world," Wharton notes, "where the real
thing was never said or done or even thought, but only represented by a
set of arbitrary signs."[49]

Wharton's rendition of *Sentimental Education* is a penetrating critique
of the genre of the nineteenth-century novel itself, which she taxonomizes
as excessively invested in the dynamics of "extra-coital" eros. Recasting
Flaubert's mid-nineteenth-century Paris of political intrigue and social
ferment as the gnarled social web of New York of the 1870s, which is for-

ever on the verge of unraveling in scandal, Wharton imagines Newland Archer and the married Countess Olenska as stand-ins for Frédéric Moreau and Madame Arnoux. Electing to forgo romantic fulfillment in favor of stoically maintained, absent devotion, Archer, like Moreau, lives a double life wherein he puts off, for a time, any lasting or binding decision. Just as in *Sentimental Education* the cynicism and banality of the counter-revolution reflects Moreau's ultimate betrayal of Madame Arnoux, so too in *The Age of Innocence* do a sequence of dishonorable financial dealings centering on reneged promises recapitulate Newland's inability to reach a romantic accord with, and to deliver on his desires for, Countess Olenska. For Wharton, erotic desire, protracted too long, creates only self-contempt. The author of *The Age of Innocence* offers a protofeminist, protomodernist recasting of the celebrated scene at the conclusion of Flaubert's novel, in which Frédéric feels repulsion before an aged Madame Arnoux as the woman at long last offers herself to him.

In an arresting revision, the hero of *The Age of Innocence* is not permitted Moreau's final paean to the day he and his friends unsuccessfully sought to enter a brothel ("That was the happiest time we ever had"), by which Flaubert's hero evokes an ideal-saturated youth of undestroyed illusions and that at the time of the novel's publication provoked enraged reactions from critics.[50] Instead of allowing Archer a moment of exquisite reflection, Wharton allows Archer only wisdom appreciated in retrospective bitterness. "The worst of doing one's duty," he concludes to himself, "was it apparently unfitted one for doing anything else."[51] In *The Age of Innocence,* Wharton offers her diagnosis of the nineteenth-century novel as obsessively, morbidly attached to an erotics of protraction that can lead only to despair. The contempt that Frédéric comes to feel for Madame Arnoux becomes Archer's self-loathing at the end of *The Age of Innocence,* casting a melancholy shadow over the entire love plot. Desires perpetuated too long, Wharton implies, lead to a self-negating hopelessness. The "belated eloquence of the inarticulate" that Archer experiences on leaving Ellen Olenska after one of their chaste outings is the belatedness of desires exhausted because they are exquisitely prolonged to the vanishing point.[52]

"Acceptable Hints of Infinity"
Dissident Desires and the Erotics
of Countermodernism

FIN-DE-SIÈCLE PRELUDE: WILDE, JAMES,
AND THE HOMOSEXUAL NOVEL OF MANNERS

In 1882, at a reception at the Washington home of Judge Edward G. Loring, Oscar Wilde met Henry James, then the toast of literary salons in America for recently having published both *Washington Square* and *Portrait of a Lady*.[1] There began the end of one of the most unlikely friendships in international letters. Wilde, appearing in knee breeches and adorned with a large, yellow silk handkerchief, introduced himself to, among other dignitaries, an American general and a United States senator. James later wrote to Isabella Gardner that Wilde, whom he termed "fatuous" and "repulsive," was ignored by everyone, although, if one can trust the testimony of Judge Loring's daughter, this was yet another of the Master's intriguing distortions. "James was so boring," wrote Loring's daughter. "Mr. Wilde was so amusing."[2]

Warmed by a favorable remark Wilde offered to a newspaper reporter regarding James's talents, James later showed up at Wilde's hotel for a chat. The meeting was evidently a disaster. "A fatuous fool, a tenth-rate cad, an unclean beast," James wailed to Mrs. Henry Adams after the encounter. (Mrs. Adams was undoubtedly relieved, as she had earlier declined to have Wilde as a guest in her home because, as she put it in her crisp, no-nonsense way, she considered him a "noodle.") Nearly fifteen years later, James's distaste for Wilde darkened into extraordinary cold-bloodedness. After the playwright's imprisonment, James refused to sign a letter asking for leniency. Writing to the French novelist Paul Bourget, he remarked that hard labor had been an inappropriate form of punishment. Isolation, insisted James, would have been more just.

I rehearse this history of the strained relations between the American novelist and the Irish playwright because that narrative is one that has dominated the extraordinary affinities linking the work of James and Wilde. The tension-producing differences between these two mavericks of modern letters would seem to have been well summed up in Richard Ellmann's remark that Wilde posed a threat to James because "James' homosexuality was latent, Wilde's patent. . . . When they come to the beautiful boy, Wilde is all atremble, James all aslant."[3] Others, such as the critic Jonathan Freedman, recently have underlined the contiguous bonds between Wilde's much-flaunted aestheticism and James's own formalist tendencies in his later fiction. As Freedman writes in his study *Professions of Taste,* "Wilde's interest in the social interplay of verbal representation of finely tuned, acutely self-aware subjectivities and—more powerfully— of the drama of influence, freedom, control and violence they enact in their interplay with each other is one that Henry James will take up and make his own."[4] Despite his astute attention to the shared stylistic strategies in the writing of James and Wilde, Freedman mostly accepts Ellmann's judgment on the contrasting sexual attitudes of these two authors, noting that the "aestheticism James shared with Pater was affronted by Wilde's extravagant sexuality and threatened by his social disgrace."[5] It would be misguided, however, to see chiefly formal resemblances between these two authors. Both writers went very far in shaping an intriguing, underestimated literary subgenre: the homosexual novel of manners.

Suggestively, Wilde's *Dorian Gray* and James's *The Tragic Muse* appeared almost simultaneously; *The Picture of Dorian Gray* was first serialized in *Lippincott's Magazine* in 1890 (and later published in book form in 1891 with six additional chapters), while *The Tragic Muse* appeared in 1890. With a polished attention to the niceties of drawing-room fiction, Wilde in the early chapters of *Dorian Gray* and James in the first third of *The Tragic Muse* strove to shape novels of dangerously assured homosexual innuendo, setting the initial terms for a novel of (partly) homosexual concerns. Some thirty years later, two other novelists with often acrimonious, entwined personal histories—E. M. Forster and D. H. Lawrence— gave that literary venture another try, although both Forster and Lawrence no longer felt obliged to situate their fictions in drawing-room settings. All four of these writers remained preoccupied with the dilemma of how to depict homoerotic relations given the loosening, but still severe, constraints placed on the representation of eroticized same-sex activity in the novel. Both *Dorian Gray* and *The Tragic Muse* tackle this problem with a recurring emphasis on allusive dialogue as opposed to substantive acts. As Wilde himself once noted of *The Picture of Dorian Gray,* "I am afraid it is rather like my own life—all conversation and no action. I can't describe action: my people sit in chairs and chatter." The languorous banter that runs through both *Dorian Gray* and *The Tragic Muse* has a way of going nowhere momentously—idle chatter that signals semi-open secrets.

What happens to fiction when the flirtation I have been characterizing as constitutive of the nineteenth-century novel becomes homosexual in kind? Is homoerotic flirting analogous to heterosexual coquetry, mimicking its strategies and rules, or does it mutate, metastasizing, through a kind of historical necessity, into a new kind of flirtatious erotics? At the most obvious level, the guarded, confidential vocabulary informing coquetry between members of the opposite sex would seem to be greatly enhanced, brought back to its irreducible essence as dangerous activity as it is forced to render its schemes more ingeniously beyond detection. Given the punitive ramifications of enacted homosexual erotics in a late-nineteenth-century context, homosexual flirtation would have to take on added dimensions. In periods of intensified legal and moral strictures, flirting with a member of one's own sex becomes a way of suggesting homosexual desire without directly conveying it, toying with same-sex carnal relations without leaving prima facie evidence.

As the novels of James Joyce, D. H. Lawrence, and to a lesser extent Virginia Woolf came to deal more forthrightly with a once off-limits sexuality, flirtation as a necessary component disappears from the novel of "high" literary art. Meanwhile, the thematics and strategies of flirting take on a preeminent place in homosexual fiction. Recent critical discussions of homosexuality at the fin de siècle have tended to consider the representation of homosexual desire in the mephitic terms of crisis, panic, and fear, in a formulation that stresses the relative impossibility of conveying homoerotic inclinations. However, in the work of James and Wilde (both figures frequently marshalled to make an argument concerning "homosexual panic"), same-sex desire also finds a place in what might be called the homosexual novel of manners. Here older males and their acolytes keep alive the notion that same-sex eroticism derives from the "influence" a worldly male has over an impressionable follower. Somewhat surprisingly, given their literary reputations, it is Wilde who abruptly changes gears in *The Picture of Dorian Gray* and comes to cast his tale a gothic penny dreadful. James, on the other hand, eschews gothic resolutions, seemingly unable to decide what to do with the bachelor Gabriel Nash, an aesthete-charmer, not unlike Wilde's Lord Henry, who dominates the first third of James's novel. Unlike Wilde, James dissipates the meaning of Gabriel's effect on his young acolyte, refusing to suggest that the "homosexual influence" spawned by the cult of aestheticism brings about deadly effects. *The Tragic Muse,* like Wilde's *Dorian Gray,* is a novel at least partly concerned with the world of the metropolitan theater. The figure of rising actress Miriam Rooth, eager to take life in a "brave, free personal way," is a more dynamic version of Wilde's blandly conceived, almost anonymous actress Sibyl Vane. James's novel famously includes an evident portrait of Wilde in the character of Nash, the elusive raconteur who, with his air of detached assurance, aphoristic tics, and rehearsed *aperçus,* very much resembles Wilde's Lord Henry. Both of these men, at once cultivated and jaded, take on roles as instructors for their young male friends. Through sheer verbal panache, Nash persuades the novel's hero, Nick Dormer, to abandon a promising political vocation, namely, an assured seat in Parliament. In each of these novels, art becomes the central subject informing conversations, yet those conversations continually refer to subtextual matters.

In *The Picture of Dorian Gray,* nature is so carnally overwrought, so comically an elaborate metaphor for wooing, that Wilde, despite his celebrated reputation as guru of aestheticism, on occasion seems to be calling on the resources of the natural world to legitimize male-male eros. Here, for example, Dorian and Lord Henry have been observing a furry bee as it creeps into the "strained trumpet" of a "Tyrian convolvulus" in Basil Hallward's garden:

> The flower seemed to quiver, and then swayed gently to and fro. . . . They rose up, and sauntered down the walk together. Two green-and-white butterflies fluttered past them, and in the pear-tree of the garden a thrush began to sing.
> "You are glad to have met me, Mr. Gray," said Lord Henry, looking at him.
> "Yes, I am glad now. I wonder shall I always be glad?"
> "Always! That is a dreadful word. It makes me shudder when I hear it. Women are so fond of using it. They spoil every romance by trying to make it last for ever. It is a meaningless word, too. The only difference between a caprice and a life-long passion is that the caprice lasts a little longer."
> As they entered the studio, Dorian Gray put his hand upon Lord Henry's arm. "In that case, let our friendship be a caprice," he murmured, flushing at his own boldness, then stepped up on the platform and resumed his pose.[6]

Although at this point Dorian has been presented to the reader as a wide-eyed ingenue, the young man is already adept at come-hither directionals with Lord Henry. His skill at coquetry predates his tutelage under experienced aesthete. Or else, *mutatis mutandis,* Dorian becomes a savvy male coquette as he confronts his challenging new friend. This partly helps to explain why, in a teasing move, Dorian feels compelled to stress the fleeting quality of his fondness for Lord Henry. Lord Henry, meanwhile, will not allow himself to be cast into the role of sentimental old goat. It is *he* who pointedly insists on the distinction between romantic ardor and capricious fun and the supremacy of the latter. Dorian, no doubt conscious of this cleverly considered retreat (and that it may well represent an "advance"), ups the ante by proffering a (slight) physical confirmation of his interest: with strategic self-assurance, he touches his companion's arm as if to acknowledge their mutual lack of seriousness and the possibilities this shared frivolity can unleash.

In *The Picture of Dorian Gray,* no extraneous matter—neither the cavorting butterflies nor the nearby bee—serves flirtation between men so much as the subject of the aesthetic realm itself. The interminable discussions of aestheticism that pervade the early section of the novel, the aphoristic repartee exploring art's precise relation to life, are the chief means of prolonging erotic desire for Dorian and Lord Henry. This displacement of homoerotic play into the domain of art is, of course, a familiar one with Wilde, but what is less noted is the way in which that displacement may be found outside the author's imaginative writing. One recalls the interrogation of the playwright at one of his trials, when the Queensberry's defense attorney Edward Carson's ferocious questioning of Wilde led to a celebrated evasion on the part of the playwright. Quoting at length a passage from *Dorian Gray* in which Basil Hallward conveys his fervent feelings on first meeting Dorian, Carson demanded, "Do you mean to say that the passage describes the natural feeling of one man for another?" Wilde responded imperiously: "It would be the influence of a beautiful personality."[7] Flirting with sexual identity, the charming oscillation between affirmation and denial, at last had become a legal strategy for the cornered, future cause celebre.

James too was especially drawn to scenarios of male-male flirtation within the context of discussions concerning late-Victorian aestheticism. The opening of *The Tragic Muse* takes place in Paris's Palais de l'Industrie, yet the matter before Gabriel Nash and Nick Dormer concerns a fondness for prettified, useless objects:

> "You do like English art, then?" Nick demanded, with a slight accent of surprise.

Mr. Nash turned his smile upon him. "My dear Mr. Dormer, do you remember the old complaint I used to make of you? You had formulas that were like walking in one's hat. One may see something in a case, and one may not."

"Upon my word," said Nick. "I don't know anyone who was fonder of generalizations than you. You turned them off as the man at the street corner distributes hand bills."

"They were my wild oats. I've sown them all."

"We shall see that!"

"Oh, they're nothing now—a tame, scanty, homely growth. My only generalizations are my actions."

"We shall see *them,* then," said Nick.

"Ah, excuse me. You can't see them with the naked eye. Moreover, mine are principally negative. People's actions, I know, are, for the most part, the things they do, but mine are all things I don't do. There are so many of those, so many, but they don't produce any effect. And then all the rest are shades—extremely fine shades."

"Shades of behavior?" Nick inquired, with an interest which surprised his sister; Mr. Nash's discourse striking her mainly as the twaddle of the underworld.[8]

The cat-and-mouse game here depends on Nash's insistence that he will not deal in actions—or, at least, visible, verifiable ones. James heightens the sense of homoerotic peril in this scene by "triangulating" the small talk of his male duo with a sudden shift to the perspective of Nick's alarmed sister, Biddy. As in *Dorian Gray,* where women are mechanically summoned in order to represent a stifling set of bourgeois conventions, Biddy listens in dismay to the two men and thereby establishes (if only out of ignorance) normative social parameters. The opening interlude at the Palais de l'Industrie allows for double and triple entendres that needle the reader with a sequence of ambiguities: what exactly are the "wild oats" to which Nash refers and that he claims to have already sown? (Sexual conquests?) And is this the very sense in which he is the "man at the street corner"? Another exchange, in which Nick asks Gabriel about his (new) absence of emotion, intensifies our sense of Gabriel as a sexual operator:

"Well, don't you show your feelings? You used to!"

"Wasn't it mainly of disgust?" Nash asked. "Those operate no longer. I have closed that window."

"Do you mean you like everything?"

"Dear me, no! But I look only at what I do like."[9]

How are we to take Nash's last remark that he only looks at what he likes, uttered as he is presumably looking directly at Nick Dormer?

Ultimately, however, *The Picture of Dorian Gray* and *The Tragic Muse* cannot sustain the homoerotic scenarios that they so daringly inaugurate. Wilde's novel abruptly shifts to a lurid register, becoming the gothic cautionary tale that has become the most well-known feature of the novel. James, unable to find a place for Gabriel Nash in his novel's larger scheme, allows him to disappear altogether from the plot. (Nash remains largely offstage for the last two-thirds of the novel, where he takes on minimal importance.) Thus both novels offer a sense that the incipient "homosexual novel" is caught in an impossible, historical cul-de-sac. Like the playful Lord Henry, beholden to caprices, *The Picture of Dorian Gray* and *The Tragic Muse* initiate scenarios that they are unable to see to fruition. The novel of homosexual concerns would have to wait another generation— and for another pair of mismatched literary confreres.

FORSTER, AUSTENIAN DESIGNS, AND LITERARY MODERNISM

"Nothing's private in India."
—Dr. Aziz, in E. M. Forster's *A Passage to India* (1924)

"India isn't a drawing room," Ronny Heaslop instructs his mother, Mrs. Moore, early in *A Passage to India* (1924), as he peevishly warns her of the dangers of a too-intimate attachment to the Indians she has met on first arriving in Chandrapore.[10] Mrs. Moore and Miss Quested, Ronny's fiancée, have just been discovered by Ronny as they have been socializing serenely in the company of Dr. Aziz and Professor Godpole on the grounds of the college where Cecil Fielding resides. The words of the pragmatic young city magistrate represent, of course, the reigning political status quo, the entrenched conservatism of the British government's overextended tenure in India. Heaslop's comment also signifies a theory of narrative in thumbnail form. For while he is a dull sahib and a reactionary pragmatist in politics, in his admonishment of his mother Ronny Heaslop could well be a modernist in his literary tastes, as he here establishes in dogmatic fashion the impossibility of projecting obsolete domestic scenarios onto late-Imperial India. Of course, Mrs. Moore, Miss Quested, and Fielding initially do attempt to recuperate in British-controlled Chandrapore the intricately elaborated personal relations suggested by all that is conjured up in the words "drawing room."

To a considerable extent, "drawing room" evokes much that is basic to

Forster's vocation as a writer, epitomizing what the novelist described, in a summary description of the world of Jane Austen's novels, as the "quiet houses, the miry lanes, the conundrums, the absence of the very rich and the very poor, the snobbery which flourishes where distinctions of income are slight." [11] The spirit of Jane Austen is never too far from Forster's deepest conceptions of the writing of fiction. "Something tremendous has happened," George Emerson tells Lucy Honeychurch in *A Room with a View* (1908), giddily exulting in his newfound love for her. Like Austen's Emma, Lucy retreats from a confrontation with a man who is her ideal mate, although George, unlike Austen's suavely secretive Knightley, forthrightly declares his feelings. And whereas *Emma* itself works toward a bemused, conservative affirmation of the need for individuals to stay within the parameters of class in making correct matches, Forster again points to the cracks in the social wall, to the now-toppling barriers that would have once separated an impoverished George from thinking of courtship with a principled middle-class young woman such as Lucy. [12] George's attentions horrify Lucy, sending Forster's fragile Edwardian ingenue into a hasty engagement with the sterile aesthete Cecil Vyse, much as Emma found herself infatuated by the captivating but thoughtless Frank Churchill.

A *Passage to India* is fairly redolent with a yearning for conceits and narrative structures that could best be described as "Austenian." Forster's longing for Austen's undestroyed universe escapes the charge of mere nostalgia, because Forster submits his Austenian allegiances to the changes in class relations that history has wrought. Both an Austenian dynamic of the novel and that dynamic's tacit inverse operate in *A Passage to India.* In the varying "plots of courtship" that inform this work, Forster not so much abandons Austen's most characteristic techniques as he honors them with allusive, slightly aslant elaborations. As if mimicking the schematics of *Emma* and *Pride and Prejudice,* for example, *A Passage to India* begins with a symbolic "marriage" for the widowed Dr. Aziz and the (twice) widowed Mrs. Moore. Most importantly, the emotional force of this unusual tie remains as absolute as any happy connubial resolution in Austen's fiction. Even the crisis of the Marabar caves cannot dissipate the power of this mystical marriage, and as is made evident in the nuptials linking Fielding and Stella that concludes the novel, this bond endures in the choices of at least one subsequent generation. Similarly, as if to duplicate the impasses that invariably begin Austen's novels, *A Passage to India* ends with an irreconcilable rupture for Aziz and Fielding.

Other details in *A Passage to India* suggest a parlor game involving a referential inversion of Austen's major texts. Thus, in a half-reversal of a key relation in *Persuasion,* Adela Quested, badly matched with the starchy Heaslop, realizes the mistake of her engagement with the young magistrate partly as a result of the "persuasion" of an urbane, older woman, Mrs. Moore. In withholding her endorsement of Adela's marriage to her son, Mrs. Moore functions as a negative variant of Lady Russell in *Persuasion.* (Indeed, her general function in the novel is that of a countermatrimonial agent.) [13] Only, unlike Anne Eliot, Adela remains unwedded at the novel's conclusion even as an "Austenian" resolution (that is, one that seems at once inevitable and satisfying) is provided via Fielding's unexpected marriage to Mrs. Moore's daughter, Stella. Again and again, the imprints of an Austenian pattern are visible in *A Passage to India* as through a deliberately askew textual palimpsest.

Perhaps Forster's deepest debt to Austen, however, lies in his updating of the "marriage fiction" so associated with Austen's pre-Victorian fictions. This Forster accomplishes by inventing either "spiritual" or erotically charged marriages for individuals who never take formal vows. In *A Passage to India,* a novel where only a single marriage occurs (and this in a geographically distant England), the major protagonists continually seem to become figures in a criss-crossing diagrammatic. It is a configuration not unlike the pattern that Forster described in his study of fiction, *Aspects of the Novel,* when he examined personal entanglements that were shaped like an "hour-glass." Thus, Mrs. Moore and Dr. Aziz are would-be lovers who elect to have a spiritualized friendship, one that, like the alliance uniting Margaret Schlegel and Mrs. Wilcox in *Howards End,* remains far more enduring than any romantic relationship evoked later in Forster's novel. The image of the hourglass is most fitting for the erotic relations informing *A Passage to India,* for the metaphor of the hourglass suggests the exhaustion of time, the pitiable passing of historical and personal opportunities, that are so basic to the theme of this novel. What Forster conveys in *A Passage to India* is the difficulty and—finally, the impossibility—of sustaining a cultural relationship that always borders on—but never ends in—consummation. The echo chamber of the Marabar caves is the sound of a repetitive conversation, a cacophony of erotic notes that strikes chords but cannot move forward. Where marriage cannot tread, *A Passage to India* intimates, flirtatious desire rushes in and becomes all-important.

A Passage to India is celebrated as a work concerning differing kinds of ambivalence—political, sexual, cultural—yet the novel is also coolly unambivalent in its viewpoint and tonally quite restrained. The initial scenes, for instance, are especially remarkable in sweepingly and instantly demonstrating just how "European" in sensibility, demeanor, and outlook both Muslim and Hindu Indians are. Forster's narrative swiftly establishes how quickly Western values give way to Eastern charms, how speedily intimacy may be established between enlightened members of the British colony and Indians of "advanced" outlooks. These early sequences of the novel insist that a potent if limited "connectedness" in fact has succeeded in British-controlled India. Although the first line of chapter 3, in which the "Bridge Party" occurs, informs us of the failure of this preposterous venture ("The Bridge Party was not a success—at least it was not what Mrs. Moore and Miss Quested were accustomed to consider a successful party"), the chapter is of ironic interest beyond its achievement as satire. Engineered by the hide-bound Turtons, the Bridge Party has as its primary aim the encouragement of harmonious relations between Indian and British subjects. But as we have seen earlier in the novel, an easy but intense intimacy already has taken place in the "union" of Mrs. Moore and Dr. Aziz. Mrs. Moore herself stumbles on the insight that Indians have come extremely close to an appreciation of Western ways when she overhears, to her delighted surprise, an Indian woman speaking English. As Fielding tells Miss Quested before the catastrophe in the caves, "You can make India in England apparently, just as you can make England in India,"[14] Fielding is referring here to the improved, internationally available technology that allows mangoes to be shipped abroad, but his point resonates.

As in much of Lawrence's fiction, cross-cultural affection in *A Passage to India* such as that animating the friendship of Mrs. Moore and Aziz is relayed as if through electromagnetic currents, rather than through anything as conventional as, say, a conversation, a suddenly intimate revelation, or a series of private gestures. Like the deliberately pared-down characters of Lawrence's *Women in Love,* Forster's protagonists often seem to be striving to transcend the conventions of language in order to transcend language itself. Both Forster and Lawrence are intensely suspicious of those refinements of "personality" so characteristic of forward-thinking individuals. In his first novel, *Where Angels Fear to Tread* (1905), for example, Lilia's death in childbirth in Monteriano brings Philip Herriton and Caroline Abbott to Italy. There, to their own incredulity, they both become smitten with Lilia's widowed husband, Gino. The death of the child, itself an event that violently upsets Austenian conventions, nonetheless provides a cautionary note that Austen would have appreciated. The death of Gino's son speaks to the danger of thoughtless acts of passion, of level-headedness failing to win out over sheer impulse. Shifting gears again, Forster undercuts this element of caution when he depicts Caroline and Philip as yearning for an absolute, passionate finale. "I love him, too!" declares Philip to Caroline, after she has revealed *her* feelings for Gino. Caroline's brusque response is a proto-Lawrentian refusal of refinement: "Get over supposing I'm refined. That's what puzzles you. Get over that." [15]

The name Forster so often gives for relations that transcend ordinary cultural categories is "friendship," but friendship carries a terrible, almost insupportable burden in all of the novelist's work. The unrequited impulses of characters such as Mrs. Moore and Dr. Aziz, too weighty to constitute infatuations, signal flirtations across boundaries of sex and class, but they also invite catastrophic results. Thus, as if in anticipation of the legal fiasco generated by the events at Marabar caves, the movement of plot in *Howards End* abruptly pauses in the midst of growing affection between Margaret Schlegel and Mrs. Wilcox and an alarming note is struck. Margaret reveals anxieties that are curiously entwined with the narrator's sweeping method of free indirect speech (and then first-person plural voice):

> Several days passed.
> Was Mr. Wilcox one of the unsatisfactory people—there are many of them—who dangle intimacy and then withdraw it? They evoke our interests and affections, and keep the life spirit dawdling around them. Then they withdraw. When physical passion is involved, there is a definite name for such behavior—flirting—and if carried far enough, it is punishable by law. But no law—not public opinion, even—punishes those who coquette with friendship, though the dull ache that they inflict, the sense of misdirected effort and exhaustion, may be as intolerable. Was she one of these? [16]

The sense of menace that Forster evokes in this passage signifies that friendship—between women, between men, across generations—has taken on a paranoia-inducing power. Most obviously, it serves as a displacement of sexual interest, harboring as much in the way of jeopardy as any erotic traffic between members of opposite classes or cultures. At once a denial and an enhancement of Austenian designs, such ties of friendship—flirtations of the senses as much of the spirit—encompass two relationships in *A Passage to India:* the heterosexually charged "mystical" accord between Dr. Aziz and Mrs. Moore as well as the homoerotic fellowship between Dr. Aziz and Cecil Fielding.

Forster's decision to inaugurate *A Passage to India* with ethereal "nuptials" for Mrs. Moore and Dr. Aziz, as well as the novel's increasing move towards a homosexually inflected crisis between Aziz and Fielding, undoubtedly grew out of Forster's response to the new claims of literary modernism. For Forster, the British modernist enterprise clearly heralded the death of those niceties of domestic manners, those hallowed rules of courtship, that he associated with the nineteenth-century novel. To the extent that he saw the "advances" of modernism as true innovations, Forster understood them as less a sustained formal experiment than as a fraudulent experimentalism. Modernism came to represent for him a new—and repellent—standard in the representation of sexual desire. In an essay that appeared the year after the publication of *A Passage to India,* he identified Virginia Woolf as a faux modernist, insisting that Woolf's claims to have forged a new aesthetic in her fiction were belied by the details of the novels themselves. Writing of Woolf's *Night and Day,* Forster characterized the work a "deliberate exercise in classicism . . . containing all that has characterized English fiction for good or evil during the last hundred and fifty years—faith in personal relations, recourse to humorous sideshows, insistence on petty social differences." This last remark echoes Forster's comments on the province he claimed was quintessentially Austenian. Indeed, Austen's work is explicitly invoked in the next sentence: "Even the style has been normalized, and though the machinery is modern, the resultant form is as traditional as *Emma.*"[17] Forster is arguing that more than a century after Austen, the modernist enterprise, supposedly advanced in its stylistic strategies, cannot escape from the shadow of Austen's influence. A year later, in a similar spirit of countermodernist skepticism, he offered a savage estimate of James Joyce, whose *Ulysses* he saw chiefly in indecent terms as a "dogged attempt to cover the universe with mud," a book that revealed an "inverted Victorianism, an attempt to make crossness and dirt succeed where sweetness and light failed, a simplification of the human character in the interests of Hell."[18]

By the time Forster published *A Passage to India,* there already had been several breakthroughs in the literary treatment of erotic themes in British literature and in literary works elsewhere in Europe. Not only had Joyce published *Ulysses* (1922), but André Gide's transparently autobiographical homosexual fictions had appeared in both France and Britain. With the exception of *Lady Chatterley's Lover* (1928), Lawrence had published all of his major work, most of it concerning incendiary sexual subject matter. It was, of course, Lawrence's fiction that represented the greatest sustained assault on a prevailing morality in the depiction of physical passion. Always in Lawrence's fiction, there is a fierce assault on the social procedures of erotic delay so central to the nineteenth-century novel, an onslaught that is forcefully dramatized in the chapter entitled "Passion" in *Sons and Lovers* (1913). Paul Morel accompanies Clara Dawes and one of her suffragette friends to Nottingham's Theater Royal to see Sarah Bernhardt in a stage version of Alexandre Dumas's *La Dame aux Camélias* and Paul becomes overwhelmed by desire:

> Only the intervals, when the light came up, hurt him expressibly. He wanted to run anywhere, so long as it would be dark again. In a maze, he wandered out for a drink. Then the lights were out, and the strange, insane reality of Clara and the drama took hold of him again.
>
> The play went on. But he was obsessed by the desire to kiss the tiny blue vein that nestled in the bend of her arm. He could feel it. His whole life seemed suspended till he had put his lips there. It must be done. And the other people! At last he bent quickly forward, and touched it with his lips. His moustache brushed the sensitive flesh. Clara shivered, drew away her arm.
>
> When all was over, the lights up, the people clapping, he came to himself and looked at his watch. His train was gone.[19]

This scene represents, in its rising physical incrementalism capped by carnal resolution, a victory over flirtatious eros, whose "intervals" cause only suffering in the ardent lover. Although Clara's withdrawal of her arm creates its own suspended tension, creating a protraction for yet another consummation, we witness a successful act whose triumphant completion receives a comic, inadvertent acknowledgment in the audience's applause.

The enactment of Paul's thrillingly successful kiss here requires several other related victories—over older, desiccated forms of representation (namely, Dumas's story of a courtesan who dies of consumption, a classic of the French stage), over a provincial public (the roaring, appreciative audience), and over time itself, depicted as a forward-moving modernity (the missed train). In Lawrence, erotic desire is constantly a sensualist's retreat from society and therefore an escape from a social ethos that demands ritualized delay. Here that retreat is staged as a battle between a real, hidden "drama" of erotic satiation that competes with and finally defeats a theatrical mode so irrelevant to the hero of *Sons and Lovers* that it is meaningless. (Significantly, this scene concludes without the slightest evocation of Bernhardt's performance, an event that we know Lawrence experienced firsthand as a young theatergoer.) Just as Woolf's subjectivist experimentalism enunciates thought, feelings, and imagination as all-determinant, Lawrence's version of modernist subjectivism insists on the momentousness of cravings consummated. It is, then, a "drama of consummation" that Paul heroically acts out in this scene in "Passion," as a new mimesis, wherein a privately exchanged kiss holds momentous meaning, trumps a hackneyed French theatrical tradition of grand gestures, wherein courtesans—and coquettes—once reigned supreme.

Deferred desire in *A Passage to India* is played out in response to Lawrence and other modernist writers predisposed to the depiction of an explicit carnality and dissident sexualities. Forster's engagement with—and disengagement from—the advanced writing of his era endures as a recurring subject in critical discussions of his fiction. Indeed, the question of Forster's precise affiliation with modernist literature remains an unresolved aspect of his literary legacy. For among twentieth-century British novelists, Forster is unique in that although partially impressed by the formal experimentalism of writers such as Woolf, he himself was committed to a formally restrained expansion of the novel of social manners. Having felt no overwhelming impulse to assimilate the avant-garde accomplishments of Joyce, Lawrence, Conrad, or Woolf, Forster is a striking case of a twentieth-century British writer who, cognizant of the effects of modernity but uninspired by modernism itself, strained to bring nineteenth-century literary values to bear on the modern novel. Of the writers identified by Virginia Woolf as comprising the radical "Georgian" movement we now understand as "modernist" (she mentioned Forster, Lawrence, Lytton Strachey, Joyce, T. S. Eliot, and by implication herself), and to which she contrasted the "Edwardians" H. G. Wells, Arnold Bennett, and John Galsworthy, it is Forster who today holds the uneasiest position as an avatar of modernism.[20]

Indeed, the features of "Edwardian" sensibility so characteristic of Forster's early fiction—sharply observed quirks of character, a demise of considerable symbolic import followed by a perfunctory nod toward a resolution by marriage, a fragile liberalism that values redemptive "feelings" over the advantages of overt political conflict, a somewhat tendentious strain of ironic didacticism—are still on exemplary display in the novelist's last major work of fiction, *A Passage to India*. Nonetheless, with this work Forster at last escaped the role of fussily Edwardian petit-maître at the margins of British letters. Nonetheless, Forster was caught in a paradox, for if he held firm allegiances to the British nineteenth-century novel, the author of *Aspects of the Novel* knew that Victorian fiction had never granted asylum to the homoerotic sublime he believed the novel must come to accommodate. Thus it was Lawrence—especially the Lawrence of *Women in Love,* where homosexual desire dominates as a theme—who could be said to have most successfully challenged Forster's aesthetics of countermodernism.

The theme of male-male love as articulated in *Women in Love* hovers over the concerns animating *A Passage to India.* Indeed, there is compelling evidence that Forster intended *A Passage to India* as a rewriting of the homoerotic scenarios so crucial to Lawrence's novel. As Forster was struggling to complete *A Passage to India,* he copied onto a sheet of his manuscript the whole concluding passage from *Women in Love.* This section includes the dialogue in which Ursula, no longer a representative of free-thinking New Womanhood but a figure of suffocating convention, confronts Birkin about his need to love Gerald. Forster's "revision" of Lawrence's passage strikes at the very heart of the question of unfulfilled versus actualized homoerotic desire.[21] In all of Lawrence's fiction, one has the sense that coquetry continually must be transcended, as flirtatious desire is invariably depicted as a merely social artifice and, therefore, an obstacle to be overcome on behalf of "blood consciousness." (The memorably malevolent bisexual artist Loerke in *Women in Love,* with whom Gudrun has an affair in the chapter "Snow," is Lawrence's emblem of an invidious masculine coquetry as he flirts with both Gudrun and his rival Gerald.) In Forster a countervailing dynamic operates even as the theme of an intensified male camaraderie holds sway.

What Forster had sought to achieve in his previous novel, *Maurice* (composed in 1913 but unpublished until 1971, the year after Forster's death) was homosexual romance, what the writer Cynthia Ozick has disparaged as a "fairy tale," capped as the novel is by an inviolate, lachrymose consummation for the reformed prig Maurice Hall and the working-class striver Alec Scudder.[22] Eschewing verisimilitude, Forster provides an uncomplicated, fortuitous resolution for Maurice and Scudder. It is as if he had rewritten the liaison between Helen Schlegel and Leonard Bast but, overwhelmed by sentiment, sought to repair the class barriers he elsewhere depicted as inviolate. The external pressure to embrace a conclusion worthy of Austen is thematized in *Maurice,* where Forster's hero is placed under a relentless expectation to adopt an "Austenian" heterosexual marriage plot that his former lover Clive, fearful of a rising tide of homosexual persecution in England, finds himself embracing. Only when that Austenian plot is adapted to the unusual terms of Maurice's love affair with Scudder does the novel find its happy conclusion. The coercions of class, unwieldy baggage inherited from the Victorian novel, are suddenly transcended easily in the neo-Victorian *Maurice*. Here Forster designed a fate for his class-breaking couple in lieu of a future he believed had been denied his own generation of homosexually inclined men. "A happy ending was imperative," Forster wrote in his 1960 "Terminal Note" to *Maurice*. "I shouldn't have bothered to write otherwise. I was determined that in fiction anyway two men should fall in love and remain in it for the ever and ever that fiction allows, and in this sense Maurice and Alec still roam the greenwood."[23] However stirring much of *Maurice* remains, it is startling to discover that Forster—even the Forster who in *Aspects of the Novel* (1927) acknowledged that the novel at times could indulge its reader's guilty "sentimentality"—discovered in a putatively novelistic solution the key to a utopian homosexual dream.[24]

What was it, then, that caused Forster to abandon, as a literary resolution, the romance scenario he had engineered for Maurice and Alec when he came to write *A Passage to India*? Was it a fear of public opprobrium that restrained Forster in this novel, keeping him from allowing Aziz and Fielding their "happy ending"? Does the ending of *A Passage to India* represent a retreat from the terrain Forster was able to explore in *Maurice*? Or was the reason that Forster prevented Fielding and Aziz from finding an Austenian resolution to their fitful friendship the novelist's awakening to the (historical) impossibility of same-sex eros? One may imagine a conclusion to *A Passage to India* that would have allowed these two friends a quaint marriage of true minds in India, perhaps away from the played-out British expatriate community that Aziz and Fielding hold in such grave contempt. Only, by literary temperament Forster was drawn not to the staging of exalted homoerotic consummations, but rather to the orchestration of sustained, sublime "disconnections."

THE USES OF DISCONNECTION: *A PASSAGE TO INDIA*

For the novelist who once declared, "I am a Jane Austenite," yet who witnessed nearly all Austenian niceties of form radically transformed in the modernist texts of Conrad, Woolf, Joyce, and Lawrence, Imperial India has become the last extant outpost for the dramatization of civilized delay in matters of the heart.[25] For Forster, the tradition represented by the author of *Emma* had to be adopted to a new fictional aesthetic, an expanded global geography, and with increasing urgency for Forster throughout the 1920s, an "unspeakable" eros that was becoming, thanks to a bold subset of modernist writers, considerably less unspeakable. There is far more preoccupying Forster in *A Passage to India* than merely the revamping of an Austenian novelistic sensibility—more, too, than the rendering of the burnished, twilight days of Anglo-Imperial relations.

From the novel's very beginning, the impulse to sustain flirtations beyond boundaries of class, country, and culture has become so acute that it approaches something outside the corporeal: a mystical knowledge transcending mere communication, an apotheosis of the senses paradoxically situated outside of the body. Certainly it is a striking feature of Forster's novel, preoccupied as it is with a sensually teeming "Orient," that the reader discovers very few physical details concerning any of the book's central characters. There is, in fact, little in the way of an evocation of actual bodies in *A Passage to India*. Beginning with the opening scene of the novel, in which Indians voluptuously inhale tobacco amidst the sweet-smelling "green blossomed champak and scraps of Persian poetry" on the veranda of Hamidullah's home, Forster's narrative is alive with lush phenomena, the detailed descriptions of nature that Virginia Woolf admired in her otherwise hostile summation of Forster's literary career. ("[B]eauty leaps from the scabbard," she wrote of certain "great scenes" in his work, "the fire of truth flames through the crusted earth; we must see the red-brick villa in the suburbs of London lit up."[26]) Furthermore, the philosophy of "Only Connect" has more meaning for the English émigrés portrayed in *A Passage to India* than for the Indians. Even the historically fraught rifts between Hindus and Moslems imbedded in Indian culture are minimized in Forster's novel in favor of a determined stress on fissures within the British middle class. When Miss Quested and Mrs. Moore arrive in Chandrapore, both women immediately find themselves disgusted with the petty snobberies of the English expatriate community. Their initial relations with the Indians whom they meet, however, take place in a realm beyond those afforded by the conventional pleasures of tourism.

The exalted encounters between open-minded English visitors and soft-voiced Indians take place outside the region of the corporeal, as the human body is again and again evaded throughout the narrative. Despite the novel's atmosphere of pervasive sensuality, the physical attributes of Dr. Aziz, for his British accusers, *the* archetypal example of the Indian male as covert erotic predator, are evoked initially in two sentences, the second of which speedily veers from the particular to the general as to suggest authorial discomfort: "He was an athletic little man, daintily put together, but really very strong. Nevertheless walking fatigued him, as it fatigues everyone in India except the newcomer."[27] (Aziz is the supreme would-be paramour in the novel, as he elicits voluptuous responses from Mrs. Moore, Miss Quested, and Fielding.) Adela Quested is introduced simply as "the queer, cautious girl whom Ronny had commissioned [Mrs. Moore] to bring from England." Although the event at the Marabar caves is obviously the locus of symbolic meaning in the novel, the fantasy animating *A Passage to India* is not the chance for an erotic showdown but rather a fantasy of refusal. The enlightened protagonists dream of deferring a sexual plot that seems to be progressing incrementally. Forster is always setting up binaries in order to erase them, nowhere more so than when writing of friends who are also would-be lovers.

This dynamic of erotic renunciation does not begin with *A Passage to India* but occurs throughout Forster's fiction. Although it is tempting to see the Forster of a novel such as *A Room with a View* as endorsing a leap into an undestroyed "primitivism," of opposing society to nature, the novelist typically erases such distinctions on behalf of a naturalized erotics of disjunction. As Ozick wrote of Forster by way of explaining the novelist's disenchantment with the Cambridge Apostles and, later, with Bloomsbury aesthetes, "He never shared their elation at smashing conventional ideas; though himself an enemy of convention, he saw beyond convention to its roots in nature."[28] By 1923, the social barriers whose fragmentation Forster had made the very material of his fiction in the years before the publication of *A Passage to India* were in tatters. The death of Gino's baby in *Where Angels Fear to Tread* puts an end to a prolonged Mediterranean fantasy, just as Leonard Bast's death in *Howards End* insists on the hazards for Helen Schlegel (and her entire class) of pursuing romantic relations in a socially downward direction.

A Passage to India transforms the problem of declaring erotic interest without an irrevocable culmination into a burning cultural problem. The Marabar caves become an evocatively suggestive metaphor for the precarious love-hate dynamic, the paralyzing ambiguities, girding the British colonial encounter with late-Imperial India. At all costs, for Forster, the disjunctive terms of that encounter must be sustained. This goes far in explaining a largely overlooked, intriguing detail in the textual history of *A Passage to India:* Forster initially imagined the incident at the Marabar caves in the unambiguous terms of a near rape, a scenario he later reformulated when he returned to his novel a decade later. In the final version of the text, the novelist conceived of the culminating scene in the caves as (depending on the perspective of his characters), a hallucination, an optical illusion, or a hysterical crisis. Adela's skirmish with a man who may or may not have been Aziz in the darkness of the cave is anything but a physical encounter. What the early drafts of *A Passage to India* reveal is that the commonplace view of Forster as a fussy Prufrockian prude who by temperament could not write about sexual matters is without foundation in fact.[29] Forster *chooses* to stress an erotics of non-consummation; they are not forced on him by sociohistorical or literary edicts alone.

It is not the possibility of romantic fulfillment in a shimmering Orient that drives Mrs. Moore, Mr. Fielding, Dr. Aziz, and Miss Quested. Like Gudrun, Ursula, Rupert, and (to a lesser degree) Gerald in *Women in Love,* all of Forster's characters of illuminated consciousness (a category that comes to include Miss Quested in the aftermath of Aziz's trial) are in marked conflict with the prevailing marriage code. Almost at the very instant in the text when Forster introduces each of these characters, the reader is alerted to their skepticism and disillusionment in the face of prescribed marital relations. Fielding, a middle-aged agnostic liberal, would seem to be an unconflicted idealist on all issues *except* relations between the sexes. Both Dr. Aziz and Mrs. Moore are veterans of previous marriages, yet both seem wholly detached from spousal and parental roles. (Significantly, their children are seldom on their minds.) Devoted to a dead wife whom he came to adore too late, Aziz keeps a photograph of her as a kind of shrine. Nonetheless, it is as if Dr. Aziz and Mrs. Moore had moved beyond mourning.

This consigning of married heterosexual relations to an irretrievable past is a much-repeated motif in Forster's novel, suggesting what might be called "postmarital fiction." World-weary yet without any traces of a defeating cynicism, Mrs. Moore is a survivor of not one but two marriages, and on her arrival in India seems as much in search of some new form of human relationship as touristic frissons. Her two previous husbands have a significantly small place in her mind. That marriage for Mrs. Moore has been a disappointment, an experience of almost banal, nontranscendent meaning—and that her two dead spouses have left her with few particular memories—are salient points in *A Passage to India*. We do not so much as learn the name of her first husband, although she is always "Mrs. Moore." Her very appellation conjures up the merest echo of an actual experience. In a curious way, too, Miss Quested is also in a process of postmarital relations, herself having arrived in India with rapidly disappearing illusions about her fiancé. Despite—or because of—their detachment from connubial allegiances, each of these four characters, equipped with varying, shifting degrees of insight into the Anglo-Indian dilemma, come to take a place in a sequence of shadow "couples." With the exception of Aziz, whose devotion to a dead wife he hardly knew appears to exempt him from the social pressure to seek a romantic partner, none of Forster's characters have pasts that weigh on the present.

Forster's keen sense of imminent cultural collapse for both India and Britain stems from a paradox that is reframed throughout the novel: it is only through the partial breakdown of communication, the continual rupture of language affirming difference, that erotic tension may be maintained. Forster is not seeking a language as unmediated, direct source of signification but as a series of scenes that must be read, deciphered, and perpetually unraveled. For Dr. Aziz, Miss Quested, Mrs. Moore, and Fielding, the unstated, central challenge is to redeem communication not so that it becomes transparent but that it can be sufficiently opaque. In being opaque, it engenders erotic frissons and a continually reanimated carnal life. "[H]e had dulled his craving for verbal truth," the narrator tells us of Fielding, "and cared chiefly for truth of mood." [30] A craving for truth of mood, as opposed to linguistic truth, imparts an erotics of deliberate imprecision.

A Passage to India continually reframes Fielding's axiom, demonstrating that verbal verities cannot be relied upon because they do not satisfy the hunger for a larger truth. We learn that Miss Quested "accepted everything Aziz said as true verbally. In her ignorance, she regarded him as 'India'." [31] When Professor Godpole sings a Hindu song to Dr. Aziz, Mrs. Moore, and Miss Quested, it is described as giving the "illusion of a Western melody. But the ear, baffled repeatedly, soon lost any clue, and wandered in a maze of noises, none harsh or unpleasant, none intelligible. It was the song of an unknown bird. Only the servants understood it." [32] Forster's British characters always seem to have fallen to a place beyond language. "Oh please—it distresses me beyond words," Mrs. Moore tells an Indian couple she has met at the Bridge Party when she learns the pair may have changed plans on her account.[33] The colloquialism echoes loudly in an Indian context in which language itself is always on the brink of stalling and dissolving. Again and again in *A Passage to India,* we witness the continual frustration of communication as connections are proffered, promised, attempted, and finally severed. It is a frustration Forster repeatedly requires as the very engine his narrative.

To be sure, the cultural distinction between the British and their Indian subjects are depicted at length by Forster, summed up in the crass Mrs. Turton's remark that "East is East and West is West" in Chandrapore. At the same time, however, even as Forster continually reintroduces conflicts into the Anglo-Indian relations of the novel so as to polemicize against Britain's colonial ambitions, the barriers described in *A Passage to India* allow, no less fundamentally, for the tacit eroticization of Anglo-Indian experience. The danger for Forster is that such barriers are always on the verge of disappearing. In narrative terms, the novelist repeatedly pulls asunder the relations between his Indian and British characters whom he has previously depicted as absolute in their degree of intimacy. Thus the catastrophe of the Marabar caves unfolds not because of a failure of communication but because the English and their Indian subjects have become *too* close in understanding; they are fundamentally alike, and at moments they are exactly the same. Adela Quested's question for Dr. Aziz before she enters the caves (inquiring as to whether Dr. Aziz indulges in polygamy), at heart is a vocalized fantasy of difference, the projection of British wishes onto a resistant East. It is little wonder, therefore, that Aziz reacts with (disguised) distaste, for he is culturally much closer to the English than they would prefer to have him.[34]

The possibility of escaping into language as a private means of communion with others and other cultures, or as a way of communing privately with oneself, has become insupportable in *A Passage to India.* This casts some light on the meaning of the Marabar caves fiasco for Mrs. Moore, who not only refuses to testify at the trial of Dr. Aziz but regards the entire episode as yet another example of the figment of intimacy encouraged by the enduring rites of courtship, marriage, and friendship. (And she, as much as Miss Quested, has left England to escape such rites, which she has come to view as both dishonest and sterile.) After the incident at the caves, Mrs. Moore is more than disconsolate; she is destroyed—and for partly selfish reasons that have little to do with her concern for the welfare of her friend Aziz: "The wonderful India of her opening weeks, with its cool nights and acceptable hints of infinity, had vanished."[35] It is the captivating mirage of a deliberately protracted erotic sublimation—"acceptable hints of infinity"—that has eluded Mrs. Moore in the wake of the Marabar caves catastrophe, rather than a dream of some final fulfillment.

Dependent on the maintenance of sexual distance, flirting requires a dynamic of separation, one that is continually undermined throughout *A Passage to India*. Despite the received wisdom among his devotees that Forster is a literary artist given over to issuing humane exhortations reducible to a philosophy of "Only Connect," in this novel, as elsewhere in his work, the divisive obstructions between classes and cultures are depicted as evaporating. Forster represents this as a historical as much as a social actuality. And in noting this shift in colonial relations, the novelist is at once more radical and more conservative than traditional critics of his writing have allowed. Similarly, Forster's dream of British-Indian homoerotic friendship is a dream of endless deferral. Unlike Lawrence, who in *Women in Love* seeks a continual, convulsive apotheosis of homoerotic feeling for Gerald and Rupert, Forster in *A Passage to India* goes so far as to summon the mute forces of nature so as to sanction scenarios of ceaseless "disconnection."

Dependent for its success on a continually suspended "racial" difference, Forster's characters partake of relations that are anchored in a conscious self-repression. It is, after all, the dowager Mrs. Moore, not the "eligible" ingenue Miss Quested, who transfixes Dr. Aziz. He is drawn to this woman because, given the tired chestnut that insists that as an older woman she is somehow beyond sexuality, Mrs. Moore is in fact "available" for him. Few think to question their relationship even after Miss Quested believes she has been attacked in the Marabar caves. Mrs. Moore therefore remains a safe friend with whom Aziz may speak with complete freedom. No doubt for this reason Mrs. Moore inspires, as well, a cult of "Emiss Moore" in the days after the trial. To remain dangerous, cross-cultural flirtations must continually become energized and redirected—through relatives, mysticism, and fraternal friendship. Significantly, Dr. Aziz's intense feelings of fellowship with Fielding reach their climax at precisely that moment in the text (the Marabar caves episode) when Anglo-Indian relations are most vexed and, indeed, at a kind of apocalyptic impasse.

Critics of Forster's work tend to perceive him as merely illustrating a need to transcend cultural barriers, to export the philosophy of "Only Connect" to the shores of Indian culture in the twilight days of Imperialism. That understanding of Forster endures in the work of many of the novelist's recent postcolonial critics, who, although they grant that Forster fully understood the limitations of nineteenth-century liberalism, nevertheless see him as a novelist of failed intimacies.[36] While it is true that in *A Passage to India*, Forster sought to demonstrate the necessity of surmounting barriers of culture, he is equally if not more absorbed in a countervailing imperative: the need to keep Indian and British subjects apart in a recurring process of endlessly eroticized "disconnectedness." As critics frequently have observed, *A Passage to India* is a novel of insurmountable barriers—between races, castes, religions, and sexes.[37] One of the more striking aspects of Forster's foray into Anglo-India relations, however, is that the divide between the local British community and its Indian subjects is not nearly as great as that between the members of the exiled British community itself. Far more than is the case with the gap dividing Dr. Aziz and Fielding (and certainly more than is true of the breach separating Mrs. Moore and Dr. Aziz), the divide segregating Mrs. Moore from her son Ronny is irreconcilable—and final. (She leaves India not having patched up the feud stemming from her refusal to testify at Dr. Aziz's trial.) As in *Howards End,* where the dying Mrs. Wilcox instantly establishes a fervent friendship with Margaret Schlegel (eventually bequeathing Margaret her beloved Hertfordshire home, Howards End), the bonds of friendly feeling in *A Passage to India* supplant familial ties. In the process, such bonds are exposed as a sham. Just as the hide-bound Ronny Heaslop increasingly seems as if he could never be the offspring of the forward-thinking Mrs. Moore, the mercenary Wilcox children appear to be mocking inversions of their mother. National bonds are similarly without a deeper emotional resonance.

As in *Howards End,* where the cultural experience separating the working-class bank clerk Leonard Bast from the high-minded Schlegels is minimal, *A Passage to India* depicts the Indian physician Aziz and the British schoolmaster Fielding as sharing tastes, attitudes, and, until the novel's penultimate pages, fantasies of British-Indian harmony. So often in Forster, the commonality that comes as a genealogical birthright is revealed as illusory, splintering into a never-ending divisiveness. "Culture" is invariably the domain in which differences and affinities are divulged.

Thus, in *Howards End,* Forster presents the artistically inclined Schlegels and the business-savvy Wilcoxes as occupying sharply stratified spheres. (The crisis Forster explores pivots on the idea that these two families might as well be from different countries.) Whereas the Schlegel sisters share literary and musical values with Leonard, it is virtually impossible to imagine the Wilcox children as having the same predilections in cultural matters as either of the Schlegel women. (The Schlegels and Leonard Bast, on the other hand, are of one mind on issues of taste; for instance, they read Meredith's novel on the theme of familial inheritance, *The Ordeal of Richard Feveral,* with shared enthusiasm.)

For Forster, cultural affinities supersede political differences. He gives keen attention to an ever-widening gap in the distinct branches of a British bourgeoisie he otherwise depicts as growing closer in their economic interests. At the very moment when, from a strictly historical perspective, the divisions between individuals of close affinities are ready to dissolve, Forster feels obliged to introduce a crisis of melodramatic proportions. Margaret Schlegel and Mrs. Wilcox are spiritual sisters in the opening chapters of *Howards End,* yet almost immediately after their meeting Forster raises—in highly overwrought terms—the threat of a fissure. Forster the literary artist and Forster the social utopian are largely at odds in *A Passage to India,* where it is the erotics of deferral—adopted from the tradition of Austen, solidified in reaction to the sexual politics of literary modernism, finally adapted to a homoerotics of permanent delay—that dominate the concerns of the novel. In *A Passage to India,* the odds against a same-sex idyll for Fielding and Aziz—indeed, for a durable establishment of a homosexual sublime—are formidable not merely because of onerous social barriers. They are insurmountable because Forster seeks to provide an anti-Lawrentian ethos of erotic distance between his male protagonists, and to do so with the consent of a distance-sanctioning, distinctly anti-Lawrentian "nature."

LAWRENCE'S *WOMEN IN LOVE* AND THE HOMOSEXUAL SUBLIME

Forster's recasting of the conclusion of *Women in Love* in *A Passage to India* highlights some of the affinities between these two novelists, not only in the broader thematic concerns of their works but in many of the details of their novels. Just as Forster was engaged in responding to Lawrence's work, so too did Lawrence write out of an acute awareness of Forster. In composing *Women in Love,* Lawrence may have been recasting elements of *Howards End,* having adopted Forster's device of pivoting his theme of England in a state of crisis on the struggles of two forward-thinking sisters.[38] In fact, Lawrence and Forster wrote in a kind of contrapuntal rhythm, with *A Passage to India* a revision of *Women in Love* much as *Maurice* stands as a homosexual anticipation of *Lady Chatterley's Lover* (although Lawrence almost certainly had not read Forster's self-suppressed novel).

Although the acquaintance between these two novelists was exceedingly rancorous, after Lawrence's death Forster generously acknowledged the author of *Sons and Lovers* and *Women in Love* as the greatest "imaginative" writer of the epoch. Not least important in the relations of these two authors is that Lawrence and Forster, far more than any other writers of the period, demonstrated an absorption in the thematics of homoerotic desire, a preoccupation that is historically notable, in part, for its shared refusal of contemporaneous Bloomsbury's attitude toward homosexual relations.[39] Forster was deeply engaged in a revision of precisely the homoerotic component of Lawrence's text—the friendship between Rupert Birkin and Gerald Crich—in his formulation of the uneasy accord between Fielding and Dr. Aziz. *A Passage to India* is as much a novel about the breakdown of communication and common culture as the novel that Lawrence achieved in *Women in Love.* Both works posit predicaments in the state of heterosexual relations, turning points that insist on the necessity—indeed, the superiority—of a *tacit* homoeroticism. Yet it is in suggesting what form such relations should take that Lawrence and Forster come to differ.

In order to distinguish his fiction from that of Lawrence, Forster was required to *surpass* the logic of Lawrentian "blood consciousness" and homoerotic "adhesiveness" as Lawrence had derived such concepts directly from Walt Whitman and, indirectly, from Edward Carpenter. When Lawrence is being most tragic about the state of heterosexual romance in *Women in Love,* he remains loyal to a love ethos that stresses an erotics of physical cohesion. Thus, in what might be characterized as a symbolic precursor of the Marabar caves episode, the drowning of Diana Crich at the Crichs' outdoor celebration in the chapter "Water Party" of *Women in Love* offers a brilliantly visual metaphor of male-female incompatibility. After the bodies of the dead newlyweds have been recovered, Lawrence provides a characteristically imagistic deathly tableau: "Diana had her arms tight round the neck of the young man," Lawrence's narrator informs the reader. Gerald's own view of the dual, nocturnal drowning ("She killed him," he bluntly informs Gudrun) is yet another salvo in a militant plea for homoerotic passion animating *Women in Love*.[40] In the subsequent chapter, "Sunday Evening," Ursula and Birkin argue viciously, a verbal duel that is followed by the novel's celebrated "Man to Man" segment. Here the strength of Gerald and Rupert's bond is established as Gerald tenderly nurses Rupert back to health, a scene that has a controlled, frenzied recapitulation in the subsequent "Gladiatorial" chapter, in which Rupert and Gerald wrestle in a pugilistic shadow play of sexual intercourse. In Lawrence's never-quite-subtextual homoerotic imaginary, male-male affection must coexist with feats of physical prowess. In this way, a homosexual sublime is achieved without the taint of effeminacy.

For Forster, the Marabar caves episode also affirms the need for an exalted male-male eroticism through an image of drastic physical separateness between heterosexuals whose flirting engenders disaster. Once the homoerotic subtext of Aziz and Fielding's friendship becomes the central story of the novel in the aftermath of the disaster at the Marabar caves, the impulse to engineer an erotically unresolved scenario is intensified in *A Passage to India*. Given that, strictly speaking, the sexual "difference" between Fielding and Aziz is relatively minimal, Forster must keep alive the rifts dividing these two men. (Earlier, the novelist stressed the closeness of Dr. Aziz's rapport with Fielding, insisting that Aziz is a man of culture, a poet, a fact that places him in the same league as both Fielding and Mrs. Moore but not, of course, with her son Ronny.) Insofar as the British novel, including Forster's own works of fiction before *A Passage to India*, concerned itself with the erotics of willful deferral, the land of the Raj presents the novelist with a fresh opportunity for the expression of feeling without culmination. Thus, with *A Passage to India*, the British novel of manners is transported to India so as to prolong a sequence of carnal renunciations that have proven untenable (in social as well as literary terms) within English culture itself. In a sort of ever-escalating tropism of sexual agitation, opportunities for retarded eros in Forster's novel encompass both heterosexually and homosexually fraught relationships.

The shared yearning for union with an exotic East on the part of Mrs. Moore, Miss Quested, and Fielding coalesces into a desire for a special male "friend," the individual with whom a sexual completion is always desirable but never possible, now sought outside of Britain. Forster's unwillingness to allow Fielding, Mrs. Moore, and Miss Quested the gravity of psychosexual pasts suggests additional links to Lawrence. Just as the trappings of nineteenth-century "character" was under assault in *Women in Love* (as we shall see, a text of formative importance for Forster's thinking in *A Passage to India),* characters in Forster's novel seem to shed the "old, stable ego" Lawrence once claimed he wished to eliminate in *Women in Love.* That modernist impulse is related, additionally, to the trouble in the Marabar caves. Just as the staging of flirtatious eros in Victorian fiction once legitimized the realist novel in its aim of endlessly decipherable, opaque encounters, Forster invents a scene of ambiguous erotic meaning as a flash point for highlighting relations dependent on a heightened subjectivity. Forster is a sort of Lawrentian manqué, whose true "Lawrentian" novel—*Maurice*—was too daring for Forster to risk publishing in his own lifetime. "We are now in a period of crisis," Lawrence announced in his preface to *Women in Love,* setting the apocalyptic tone for his novel. "Every man who is acutely alive is acutely wrestling with his own soul." [41] Forster resisted this end-of-worldism for a sanguine surrender to the inevitability of a political solution in India.

More explicit traces of Lawrence's *Women in Love* may be located elsewhere in *A Passage to India,* in such seemingly minor details as Cecil Fielding's vocation as a schoolmaster, a role that duplicates Rupert Birkin's role as rabble-rousing inspector of schools. At an even deeper level, both works begin by making marriage a question that is up for grabs. After an initial overture in which the Marabar caves are described as the sole interesting detail of Chandrapore's otherwise unexceptional landscape, the novel takes off with a conversation at the home of Dr. Aziz's friend, Hamidullah, in which Dr. Aziz and his cohorts lament the decline of an old British social ethos as they question the point of marriage. Here it is the men who express skepticism toward marital relations, while the one woman who is present deplores the disappearance of eligible young Indian men. For these contemplative Indians, an historical epoch has disappeared, and they nostalgically recall an undestroyed past in which Queen Victoria emerges as a rare, legitimate icon. When a friend of Aziz nostalgically recalls that a certain Mrs. Bannister demonstrated great "goodness" toward him, causing yet another friend to recall that Queen Victoria herself was "different," Aziz is an unflappable realist, declaring: "Queen Victoria and Mrs. Bannister were the only exceptions, and they're dead." [42] (At such moments Aziz and his friends, discoursing pleasantly on the decline of

British manners, might well be the members of an eccentric, retrograde
London Club.) Mrs. Moore's encounter with Dr. Aziz in a mosque occurs
within days of her arrival in India, a meeting that sets a standard of sublime deferral (the kind of encounter that, when replicated by Aziz and
Adela Quested, turns calamitous).

> "I think you ought not to walk at night alone, Mrs. Moore. There are bad
> characters about and leopards may come across from the Marabar Hills.
> Snakes also."
> She exclaimed; she had forgotten about the snakes.
> "For example, a six-spot beetle," he continued. "You pick it up, it bites,
> you die."
> "But you walk about yourself."
> "Oh, I am used to it."
> "Used to snakes?"
> They both laughed.[43]

Only the last line in this exchange shifts this superficially "Lawrentian"
conversation into a distinctly un-Lawrentian droll register. Dr. Aziz and
Mrs. Moore must retreat from, and even tame, the primitive elements
around them, whose symbolic weight could sink the inaugural scene of
their friendship. The effect on Mrs. Moore is immediate and magical,
echoing the "Moony" chapter of *Women in Love,* in which Birkin shatters
with stones the reflection of the moon in a pool of water (a scene that
Forster had specifically praised in the "Prophecy" section of *Aspects of the
Novel* as wonderfully "irradiating nature from within"). In Forster, the
moment of nocturnal communion is linked to Mrs. Moore's self-exile
from national identification:

> Mrs. Moore, whom the club had stupefied, woke up outside. She watched
> the moon, whose radiance stained with primrose the purple of the surround-
> ing sky. In England the moon had seemed dead and alien; here she was
> caught in the shawl of night together with earth and all the other stars. A sud-
> den sense of unity, of kinship with the heavenly bodies, passed into the old
> woman and out, like water through a tank, leaving a strange freshness be-
> hind. She did not like "Cousin Kate" or the National Anthem, but their note
> had died into a new one, just as cocktails and cigars had died into invisible
> flowers.[44]

The writing here is far more subdued than in Lawrence, yet, as with the
central protagonists of *Women in Love,* Mrs. Moore is less a conventional
character than a suddenly awakened consciousness. Immediately transformed by her meeting with Aziz, she loses the detritus of a personal

history. She has been transformed into a sheer conduit of energy. Just as Lawrence had hoped to eliminate the "old stable ego" from his novel, so too has Forster subtracted from Mrs. Moore a foundation in a stable ego that might have kept her from giving herself up to the new experience in the mosque.

Forster's most strenuous engagement of Lawrence in *A Passage to India* comes with the final gesture toward a state of "disconnection." Both novelists favor crises of cathartic power in their narratives, but for Lawrence it lies in the very nature of human sexuality, as opposed to Forster's relegation of cathartic eroticism to moments in time (the encounter in the Marabar caves, for example). In place of Lawrence's reach for a Whitmanesque "adhesiveness" in male-male relations, stemming from a catharsis of encounter and release, Forster strives for a homoerotic sublimity in which men seek a union that they are never granted. Out of a radical skepticism regarding conventional heterosexual relations, both Lawrence and Forster reach for solutions that find their sanctification in differing conceptions of nature.

Here the conclusion of *A Passage to India* is worth quoting in full, for in it Forster was unequivocal in detailing those factors he believed restrained Fielding and Aziz:

> "Why can't we be friends now?" said the other, holding him affectionately. "It's what I want. It's what you want."
> But the horses didn't want it—they swerved apart; the earth didn't want it, sending up rocks through which the riders must pass single file; the temples, the tank, the jail, the palace, the birds, the carrion, the Guest House, that came into view as they issued from the gap and saw Mau beneath; they didn't want it, they said in their hundred voices, "No, not yet," and the sky said, "No, not there."[45]

An absolute fulfillment is denied Fielding and Aziz by nature in its many incarnations—through allusions to horses, earth, and sky. The passage stands too as a deliberate recasting of the conclusion of *Women in Love*; in the last pages of Lawrence's novel, the tragedy of Gerald's death is undercut by the *Women in Love's* extraordinary concluding endorsement of bisexuality. "You can't have two kinds of love," Ursula insists to Birkin after Gerald's body has been buried, as she dismisses Birkin's ideas as "an obstinacy, a theory, a perversity." Rupert's response and *Women in Love's* final sentence is a refusal to accept a delimited heterosexual arrangement: "I don't believe that."[46] Lawrence's genius consists in his emphasis on the barely articulated, unconscious dynamics of homoerotic relations as they move in a state of crisis, flux, and cathartic confrontation. It was his willingness to transcend the conventions of the nineteenth-century novel, subverting what he called the "old, stable ego," and, in turn, the stable sexual self, that enabled him at his best to depict the experimental excitement of same-sex relations.[47] Despite the potential for true passion and tenderness between men, real devotion between males is stymied by a failure of nerve. For the Forster of *A Passage to India,* however, nature authorizes a homoerotics of endlessly suspended separation.

Notes

INTRODUCTION

1. Kundera, *Immortality,* 196–97.

2. Brooks, *Reading for the Plot,* 29.

3. Bersani, *A Future for Astyanax,* 76.

4. Polhemus, *Erotic Faith,* 4. For an earlier articulation of this theme, see Polhemus, *Comic Faith: The Great Tradition from Austen to Joyce* (Chicago: University of Chicago Press, 1980).

5. Mikhail Bakhtin, "Discourse on the Novel," in *The Dialogic Imagination,* 338.

6. For example, Michael Mason has argued that the commonplace perception of nineteenth-century sexual culture as fostering prudery and hypocrisy is misguided. In what he claims is less a refutation of Foucault than an exploration of the "field of bodies and pleasures" ignored by Foucault, Mason's study contends that Victorian sexual moralism, embraced by members of the upper class and the poor, encouraged citizens to be agnostic, radically minded, and sexually contingent. Mason, *The Making of Victorian Sexuality.*

7. D. A. Miller, *The Novel and the Police,* 76, 85. Miller's theory of the panopticon has even been employed for eighteenth-century fiction in the work of John Bender.

8. Miller, *The Novel and the Police,* 21.

9. Sedgwick, *Between Men;* Sedgwick, *Epistemology of the Closet.* For a similar perspective, see Joseph Litvak, *Caught in the Act.*

Lately Sedgwick has expressed partial regret at what she now calls a "paranoid position" in queer readings of the novel, endorsing what she terms a "reparative reading position," in which "selves and communities succeed in extracting sustenance from the objects of a culture—even of a culture whose avowed desire has often been not to sustain them." See Sedgwick's "Paranoid Reading and Reparative Reading; or, You're So Paranoid, You Probably Think This Introduction is About You," introduction to *Novel Gazing: Queer Readings in Fiction,* 35.

10. Henry James, Review of Hardy's *Far from the Madding Crowd* (Dec. 24, 1874), in *Henry James: Literary Criticism* (New York: Library of America, 1984), 1048.

11. Barbara Leckie's recent path-breaking study, *Culture and Adultery,* which demonstrates, *pace* the literary critic Franco Moretti, that between 1847 and 1914 adultery was neither invisible in the English novel, as Moretti claims, nor absent in other cultural formations, inevitably finds its study dealing with the legal inflections of adulterous desire. Indeed, Leckie brilliantly explores the relation between Victorian trials, censorship legislation, sensation fiction, and modernist texts such as James's *The*

Golden Bowl to argue that in serious fiction adultery emerged as a question of epistemology rather than a matter of passion. Flirtation, however risky, seldom falls within
the purview of the law, and it is one of the features of flirtation that allows it to retain
its radical force. Adultery lends itself to surveillance and legal strictures; flirtation, ex-
pertly deployed, renders them meaningless.

12. Foucault, *Discipline and Punish,* 308.

13. Jürgen Habermas, "Georg Simmel on Philosophy and Culture: Postscript to
a Collection of Essays." Translated by Mathieu Deflem, *Critical Inquiry* 22 (spring
1996), 405.

14. For a penetrating analysis of Simmel's preoccupation with neurotic forms of
urban behavior owing to an aversion to excessive stimulation in the metropolis, see
David Frisby, *Fragments of Modernity: Georg Simmel, Siegfried Kracauer, Walter Benjamin* (London: Heinemann, 1985), 72–77.

15. Baudelaire, "Le Peintre de la vie moderne," 214; Benjamin, "Paris: Capital of the
Nineteenth Century," 173.

16. Baudelaire, "Le Peintre de la vie moderne," 217.

17. Beerbohm, *Zuleika Dobson,* 158.

18. Robert Darnton, *The Hidden Bestsellers of Pre-Revolutionary France* (New York:
W. W. Norton, 1995).

19. For a discussion of time as it operates in eighteenth-century pornographic literature, see Jean-Marie Goulemot, *Forbidden Texts: Erotic Literature and Its Readers in
Eighteenth-Century France,* trans. James Simpson (Oxford: Oxford University Press,
1995).

20. Albert Smith, *The Natural History of the Flirt* (London: Armitage, 1851), 103.

21. Charles Dickens, *David Copperfield* (1849–50; reprint, New York: Penguin,
1986), 140.

22. See, for example, Yeazell's *Fictions of Modesty,* which I discuss later in this introduction as well as in my chapter on Darwin's theory of sexual selection.

23. *Le nouveau petit Robert* (Paris: Maury, 1993), 936. There are no direct citations
given for these usages.

24. A sentence from Swift that Johnson provided to illustrate the word's meaning
lent support to this sense of coquetting as crossing lines of gender: "You are coquetting
a maid of honor, my lord looking on to see how the gamesters play, and I railing at you
both." Quoted in Samuel Johnson, *Johnson's Dictionary: A Modern Selection,* ed. E. L.
McAdam Jr. and George Milne (New York: Pantheon, 1963), 185, 130. Alvin Kernan sees
Johnson's dispute with Chesterfield over these and other terms as indicative of the tensions between an aristocratic attempt at influencing language and the new sovereignty
of the professional writing class represented by Johnson. See Kernan, "The Battle for
the Word: Dictionaries, Deconstructors, and Language Engineers," in *The Death of Literature* (New Haven, Conn.: Yale University Press, 1990), 152–61.

Johnson offered a definition of the noun "flirt" as "a pert young hussey," but his
definition of "to flirt" as a "quick, sprightly motion," while minimizing the erotic nature of the coquetry, implied that activity could conceivably be initiated by members
of both sexes. Despite his patron's urging, Johnson had pointedly rejected from his dictionary an amorous or erotic sense of the verb "to flirt" in favor of two definitions ("To
jeer; to jibe at one," and "To run about perpetually; to be unsteady and fluttering").
Despite Chesterfield's pleas, Johnson concluded that such a connotation was too

fashionable, as although the word "flirtation" was included, like the noun, it was gendered as female: "A quick sprightly motion; a cant word among women." Johnson, *Johnson's Dictionary: A Modern Selection*, 130.

25. David Garrick, *The Male-Coquette: or Seventeen Hundred Fifty-Seven* (London: Vaillant, 1757), 15, 22. The play as originally performed at London's Drury Lane Theater was entitled "The Modern Fine Gentleman."

26. Amelia Opie, *Dangers of Coquetry: A Novel,* 2 vols. (London: W. Lane, 1790), 41.

27. Austen, *Lady Susan,* 53.

28. In a similar vein, the author of the popular *Reveries of a Bachelor: A Book of the Heart* (1850), Ik Marvel, implied that both coquetry and flirtation involved the captivation of a once-stalwart, soon-to-be-smitten male. For Ik Marvel, coquettish gestures were a necessary stage in the process of lovemaking, while flirtatious actions represented a mockery of amorous desire: "Coquetry whets the appetite," he flatly admonished, "flirtation depraves it. Coquetry is the thorn that guards the rose—easily trimmed off once plucked. Flirtation is like the slime on water-plants, making them hard to handle, and when caught, only to be cherished in slimy waters." Ik Marvel (Donald G. Mitchell), *Reveries of a Bachelor: A Book of the Heart* (1850; reprint, New York: Charles Scribner's Sons, 1889), 59. This stridently articulated naturalized vocabulary of purity and pollution at times gives way, however, to a more sensitive appreciation of flirting as an intricate, elevated enterprise. Such a notion relied on an earlier understanding of the activity as feminine artistry, artful sexuality, as practiced by cunningly intelligent females of superfine discriminations. Thus *The Saturday Review* of 1863 refers to "the flirtational element and its kindred infinitesimal phases," while Walter Besant's novel *The Golden Butterfly* speaks of the "great art of flirtation." *The Saturday Review* (May 3, 1863); Walter Besant, *The Golden Butterfly: A Novel* (London: John Tammel, 1876).

29. As early as 1688, the French aphorist Jean de la Bruyère imagined with distaste the possibility of males taking on a coquette's role. "Gallantry in a woman seems to add to coquetry," he hazarded in his epigrammatic essay "Des femmes," without quite explaining of what female gallantry consisted. "A male coquette, on the contrary, is something worse than a gallant. A male coquette and a woman of gallantry are pretty much on a level." Jean de la Bruyère, "On Women" ["Des femmes"] (1688), in *Characters,* trans. Henri Van Laun (New York: Howard Fertig, 1992), 63.

30. Stendhal (Marie Henri Beyle), *Love,* trans. Gilbert and Suzanne Sale (1822; reprint, London: Penguin, 1975), 88.

31. Mrs. S. S. Ellis, *The Daughters of England, Their Position in Society, Character, and Responsibilities* (London: Fisher, Son & Co., 1842), 302–3.

32. Charles Maurice de Talleyrand, in *Le miroir de Talleyrand: lettres inedites à la Duchesse de Courlande pendant le Congrés de Vienne,* ed. Gaston Palewski (Paris: Perrin, 1976), 178.

33. Bourget, *Physiologie de l'amour moderne,* 156. My translation.

34. Bourget, "Flirting Club," in *Profils perdus* (Paris: Alphonse Lemerre, 1901). My translation.

35. No doubt because of a seeming misunderstanding about the meaning of the word "le flirt"—it is close in meaning to the English word "flirtation"—Hervieu's novel has been somewhat inaccurately translated into English by Hugh Craig as *Flirt: A Novel of Parisian Life* (New York: Worthington Company, 1890).

36. "Though Speaking Softly, Still Look for the Mike," *The New York Times* (Aug. 20, 1992).

37. James Reston, "Adlai and Mario and Ike and George," op-ed piece, *The New York Times* (Nov. 11, 1991).

38. Phillips, *On Flirtation*.

39. Austen, *Northanger Abbey*, 54.

40. Simmel, "Flirtation," in *On Women, Sexuality, and Love*, 135. This essay first appeared in 1923 in the third edition of *Philosophische Kultur: Gesammelte Essais [Philosophic Culture]*. A preliminary version of "Flirtation" was published in 1909 as "Psychologie der Koketterie," *Der Tag*, Berlin, (May 11–12, 1909).

41. Simmel, "Sociability," from *Fundamental Problems of Sociology: Individual and Society* (1917) in *The Sociology of Georg Simmel*, 51.

42. Simmel, "The Metropolis and Mental Life," in *The Sociology of Georg Simmel*, 409–10.

43. Ibid., 410.

44. For a superb discussion of Simmel and modernity, with particular attention to Benjamin, see Frisby, *Fragments of Modernity,* cited above.

45. Habermas, "Georg Simmel on Philosophy and Culture," 413.

46. In its articulation of the civilizing function of the "play element" in romantic relations, Simmel's discussion resembles Johan Huizinga's 1950 cultural study *Homo Ludens: A Study of the Play Element in Culture* (Boston: Beacon Press, 1970).

47. Emile Batault, *Contribution a l'étude de l'hystère chez l'homme* (Paris, 1885), 48.

48. Otto Weininger, *Sex and Character* (1906; reprint, New York: AMS Press, 1975), 232.

49. Sigmund Freud, "Thoughts for the Times on War and Death" (1915), paper delivered to the B'Nai B'rith Club of Vienna, in Sigmund Freud, *The Standard Edition of the Complete Psychological Works of Sigmund Freud,* ed. and trans. James Strachey (London: Hogarth Press and the Institute of Psychoanalysis, 1915), vol. 7.

50. Brooks, *Reading for the Plot,* 109.

51. Ibid., 54.

52. Caryl Emerson and Gary Saul Morson, "Penultimate Words," in *The Current in Criticism: Essays on the Present and Future of Literary Theory,* ed. Clayton Koelb and Virgil Locke (West Lafayette, Ind.: Purdue University Press), 49.

53. Bourget, *Physiologie de l'amour moderne,* 62.

54. Christopher Isherwood, *A Single Man* (1948; reprint, New York: Avon, 1964), 147.

55. Henry James, *Washington Square* (New York: Library of America, 1985), 14.

56. Thackeray, *Vanity Fair,* 844–45.

57. Thackeray, *Vanity Fair,* 677.

58. Eugene Fromentin, *Dominique,* trans. Edward Marsh (1862; reprint, New York: Chanticleer Press, 1962).

59. Anthony Trollope, *Miss MacKenzie* (1865). In his autobiography, Trollope further confessed that his effort to produce such a novel eventually "breaks down before the conclusion." (Miss MacKenzie eventually accepts one of her suitors.)

60. Stendhal (Marie Henri Beyle), *The Charterhouse of Parma,* trans. Margaret Shaw (1839; reprint, New York: Penguin, 1958), 152.

61. Barthes, *A Lover's Discourse,* 67.

62. Armstrong, *Desire and Domestic Fiction*. See also, Spacks, *Desire and Truth*.

63. Boone, *Tradition Counter Tradition,* 10.

64. There are problems, as well, entailed in Boone's forced diagrammatics of literary history, in which, for example, Hardy's *Tess of the D'Urbervilles* emerges as a "traditional text" but Woolf's *To the Lighthouse* (1927) is "countertraditional." And despite the attention to the subversive energies of such supposedly "form-breaking" counter-traditional novels as *Daniel Deronda* and *Cranford* (1853), Boone often evinces a bleakly reductive view of the possibilities for individual freedom in nineteenth-century fiction. This requires him to conclude at one point, for example, that "In psychological as well as geographical terms, the place allotted to women—married or single—in nineteenth-century English and American patriarchy was essentially static." An unstated but key assumption of *Tradition Counter Tradition* is its recurring faith in the novel's progressive "evolution" toward an *écriture feminine,* supposedly antipatriarchal twentieth-century texts, much as early theorists of the novel such as Ian Watt and Georg Lukács once understood eighteenth-century texts as "rising" toward the nineteenth-century novel. (In his updated teleological schema, Boone relies on Nina Auerbach's *Communities of Women,* which locates a lost female homosocial tradition in the British and American novel, rather than on Auerbach's more revisionist *Woman and the Demon* and *Romantic Imprisonment.* These later works powerfully undermined then-standard feminist literary histories by insisting that the Victorian novel encouraged deeply grained antipatriarchal energies.) Other fundamental points made by Boone—that the male is presented as complete at the outset of the "traditional" novel whereas the female typically is presented as needing to develop (a process capped by marriage)—places too high a premium on completion over development, when both are ethically neutral. To state this point another way, Tom Tulliver's "completeness" is a mark of his know-nothing rigidity, and thus, paradoxically, of his "incompleteness" (just as his sister Maggie—and even Stephen—are magnificently "incomplete"). Madame Merle is monstrously "finished" in James's *The Portrait of a Lady* (1881), although there should be little doubt that she is, morally speaking, debased. Boone's scheme inadvertently mimics a component of bourgeois ideology, by defending self-realized "wholeness" as an unquestioned human good and condemning a shifting, indeterminate social self.

65. Eliot, *The Mill on the Floss,* 485.

66. Kucich, *Repression in Victorian Fiction,* 14 – 15.

67. Ibid., 40.

68. As Kucich comments, "'Power' for Foucault is a kind of mystified, ontological absolute though it masquerades as the end of ontology." Kucich, *Repression in Victorian Fiction,* 14 – 15.

69. *The Mikado* ran at the Savoy Theater for 674 consecutive performances, a record that was not to be broken at that theater for thirty-five years. Christopher Hibbert, *Gilbert and Sullivan and Their Victorian World* (New York: American Heritage, 1976), 184.

70. Gore Vidal, *Myra Breckinridge* (New York: Bantam, 1968), 1.

71. Irving Howe, *Politics and the Novel* (1957; reprint, New York: Avon, 1967), 117.

72. Almost all of the major critics of Wharton's fiction have emphasized the novelist's allegiance to the American literary tradition.

73. Bruce R. Smith, *Homosexual Desire in Shakespeare's England: A Cultural Poetics* (Chicago: University of Chicago Press, 1991), 16 – 17.

74. Vladimir Nabokov, "Spring in Fialta" [1938], in *Spring in Fialta* (New York: Popular Library, 1959), 20.

75. Nicholson Baker, *Vox,* (New York: Random House, 1992).

76. Forster, *A Passage to India,* 197.

1. DIALECTICAL DESIRES

1. Harth, *Cartesian Women.*

2. As a subject of intense intellectual discussion, coquetry emerges as part of a sometimes-feverish debate on the role and habits of aristocratic *salonistes.* Such a discussion has its origins in seventeenth-century French culture. In his celebrated *Maxims* (1665–68), La Rochefoucauld saw in flirtation a distinctly feminocentric enterprise, a kind of all-female plot militantly opposed to the erotic interests of men, when noting that the "women of Paris would much more be willing to give up adultery than coquetry." In 1660, the Abbé d'Aubignac (1604–72), acclaimed for a treatise on the French theater, composed a cautionary *voyage imaginaire* to "The Island of Coquetry" (located, appropriately enough, near the Cape of Good Hope), whose inhabitants conducted their lives on a single principle: wanton insincerity. D'Aubignac's island is a comic dystopia—local schools, for example, instruct children in the "art of speaking well while doing poorly"—where a lack of earnestness is everywhere rewarded. This "impertinent kingdom" is a place of "little faith but many churches, where congregants go to be seen." L'Abbé d'Aubignac, "La relation du royaume de coquetterie" (1660) in *Voyages imaginaires, songes, visions, et romans cabalistiques,* vol. 28 (Amsterdam: Rueet Hotel Serpente, 1788), 330. The social critique implicit in d'Aubignac's allegory is unmistakable, forming a biting send-up of a French high society aggressively committed to noncommitment.

3. Pierre Choderlos de Laclos, *Les liaisons dangereuses,* trans. P. W. K. Stone (1782; reprint, New York: Penguin, 1985), 150.

4. Laclos, *Les liaisons dangereuses,* 47.

5. Wollstonecraft, *The Vindication of the Rights of Woman,* 108.

6. Amelie Opie, *Dangers of Coquetry,* 108.

7. George Meredith, *Beauchamp's Career,* ed. Margaret Harris (1876; reprint, Oxford: Oxford University Press, 1988), 50.

8. Lady Charlotte (Campbell) Bury, *The History of a Flirt (As Told by Herself),* 3 vols. (London: Henry Colburn, 1841), 1:4–5.

9. Wollstonecraft, *The Vindication of the Rights of Woman,* 108.

10. One recent effort at locating "perverse" desire in Austen's work—and one that has generated considerable resistance among some scholars of Austen's work—is Terry Castle's review of a new edition of Austen's letters. Castle illuminates the "homophilic" strand in the novelist's relations with her sisters as evinced in Austen's correspondence. Terry Castle, "Sister," *The London Review of Books* (Aug. 15, 1995).

11. The representation of the female flirt as glitteringly malevolent stemmed from her associations with theatricality. In her discussion of eighteenth-century masquerade, Terry Castle argues that the theatrical impulse has frequently been constituted as demonic, mysterious, and female by definition. Terry Castle, *Masquerade and Civilization.*

12. Austen, *Lady Susan,* 55.

13. Bersani, "Realism and the Fear of Desire," in *A Future for Astyanax,* 67.

14. Although my discussion here is largely taken up with representations of the coquette in an English context, there is a corresponding and contemporaneous representation of the coquette in French theater. Pierre Carlet de Chamberlain de Marivaux's *The Triumph of Love* (1732), close in comic spirit to Congreve's *The Way of the World,* presents in its portrait of the captivating Leonide a coquette whose linguistic prowess earns her a position in the play equal to that of Millamant. In a Gallic turn on a Shakespearean confusion of identity, Leonide dresses as a man, "Phocion," and wins the affection of the dispossessed prince Agis (who thinks he is falling in love with a man). Unlike *The Way of the World,* however, Marivaux's play exploits the coquette's power to inspire erotic interest in both men and women.

15. George Meredith, *An Essay on Comedy and the Uses of the Comic Spirit* (1897; reprint, Ithaca, N.Y.: Cornell University Press, 1956), 98.

16. Congreve, *The Way of the World,* 293–94.

17. Peters, 121; Kenneth Muir, "The Comedies of William Congreve," in *Restoration Theater,* ed. John Russell Brown and Bernard Harris (New York: Capricorn, 1967), 234.

18. For a discussion of Millamant's debt to the rhetoric of the Cavalier poets, with special attention to the question of flirtation, see Donald Williams Bruce, "Why Millamant Studied Sir John Suckling," *Notes and Queries,* vol. 34 (Sept. 1987), 334–35.

19. William Hazlitt, *Lectures on the English Comic Writers,* in *The Collected Works of William Hazlitt,* ed. A. R. Waller and Arnold Glover (London: J. M. Dent and Co., 1903), 72.

20. This displacement of an aesthetic will into the erotic domain is reminiscent of Alexander Pope's "The Rape of the Lock," where the "belles" are coquettes.

21. Edward Burns, *Restoration Comedy: Crises of Desire and Identity* (London: Macmillan, 1987), 207.

22. Burns, *Restoration Comedy,* 203.

23. Hazlitt, *Lectures on the English Comic Writers,* 74.

24. When writers removed the coquette from the domain of the theater, she became shorn of her indomitable brilliance. In an essayistic and fictional commentary published in the *Tatler,* the coquette is presented as deliberately generating perverse forms of behavior. The fictitious astrologer Isaac Bickerstaff, under whose name Joseph Addison and Richard Steele offered their thrice-weekly commentaries, devoted his periodical article to what he suggested were two culturally pervasive and curiously analogous types of women, Castabella, a Prude, and Lydia, a Coquet: "The Prude and Coquet (as different as they appear in their Behaviour) are in Reality the same kind of women: the Motive of Action in both is the Affectation of pleasing men. They are Sisters of the same Blood and Constitution, only one chose a grave and the other a light, Dress." The *Tatler* erases the line dividing those who deny libidinal impulses and those who try to inspire them:

> The Prude appears more virtuous, the *Coquet* more vicious, than she really
> is. The distant behavior of the Prude, tends to the same Purpose as the Advances of the Coquet; and you have as little Reason to fall into Despair from
> the Severity of the one, as to conceive Hope from the familiarity of the other.
> What leads you into a clear Sense of their Character Is, That you may observe each of them has the Distinction of Sex in all her Thoughts, Words and

Actions. You can never mention any Assembly you were lately in, but one asks you with a rigid, the other with a sprightly air, Pray, what men were there? As for Prudes, it must be confessed, that there are several of them, who, like Hypocrites, by long practice of a false Part, become sincere; or at least delude themselves into a Belief that they are so.

The paradox identified by the *Tatler* stems from the coquette and the prude's shared distance from the standard rules of courtship; both female types disengage from sexual practice, acknowledging the power of erotic activity even as they refuse to surrender to the dictates of eros.

In the last part of the *Tatler*'s account the Coquet takes on the role of cross-dressing generator of (homo)sexually perverse plots. A young "Coquet Widow" in France, angry with a "Gascon of Quality" for boasting to his companions that he has partaken of "some favours which he never received," takes a curious revenge on him. Summoning the fellow, she tells him that she has a friend, Belinda, who has another engagement and therefore must be away from her husband for a night. The Coquet Widow asks if the Gascon might therefore spend a night dressed up as Belinda next to her "husband" and pretend to sleep. Agreeing to do so, the young Gascon spends a dreadful night next to the man he imagines is Belinda's spouse, as the narrator winkingly informs us that the "person who went to bed with him . . . was our young Coquet Widow. The Gascon was in a terrible Fright every Time she moved in the Bed, or turned towards him, and did not fail to shrink from her till he had conveyed himself to the very Ridge of the Bed." The anecdote ends with the Coquet Widow and three companions (the very companions to whom the Gascon had once boasted of favors) "joined with the rest in laughing at this man of Intrigue." A remarkable depiction of female vengeance, this anecdote goes well beyond the distinction between Prude and Coquet that the *Tatler* article initially established. The coquette here takes inordinate pleasure in staging perversity between men. With the *Tatler*'s rakish Coquet Widow, we witness the devolution of the eighteenth-century coquette into a willfully perverse antiheroine.

25. Austen, *Lady Susan*, 44.

26. Ibid., 55.

27. Ibid., 49.

28. Ibid., 47.

29. Balzac, "La Duchesse de Langeais," 217.

30. Brontë, *Villette*, 106.

31. Austen, *Northanger Abbey*, 217.

32. Brontë, *Villette*, 590.

33. Literary critics indebted to the work of Michel Foucault, such as D. A. Miller, John Bender, Mark Seltzer, and Joseph Litvak, have argued that the depth model so essential to Enlightenment thought and implicit in Victorian fictional identity is tied to an increasingly vigilant culture of surveillance throughout the nineteenth century. The novel, we are instructed, is complicit in the cultural practices of surveillance, while "interiority" itself is reactively produced by such practices. Michel Foucault, *Discipline and Punish*; D. A. Miller, *The Novel and the Police*; John Bender, *Imagining the Penitentiary: Fiction and the Architecture of Mind in Eighteenth-Century England* (Chicago: University of Chicago Press, 1987); Mark Seltzer, *Henry James and the Art of Power*, (Ithaca, N.Y.: Cornell University Press, 1984); Litvak, *Caught in the Act*.

I would suggest, however, that Austen, Brontë, and Thackeray, through their coupling of high-minded heroines with empty-headed coquettes, intimated that interiority was simply one available (although superior) conception of fictive character among several. For if it is a truism that interiority of character is a key constitutive element of Victorian fiction, then it is also the case that the antitheses of interiority of the self—emptiness, shallowness, "exteriority," multidimensionality of character—also find a place in the Victorian novel in the coquette-demons I explore here.

34. Georg Lukács, "The Intellectual Physiognomy in Characterization" (1936), in *Writer and Critic and Other Essays,* ed. and trans. Arthur D. Kahn (New York: Grosset and Dunlap, 1970), 154.

35. Simmel, "Flirtation," 135.

36. Austen, *Lady Susan,* 96.

37. Austen, *Northanger Abbey,* 217.

38. Tony Tanner, "Reading Reality in *Villette,*" in *Villette: New Casebooks,* ed. Pauline Nestor (New York: St. Martin's, 1992), 64. According to Tony Tanner, in Brontë's novel *Shirley* the author's "attempt to broaden the landscape of her novel, to provide a larger social context for the love stories, in many ways did not succeed nor did it make the novel more successful than, say, *Jane Eyre.*" Tanner, *Jane Austen,* 67.

39. Ronald Blythe, introduction to *Emma,* by Jane Austen (London: Penguin, 1966), 14.

40. Johnson, *Jane Austen,* 24.

41. Austen, *Northanger Abbey,* 217.

42. Austen, *Lady Susan,* 93.

43. Ibid., 58.

44. Ibid., 51.

45. See Sally Shuttleworth, "Demonic Mothers: Ideologies of Bourgeois Motherhood in the Mid-Victorian Era," in *Rewriting the Victorians: Theory, History, and the Politics of Gender* (New York: Routledge, 1992), 31–51.

46. Austen, *Lady Susan,* 47.

47. Austen, *Northanger Abbey,* 158–59.

48. Austen, *Emma,* 90.

49. Ibid., 361–62.

50. Lewes, *Ranthorpe,* 88–89.

51. That men might recognize flirts but choose to submit to loving them, albeit in secrecy, is a scenario entertained in Anthony Trollope's short story "Miss Sarah Jack, of Spanish Town, Jamaica" (1860), in which the character of Maurice Cumming "dearly, ardently loved that little flirt," a woman named Marian, "but seeing that she was a flirt, that she had flirted so grossly when he was by, he would not confess his love to a human being." Anthony Trollope, "Miss Sarah Jack, of Spanish Town, Jamaica," in *Early Short Stories* (New York: Penguin, 1994), 145.

52. Charlotte Brontë's fictional interest in the coquette was protracted over the course of an entire literary career. With the juvenilia of the *Glass Town Saga* (1826–32), she introduced such a figure in the character of the glamorous Lady Maria Sneachie, the chief Glass Town flirt, who finds her double in Mr. Myrtillus Ellrington, a coquettish fop whose feminized role is evinced in his sporting of salmon-pink "cambric trowsers." Brontë, *The Early Writings of Charlotte Bronte: Volume 1, The Glass Town Saga 1826–1832* (Oxford: Blackwell/Shakespeare Head, 1992).

With Brontë's first novel, *The Professor,* the reader is introduced to a classroom of coquettish girls who dog the repressed Crimsworth, comprising a cumulatively irksome erotic force and reminding him of a passion he cannot countenance. The heroine of *Jane Eyre*, meanwhile, encounters several key flirts in her move toward independence, including Rosamond Oliver, the dynamic socialite Blanche, and, most significantly, the doomed Bertha Mason, a society flirt whose feminine wiles help doom her to insanity. (Or so Rochester claims ex post facto in order to regain the "norms" he lost as rake manqué.) Such figures teach an unconscious lesson to Jane Eyre; at a pivotal point in her relations with Rochester, she visits St. John Rivers, in the process solidifying Rochester's romantic interest in her through coyly delivered references to Sir John (which he duplicates in kind through references to Blanche).

53. Brontë, *Villette*, 360.

54. Ibid., 69.

55. Kucich, *Repression in Victorian Fiction*, 106.

56. Brontë, *Villette*, 196.

57. Nina Auerbach, "Charlotte Brontë: The Two Countries," in *Romantic Imprisonment*, 339.

58. Thackeray, *Vanity Fair*, 34.

59. Ibid., 844.

60. Ibid., 754.

61. Ibid., 29.

2. THE FLIRTATION OF SPECIES

1. Darwin, *The Descent of Man*, 273.

2. The evolutionary biologist Tim Birkhead recently has written of "cryptic female choice" in the comb-jelly in the wild off the coast of Coburg Island in the Canadian Arctic, offering photographs demonstrating how the nucleus of the female's egg appears to deliberate as it "decides" between two sperm, finally fusing with one to create a baby comb-jelly. Tim Birkhead, *Promiscuity: An Evolutionary History of Sperm Competition and Sexual Conflict* (London: Faber, 2000).

3. See Malte Andersson, *Sexual Selection* (Princeton, N.J.: Princeton University Press, 1994). Andersson's overview of research on sexual selection (the most comprehensive to date) concludes that only in the last decade has Darwin's theory widely been substantiated, owing to what Andersson deems an overwhelming number of empirical studies confirming the basic outline of *The Descent of Man*. For a history of the reception of Darwin's theory in the years following the publication of *The Descent of Man*, see also C. J. Bajeema, *Evolution by Sexual Selection Theory Prior to 1900* (New York: Van Nostrand Reinhold, 1984). For a critique of Darwinian sexual selection based on anthropological work with female primates (specifically, prosimians, monkeys, and apes), see Meredith F. Small, *Female Choices: Sexual Behavior of Female Primates* (Ithaca, N.Y.: Cornell University Press, 1994).

4. Levine, *Darwin and the Novelists*. Trollope is an especially good subject for a consideration of the theory of sexual selection theory, given that the preoccupations of *The Descent* pervade and even dominate such novels as *Miss MacKenzie* (1865) and *Can You Forgive Her?* (1864–65).

5. Beer, *Darwin's Plots*, 211.

6. Armstrong, *Desire and Domestic Fiction.*

7. Philip Barrish, "Accumulating Variation: Darwin's *On the Origin of Species* and Contemporary Literary and Cultural Theory," *Victorian Studies* (summer 1991), 450.

8. Ruth Bernard Yeazell, "Nature's Courtship Plot in Darwin and Ellis," *Yale Journal of Criticism,* vol. 2, no. 2 (spring 1989), 42. Yeazell points out that sexual selection can only work if "males who happen to possess the traits females admire manage to produce more offspring than the others." According to Yeazell, Darwin assumes, without marshalling much evidence, that the most attractive males are always the most "vigorous" (and therefore, presumably, the most fertile). What Darwin cannot see, she writes, is the conclusion modern biologists have made, which is that sexual selection is confined largely to polygynous or so-called promiscuous species. "By focusing on the choosing female rather than the sexual activity of the male," argues Yeazell, "*The Descent* effectively manages to evade the issue."

9. Charles Darwin, *The Autobiography of Charles Darwin 1809–1882,* ed. with appendix and notes by Nora Barlow (1887; reprint with original omissions restored, New York: Norton, 1993), 138–39. One might well ask, however, if Darwin's depreciation of his own aesthetic powers did not arise from his own characterization in *The Descent* of aesthetic decision-making as largely a female enterprise.

10. Rosemary Jahn, "Darwin and the Anthropologists: Sexual Selection and Its Discontents," *Victorian Studies* (winter 1994) vol. 37:2, 302, 301.

11. In Darwin's notebooks, the works of Jane Austen outnumber those of any other novelist mentioned by the evolutionist. Noted in Gillian Beer, "Darwin's Reading and the Fictions of Development," in *The Darwinian Heritage,* ed. David Kohn (Princeton, N.J.: Princeton University Press, 1985), 543–88.

12. Both Huxley's and Eliot's comments are quoted in J. W. Burrow's introduction to Darwin, *The Origin of Species,* 14.

13. Such critiques of the theory of sexual selection are compatible with recent appraisals of other aspects of Darwin's work that have viewed the Victorian evolutionist as a sanguine defender of an increasingly beleaguered conservative political and social ethos. Adrian Desmond, for example, has alerted us to the ways in which Darwin deliberately evaded the radical, working-class implications of incipient Victorian evolutionism. Adrian Desmond, "Robert E. Grant: The Making of Institutional Biology in London, 1822–36," *History of Science* 23: 153–85, 223–50. Similarly, James R. Moore has maintained that Darwin's work, although unremittingly materialist in its foundational assumptions, nonetheless conserved the structure of the world it displaced, substituting "nature" for "God," thereby replacing a theological hierarchy for a scientific one. James R. Moore, "1859 and All That: Remaking the Evolution-Religion," in *Charles Darwin, 1809–1882: A Centennial Commemorative,* ed. R. Chapman (Wellington, New Zealand, n.p., 1982).

14. Darwin, *The Origin of Species,* 75.

15. Quoted in James Meek, "Sex Is Best When You Lose Your Head," review of *Promiscuity: An Evolutionary History of Sperm Competition and Sexual Conflict* by Tim Birkhead, *London Review of Books* (Nov. 16, 2000), 10.

16. George Levine, "Charles Darwin's Reluctant Revolution," *South Atlantic Quarterly,* 91:3 (summer 1992), 546.

17. Beer, *Darwin's Plots,* 63.

18. None of the better recent theoretical accounts dealing with the construction of

homosexuality provide more than a passing account of Darwin, usually seeing him as a part of the same "medicalizing" continuum that reaches its culmination in Freud. See, for example, Jeffrey Weeks, *Sexuality and Its Discontents: Meanings, Myths and Modern Sexualities* (London: Routledge and Kegan Paul, 1985).

19. The implications of Darwin's theory of sexual selection, in which natural phenomena teeter off into an endless array of disparate phenomena, suggest that in the work of the evolutionary theorist we may locate a way of finding in nineteenth-century culture means of avoiding the pitfalls of the "subversion hypothesis" that D. A. Miller has criticized as underpinning critical studies of Victorian narrative. For Miller, as I've noted earlier, all insurgent gestures, erotic or otherwise, collapse into a substantiation of power. Darwin provides, however, a depiction of the natural world where, while nature is scrutinized with ever-heightened tools of scientific surveillance, all phenomena fall under the rubric of the "natural," and questions of power are eclipsed by matters of survival and endurance.

20. For the location of a "counterworld" in the work of Wilkie Collins, see U. C. Knoepflmacher, "The Counterworld of Victorian Fiction and *The Woman in White,*" in *The World of Victorian Fiction,* ed. Jerome H. Buckley (Cambridge, Mass.: Harvard University Press, 1975), 351–69.

21. Pater, *The Renaissance,* xxix.

22. Ibid.

23. For a study of Pater as a writer of protohomosexual ideas, see Dellamora, *Masculine Desire.*

24. Marcel Proust, "Cities of the Plain", in *Remembrance of Things Past, Vol. 2,* trans. by C. K. Scott Montcrieff and Terence Kilmartin (New York: Random House, 1981), 653.

25. Gillian Beer, "Descent and Sexual Selection: Women in Narrative," in *Darwin's Plots,* 213.

26. To briefly consider two central yet strikingly dissimilar "pre-Darwinian" Victorian novels is to illustrate this point: *Wuthering Heights* (1847) and *Vanity Fair* (1847–48) both give considerable weight not only to the paramount place of female choosing but to a particular conception of romantic eros as existing in tension with flirtatious desire. Although Catherine Earnshaw is described by Nelly Dean as "not artful, never playing the coquette," her misguided choice of Edgar Linton over Heathcliff is a momentous act that dooms her and the woeful figures of *Wuthering Heights* to a lamentable fate. In *Wuthering Heights,* the female's decision leads to at least a generation of familial chaos, as a domestic order is undermined on behalf of the imagined civilizing processes of a class-compatible marriage. Significantly, before Catherine's fateful decision actually is enacted, it is verbally contemplated by Catherine in a conversation with Nelly Dean that, disastrously, is overheard in part by the rejected Heathcliff. Thus Catherine's seeming decisiveness is actually a form of prolonged feminine "coyness" in lieu of decisive action. (True decisiveness comes only with the acceptance of her future husband.) It is Heathcliff, however, who most completely embodies the distinction between an all-consuming amorous devotion and flirtatious eros. Heathcliff flirts heartlessly with Isabella precisely because, for him, desire for anyone other than his "heart's darling" is inconceivable.

Becky Sharp's indulgence in all of the advantages of female prerogative, meanwhile, is independent of her love for Rawdon Crawley, superseding vows of marriage as her indulgence becomes an engine for the functioning of narrative in *Vanity Fair* as well as the culmination of an entire class's entrepreneurial aspirations. For Becky, orthodox romantic love is an impediment to a Darwinian design in which desire forms the currency of exchange in a war of survival. Paralleling Becky's Machiavellian trajectory is the kind-hearted Dobbin's long-unfulfilled yearning for Amelia, expressed through countless demure acts of boyish flirtation.

27. Eliot, *The Mill on the Floss,* 364.

28. "A Duet in Paradise" is Eliot's title for chapter 1 of the sixth book of her novel, a book that is itself entitled "The Great Temptation."

29. Darwin, *The Descent of Man,* 372.

30. Stephen Jay Gould, "The Confusion Over Evolution," *New York Review of Books* (Nov. 19, 1992), 47–54.

31. Darwin, *The Descent of Man,* 1:273. J. Hunter, author of *Essays and Observations,* was an evolutionary scientist cited by Darwin throughout *The Descent.*

32. Darwin, *The Descent of Man,* 1:262.

33. Beer, *Darwin's Plots,* 213.

34. Darwin, *The Descent of Man,* 1:279.

35. Gertrude Himmelfarb, *Darwin and the Darwinian Revolution* (New York: W. W. Norton, 1968), 314.

36. T. H. Morgan, *Evolution and Adaptation* (New York: Macmillan, 1903).

37. Gould, "The Confusion Over Evolution," 37–44.

38. Patrick Geddes and J. Arthur Thomson, *The Evolution of Sex* (London: Walter Scott, 1889).

39. Herbert Spencer, *Principles of Ethics,* 3 vols. (London: Williams and Norgate, 1892–93), 2:197. For a discussion of Spencer's shift from progressive supporter of feminist causes (largely owing to his Individualist philosophical beliefs) to conservative opponent of women's emancipation (derived from biological justifications for women's inherent inferiority and subordinate position within the structure of the family), see Nancy Paxton, "Beauty, Sexuality and Evolutionary Process: *Adam Bede* and Personal Beauty, " in *George Eliot and Herbert Spencer,* 43–68.

40. Darwin's remark is quoted in Russett, *Sexual Science,* 13–14.

41. Gamble, *The Evolution of Women,* 44.

42. Charlotte Perkins Gilman, *Women and Economics: A Study of the Economic Relations between Men and Women as a Factor in Social Evolution,* ed., Carl N. Degler (New York: Harper and Row, 1966), 111.

43. Ibid.

44. Havelock Ellis, *Women and Marriage* (London, 1888), 13.

45. Levine, *Darwin and the Novelists,* 93. Levine offers a detailed discussion of the implications of Darwinian chance in the Victorian novel.

46. Darwin, *The Descent of Man,* 1:64

47. Darwin to John Morley (March 24, 1871), in Francis Darwin, ed., *More Letters of Charles Darwin,* 2 volumes (New York: D. Appleton, 1903) 1:325.

48. Darwin, *The Descent of Man,* 2:141.

49. Darwin, *The Descent of Man and Selection in Relation to Sex* (New York: A. L. Burt Company, 1874), 479.

50. Darwin, *The Descent of Man,* 2:124.

51. Darwin, *The Descent of Man,* 2:230.

52. Quoted in Bajeema, *Evolution by Sexual Selection Theory*, 12.

53. Charles Darwin, "Sexual Selection in Relation to Monkeys" (1876), reprinted in *The Portable Darwin*, ed. Duncan M. Porter and Peter W. Graham (New York: Vintage, 1993), 456.

54. Shaw, *Candida*, 48.

55. That an operetta should be the ideal vehicle for the satirizing of subject matter that elsewhere in the culture generates enormous anxiety is explored by the philosopher Karl Kraus in an essay on the operetta. In his study *Sprüche und Widersprüche*, Kraus argues that in operettas (which he holds to be generically superior to opera), the musical and theatrical elements come into conflict and the resulting juxtaposition results in heightened comedy. Folly, according to Kraus, is the necessary ingredient for this transformation, in which causality is suspended and no rationality expected. For a discussion of Kraus's view of operetta, see Harry Zohn, *Karl Kraus* (New York: Twayne, 1971), 116.

56. William Schwenk Gilbert and Arthur Sullivan, "*The Mikado*, or the Town of Titipu" (1885), in *The Complete Plays of Gilbert and Sullivan*, 321.

57. Gilbert and Sullivan, *The Mikado*, 302.

58. Alfred Russell Wallace, *Darwinism* (London: Macmillan, 1989), 286. For a discussion of Wallace's disagreements with Darwin, see M. J. Kottler, "Darwin, Wallace, and the Origin of Sexual Dimorphism," *Proceedings of the American Philosophical Society* 124 (1980): 203–26.

59. John R. Durant, "The Ascent of Nature in Darwin's *Descent of Man*," in *The Darwinian Heritage*, ed. David Kohn (Princeton, N.J.: Princeton University Press, 1985), 299.

60. Robert W. Buchanan, *A Look Round Literature*, (London, 1887), 197.

61. Charles Darwin, *Voyage of the Beagle: Journal of Researches*, ed. Janet Browne and Michael Neve (1839; reprint, London: Penguin, 1989), 66–68.

62. Darwin, *Voyage of the Beagle*, 67.

63. A. Dwight Culler notes, en passant, the philosophical connections between Darwin and Pater. In an essay exploring how the form of Darwinian explanation has influenced, or is analogous to, forms of literary expression in the post-Darwinian world, Culler notes that the basis of Darwin's and Pater's commonality consists in the "relativism, the atomism, the materialism of both fields—ultimately, their dependence on sensation." Culler notes too that in Wilde's *The Picture of Dorian Gray*, Lord Henry continues to maintain (like Darwin) the "supremacy of form over matter" and "style in the true Darwinian way." A. Dwight Culler, "The Darwinian Revolution and Literary Form," in *The Art of Victorian Prose*, ed. George Levine and William Madden (New York: Oxford University Press, 1968), 241.

64. In his memoirs of the late-Romantic aestheticist movement, Richard Le Gallienne recalled Allen as a disciple of Herbert Spencer, calling Allen "one the most barometric minds of the time, and one of the most vigorous and persuasive trumpeters of 'advance' in every form." Le Gallienne, *The Romantic 90s* (New York: Doubleday, Page, and Co., 1925), 59–60, 147. Although today almost entirely neglected as a scientific thinker and as a theorist of aestheticism, Allen's position as the author of the popular novel *The Woman Who Did* (1895), which concerns Herminia Barton, who lives in sin and after refusing to marry on ethical grounds suffers a tragic death, has given Allen a key place in the history of fin-de-siècle fiction dealing with the theme of the "New Woman." Elaine Showalter has explored the novel's historic influence as well

as its conflicted attitude toward the "women's question," pointing out that elsewhere in his writing Allen opposed female gains in the social and political sphere. See Showalter, *A Literature of Their Own.*

65. Beer is quoting Allen's 1880 article on "Aesthetic Evolution in Man" published in *Mind 5.* Beer, *Darwin's Plots,* 212.

66. Allen, "Falling in Love," in *Falling in Love with Other Essays on More Exact Branches of Science,* 3.

67. Ibid., 7.

68. Unpublished letter from Grant Allen to Oscar Wilde (Feb. 6, 1891), J. Harlin O'Connell Collection, Firestone Library, Princeton University.

69. Allen, "Falling in Love," 8.

70. Allen, *Charles Darwin,* 147–48.

71. Grant Allen, "The Decline of Marriage," in *Post-Prandial Philosophy* (London: Chatto and Windus, 1894), 115.

3. GEORGE ELIOT AND THOMAS HARDY

1. See Shuttleworth, *George Eliot and Nineteenth-Century Science.*

2. The exception, as I note in chapter 3, is Gillian Beer's discussion of sexual selection in the work of Eliot and Darwin in *Darwin's Plots.*

3. Darwin, *The Descent of Man,* 372.

4. George Eliot, *Felix Holt, The Radical.* Reprint (Oxford: Oxford University Press, 1980), 352.

5. Austen, *Emma,* 90–91.

6. Eliot, *The Mill on the Floss,* 478.

7. For a discussion of Ladislaw as a forerunner of Pater's "New Hedonist," see Knoepflmacher, *Religious Humanism and the Victorian Novel.*

8. Nancy Miller, "Emphasis Added: Plots and Plausibilities in Women's Fiction" in *The New Feminist Criticism: Essays on Women, Literature and Theory,* ed. Elaine Showalter (New York: Pantheon, 1985), 354.

9. In her study of George Eliot and nineteenth-century science, Sally Shuttleworth does not consider Darwin's theory of sexual selection, in an otherwise thorough examination of Eliot's reliance on scientific beliefs of the period. Shuttleworth, *George Eliot and Nineteenth-Century Science.*

10. Sir Edward Bulwer-Lytton to John Blackwood, Letter (April 14, 1860), reproduced in *George Eliot: The Critical Heritage* (New York: Barnes and Noble, 1971), 121. An 1839 cartoon in a British periodical drew Bulwer-Lytton and Benjamin Disraeli as dandy doubles of one another. For a discussion of Bulwer-Lytton's early career as a dandy of Byronic affectations, see Andrew Elfenbein, *Byron and the Victorians* (New York: Cambridge University Press, 1995), 206–46.

11. George Eliot to John Blackwood, Letter (July 9, 1860), in *The George Eliot Letters,* vol. 3, ed. Gordon S. Haight (New Haven, Conn.: Yale University Press, 1954–1978), 317–18.

12. Unsigned review, *The Guardian* (April 25, 1860) and E. S. Dallas, unsigned review, *The Times* (May 19, 1860), both reproduced in *George Eliot: The Critical Heritage,* 131.

13. Swinburne's comment first appeared in the poet's *A Note on Charlotte Brontë*

(1877) and is reprinted in George Eliot, *The Mill on the Floss: An Authoritative Text,* ed. Carol T. Christ (New York: W. W. Norton, 1993), 466.

14. Leslie Stephen, *George Eliot* (London: Macmillan, 1902), 101–4.

15. F. R. Leavis, *The Great Tradition: George Eliot, Henry James, Joseph Conrad* (1948; reprint, London: Penguin, 1962), 55–57. Leavis's negative estimate of a relationship in *The Mill on the Floss* I have chosen to term "Lawrentian" is of ironic interest given Leavis's role as one of the first scholars to make a sustained case for Lawrence as a major novelist whose novels continued, Leavis maintained, a literary genealogy that begins with George Eliot.

16. Tanner, *Adultery in the Novel.*

17. Knoepflmacher, *George Eliot's Early Novels,* 216, 219.

18. George Levine, "Intelligence as Deception: *The Mill on the Floss,*" *PMLA,* 80 (Sept. 1965), 402–9.

19. Gillian Beer, *George Eliot* (London: Harvester Press, 1986), 99–100.

20. Nancy Miller, "Emphasis Added," 356.

21. For details of Eliot's response to Pater, see Gordon S. Haight, *George Eliot: A Biography* (1968; reprint, New York: Penguin, 1978).

22. Eliot, *Daniel Deronda,* 147, 361.

23. Eliot, *The Mill on the Floss,* 433.

24. Ibid., 480.

25. Knoepflmacher, *George Eliot's Early Novels,* 215.

26. Eliot, *The Mill on the Floss,* 448.

27. Ibid., 400.

28. Ibid., 367.

29. Ibid., 431.

30. Ibid., 433.

31. Ibid., 406.

32. Ibid., 378.

33. In Austen's *Emma,* for example, dance is an illusion-creating rite of flirtation. Frank Churchill is a success for waltzing splendidly, yet he does so as part of his dual toying with two female rivals—Emma, the heroine, and Jane Fairfax, the woman to whom he is secretly engaged. (He privately informs Emma, however, that she is by far the superior dancer of the two women.)

34. Eliot, *The Mill on the Floss,* 440.

35. Ibid., 440.

36. Ibid., 449.

37. As more than one critic has observed, the erotic chords struck by such encounters are intensely proto-Lawrentian; Knoepflmacher mentions *Lady Chatterley's Lover* as a literary offshoot, while Beer invokes *Women in Love.* Knoepflmacher, *George Eliot's Early Novels,* 214; Beer, *George Eliot,* 103. Beer compares the flood scene that ends Eliot's novel with the drowning scene in the "Water Party" chapter of Lawrence's novel, although *The Rainbow* could just as easily be evoked for the encounters between Maggie and Stephen. The pair's on-again, off-again dynamic of sensuality and torment suggests the anguished affair of Ursula Brangwen and Anton Skrebensky of *The Rainbow.* (Skrebensky has some of Stephen's commingling of passion and weakness.)

38. Eliot, *The Mill on the Floss,* 490.

39. Ibid., 459.

40. Ibid., 441–42.

41. Ibid., 490.

42. Henry James, "The Novels of George Eliot," *The Atlantic Monthly*, Oct. 1866, 90.

43. Eliot, *Middlemarch*, 335.

44. Ibid., 300.

45. Ibid., 301–2.

46. Eliot's idea here of a "crystallizing feather-touch" whereby coquetry becomes love no doubt originates with Stendhal's *De l'amour* (1822), the novelist's treatise on love, in which Stendhal adopted the metaphor of the Salzburg bough to designate a process of love-formation he termed "crystallization." According to Stendhal, it is customary in the salt mines of Salzburg to throw a leafless wintry bough into one of the abandoned workings. "Two or three months later they haul it out covered with a shining deposit of crystals. The smallest twig, no bigger than a torn-tit's claw, is studded with a galaxy of scintillating diamonds. The original branch is no longer recognizable." The lover analogously, according to Stendhal, "crystallizes" his beloved with imaginary perfections. This is, of course, an appropriate way for Eliot to describe Lydgate's infatuation with a future wife who will later prove unworthy of his idealism. Stendhal, *Love*, trans. Gilbert and Suzanne Sale (New York: Penguin, 1975), 45.

47. Eliot, *Middlemarch*, 474–75.

48. Although, in making my point concerning a widespread pre-*Descent of Man* preoccupation with the principles of sexual selection I have here considered three of the more celebrated novels of the mid-Victorian period, the concerns and schemes I have outlined attracted a host of other authors whose narratives preceded Darwin's full articulation of sexual selection in *The Descent of Man*. Even a novelist as socially conservative as Trollope comically calibrated the success of female choice over convention in *Miss MacKenzie* (1865). Long after she should have been ineligible for the marriage market, the sensible, middle-aged heroine of Trollope's novel, "overwhelmed with money troubles," elects to suspend the fates of four suitors as she seeks to assess their economic worth. Trollope's statement concerning his intentions in *Miss MacKenzie* (composed, he claimed, "to prove that a novel may be produced without any love") evokes Darwin's project of distilling basic natural laws while unsentimentally implying a link between the human and the nonhuman.

49. Eliot, *Middlemarch*, 104.

50. Ibid., 583.

51. This is the characteristic "labour of choice" described (in non-Darwinian terms) by Rosemarie Bodenheimer as dominating the moral and romantic struggles of so many of Eliot's heroines. Rosemarie Bodenheimer, *The Real Life of Mary Ann Evans: George Eliot, Her Letters and Fiction* (Ithaca, N.Y.: Cornell University Press, 1994).

52. Eliot, *Middlemarch*, 832.

53. It is likely that Henry James had in mind either or both of these scenes from *Middlemarch* and *Daniel Deronda* when writing Chapter 49 of *The Portrait of a Lady* (1881), when Isabel Archer comes to grasp that Osmond and Madame Merle have been lovers based on a memory of having witnessed her husband seated while Madame Merle stands as the two talk alone. It is notable that James, a novelist celebrated for his calculated literary ambiguities as a matter of modernist principle, depicts this scene in unambiguous terms. At this moment Isabel's "point of view," quite demonstrably, is the truth itself. In a reversal of conventional conceptions of Eliot's and James's most

characteristic narrative strategies, it the Victorian novel that here eschews an all-seeing omniscience, the modernist text that forgoes ambiguity of effect.

54. Eliot, *Daniel Deronda,* 594, 611.

55. Having published *Daniel Deronda* five years after *The Descent of Man,* Eliot may have been acknowledging Darwin explicitly when she entitled her chapter detailing Gwendolen's decision to marry Grandcourt "Maidens Choosing."

56. Eliot, *Daniel Deronda,* 610.

57. Nancy Paxton supplies a powerful reading of *Daniel Deronda* in the light of Herbert Spencer's theory of "degeneration" in his later writings. See Paxton, *George Eliot and Herbert Spencer.*

58. See Elliott B. Gose, "Psychic Evolution: Darwin and Initiation in *Tess of the D'Urbervilles,*" in *Nineteenth-Century Fiction,* vol. 18, no. 3, Dec. 1963, 261–72.

59. Stephen's remark is quoted in Robert Gittings, *Young Thomas Hardy* (1975; reprint, New York: Penguin, 1986), 244.

60. Hardy, *Under the Greenwood Tree,* 33.

61. Ibid., 155.

62. Ibid., 78.

63. Ibid., 133.

64. Ibid., 71.

65. Ibid., 75–76.

66. Ibid., 207.

67. Ibid., 208.

68. Hardy, *Tess of the D'Urbervilles,* 49.

69. Hardy, *Far from the Madding Crowd,* 252.

70. Thomas Hardy, *Jude the Obscure* (New York: Penguin, 1978), 429.

4. DEADLY DEFERRALS

1. The phrase comes from Wharton's posthumously published autobiographical sketch, "Life and I" in *Novellas and Other Writings* in *The Library of America Edith Wharton* (New York: Harper and Row, 1975).

2. Quoted in Tony Tanner, *Henry James: The Writer and His Work* (Amherst: University of Massachusetts Press, 1985), 4.

3. James, "Gustave Flaubert," 322.

4. James, *Daisy Miller,* 14–15.

5. Writing in 1850, the popular writer "Ik Marvel" vociferously insisted on the differences between these two types of women, maintaining that the flirtatious woman is the "prostitute of fashion, the bauble of fifty hearts idle as hers, the shifting makepeace of a stage scene, the actress, now in peasant, and now in princely petticoats. How it would cheer an honest soul to call her—his." Ik Marvel (Donald G. Mitchell), *Reveries of a Bachelor,* 58.

6. Walter Benjamin, "On Some Motifs in Baudelaire," in *Illuminations,* ed. and with an introduction by Hannah Arendt (New York: Schocken, 1973), 172.

7. In Gertrude Stein's novel *Q.E.D.* (1903), the physique of an American coquette is described as suggestive of a pleasure-seeking spirit while actually masking a repressed Puritan self. Observes Stein's narrator: "It is one of the peculiarities of American

womanhood that the body of a coquette often encloses the soul of a prude and the angular form of a spinster is possessed by the nature of the tropics." As with *Daisy Miller,* nineteenth-century phrenology is subsumed by an updated, Freudian understanding of unconscious drives. Gertrude Stein, *Q.E.D.,* in *Fernhurst, Q.E.D. and Other Early Writings* (New York: Liveright, 1971), 55.

8. Winterbourne's fitful attempts at understanding Daisy through physiognomic "hard evidence" may suggest a larger cultural crisis in epistemology, a playing out in social relations of the issues discussed by Alexander Welsh in his study of circumstantial evidence and narrative. Welsh argues that a large part of eighteenth- and nineteenth-century writing aims to discover "strong evidence" for that which is hidden from view. Welsh, *Strong Representations: Narrative and Circumstantial Evidence in England* (Baltimore: John Hopkins University Press, 1992).

9. Wharton's fondness for disturbing the smooth-running workings of conventional courtship plots through the staging of scenarios of flirtatious "misconduct" may have had a foundation in her early years as a New York debutante. Recalling the social rituals of her youth, Wharton remembered the "only 'flirtation' I have ever indulged in," an "innocent enough adventure" in which the young Edith Newbold flirted with a "very good looking & amusing" young man who had been pursuing a heiress and was now engaged to a young lady from a wealthy New York family. Calling this comic episode "the only one on which I embarked with malice prepense," Wharton claimed that it was "visible at a glance that [the young woman] loved him & the situation appealed to my sense of humor, as one which it might be amusing to complicate a little." Wharton, "Life and I," in *Novellas and Other Writings,* 1096.

10. Alexandra Johnson, *The Nation,* (July 8, 1991), 59–61.

11. Wharton registered not so much the prevalence of male same-sex erotics as the ongoing possibility of erotic experimentation on the male's part that is free of punitive regulation. In *The Reef* (1912), the diplomat George Darrow, whose mildly contrite attitude toward his carnal past lends the novel its thematic thrust, initiates a traumatic crisis in which his fiancée, Anna Leath, is transformed from an anxious Puritan witness before illicit sexuality into a partially accommodating partner in her lover's (perversely defined) eros. Darrow's desires reflect Anna's own "illicit," incestuous attraction to her stepson. (The novel undoubtedly represents Wharton's updating of Racine's *Phèdre.*) In addition to casting the subject of erotic relations in markedly transcultural terms, Wharton's characterization of scandalous male eros—as finding its analogue in a socially unauthorized female eros, defined in *The Reef* as incestuous desire— significantly disturbs a Sedgwickian model of "homosexual panic" in which male same-sex desire is mediated through, rather than mirrored by, a woman's own compromising erotic impulses.

The theoretical lacunae in Sedgwick's model, in which female erotic agency invariably is eclipsed, become unusually evident in a modern French context (the setting of the greater part of *The Reef*), where existing legal codes treated all same-sex sexual activity much as the British Parliament dealt with lesbian sexuality, which was by ignoring its legal ramifications. For it is precisely in its disinclination to conceive of a female erotic subjectivity (let alone one understood as disreputable in social terms) that Sedgwick's "homosocial" model is most vulnerable, particularly, as in *The Reef,* where one discovers a female character's erotic "perspective" The first third of this novel is narrated from the position of Darrow, and then, in an abrupt shift after Darrow conducts his assignation with a "boyish" young woman, Wharton provides the viewpoint of the novel's heroine. In presenting these juxtaposed angles, Wharton insists on an appreciation of female desire as it impinges on the dynamics of subtextual male homoeroticism. See Kaye, "Edith Wharton and the 'New Gomorrahs' of Paris."

12. Wharton, *The Age of Innocence*, 309.

13. Wharton, *The Age of Innocence*, 351.

14. Carol J. Singley, "Gothic Borrowings and innovations in Edith Wharton's 'A Bottle of Perrier,'" in *Edith Wharton: New Critical Essays*, Alfred Bendizen and Annette Zilversmitt, eds., 271–87. See also Richard A. Kaye, "'Unearthly Visitants': Wharton's Ghost Tales, Gothic Form, and the Literature of Homosexual Panic," in *The Edith Wharton Review* (spring 1994), vol. 11, no. 1., 10–18.

15. In her autobiography, Wharton noted her great debt to Darwinian thought. Wharton, *A Backward Glance*, 65.

16. Simmel, "Flirtation," 133–52.

17. Cathy N. Davidson, introduction to Foster, *The Coquette*, xx. *The Coquette* was one of the two best-selling novels of the eighteenth century. The story was based on an actual case involving a distant relation of the author, which detailed through a series of letters the tortuous courtship of the heroine by two men. After she is impregnated by one of them and then abandoned by both (each marries another woman), she dies in childbirth at a roadside inn.

Another eighteenth-century American author, William Hill Brown, also turned to female coquetry as viable material. In what is often cited as the first American novel, Brown's anonymously published *The Power of Sympathy: Or, the Triumph of Nature* (1789) (a work that Brown himself did not call a novel) the heroine Elizabeth Whitman is described as a "great reader of novels and romances and having imbibed her ideas of *the characters of men* from these fallacious sources, became vain and coquettish, and rejected several offers of marriage, in expectation of receiving one more agreeable to her fanciful idea."

18. George Eliot, Letter to Madame Bodichon, Dec. 5, 1859, in *The George Eliot Letters*, 1:227. For a discussion of George Eliot and Darwin, see Shuttleworth, *George Eliot and Nineteenth-Century Science*.

19. Edith Wharton, Letter to Charles Eliot Norton (March 2, 1908), in *The Letters of Edith Wharton*, ed. R. W. B. Lewis and Nancy Lewis (New York: Charles Scribner's Sons, 1988), 136.

20. Wharton credited her friend Egerton Winthrop with introducing her to evolutionary theory. Wharton, *A Backward Glance*, 94. In a letter to Charles Eliot Norton, she mentioned Vernon Kellog's 1907 *Darwinism Today: A Discussion of Present-Day Scientific Criticism of Darwinian Selection Theories*, although she claimed not to have read it, adding, "I am told it is admirable." *The Letters of Edith Wharton*, 131. There have been several discussions on the effect of Darwin's thinking on Wharton's work. See, for example, James W. Tuttleton, "Edith Wharton: The Archeological Motive," *The Yale Review* (summer 1972), 61. Tuttleton argues that the notion of evolutionary development, advanced or implied in the work of evolutionary scientists, profoundly influenced Wharton's idea of individual identity and of the cultural traditions that shape it. Also see Jeraldine Parker, "'Uneasy Survivors': Five Women Writers: 1886–1923," Ph.D. dissertation, University of Utah, 1973. Parker suggests that Wharton is one of a group of women writers, including Sarah Orne Jewett, Mary Wilkins Freeman, Willa

Cather and Ellen Glasgow, who bridge the "sentimentalism of the genteelists and the factualism of the naturalists." She further argues that these writers' experimental techniques contributed to a world altered by Darwinian biology and Freudian psychology but that they "became, paradoxically, guardians of the traditional values that were being displaced."

21. Edith Wharton, "Tendencies in Modern Fiction," *Saturday Review of Literature* (Jan. 27, 1934), vol. 10, no. 28, 433–34.

22. Edith Wharton, "The Criticism of Fiction," *Times Literary Supplement* (May 14, 1914), 229–30. Wharton's theory of fiction, elaborated in numerous essays but most fully in *The Writing of Fiction* (1924), strove to accentuate the links between scientific and literary aspirations. According to Wharton, the novelist, no less than the evolutionist, must seek a form that attempts to reproduce with accuracy the plot of nature. The short story, for example, depended for its power on the "precious instinct of selection by that long patience which, if it be not genius, must be one of genius's chief reliances in communicating itself." Wharton, "Telling a Short Story," in *The Writing of Fiction*, 54.

In a 1902 review of Leslie Stephen's biography of George Eliot, Wharton defended the author of *Middlemarch* from the charge that Eliot had "sterilized her imagination and deformed her style by the study of biology and metaphysics." Pointing out that "there is more than one way of studying the phenomena of life," she noted that "no one can deny the poetic value of the evolutionary conception." And she added that "Goethe the poet was nourished, not stunted, by the scientific inductions of Goethe the morphologist; and Milton's allusion to Galileo's 'optic glass' shows how early the poetic mind was ready to seize on any illustration furnished by the investigations of science." Edith Wharton, "George Eliot," *The Bookman* (May 1902), 247–48. In the same essay, however, she maintained that the "evolution" of George Eliot's plots, so "simple and natural" in *Adam Bede, Silas Marner,* and *The Mill on the Floss,* had become "more complicate [*sic*] and obstructive" with the later fiction, by which Wharton presumably meant *Middlemarch* and *Daniel Deronda.*

23. Thackeray, *Vanity Fair,* 866.

24. Lee Clark Mitchell, *Determined Fictions: American Literary Naturalism* (New York: Columbia University Press, 1989), 11.

25. Wharton, "The Criticism of Fiction," 229–30.

26. What might be termed "normative psychological criticism" often has elected to judge Wharton as fatally drawn to chronically indecisive males in both her fiction and her romantic life. Such critiques (typically viewing the archetypal Wharton bachelor as immature, excessively refined, and sexually repressed or underdeveloped) inadvertently partake of the language of conservative psychological discourse on homosexuality.

Edmund Wilson set the tone for such an approach in 1941 when he discussed the fictional Wharton male as a genuine historical figure, drawn from "stunted and thwarted" men who comprised "a very common phenomenon of the America after the Civil War," figures such as "Selden, the city lawyer, who sits comfortably in his bachelor apartment with his flowerbox of mignonette and his first edition of La Bruyère and allows Lily Bart to drown" [*sic*]. Edmund Wilson, "Justice to Edith Wharton," in *Edith Wharton: A Collection of Critical Essays,* ed. Irving Howe (Englewood Cliffs, N.J.: Prentice Hall, 1962), 27. Elizabeth Ammons in *Edith Wharton's Argument with America*

(1980), argues that for Wharton the "erotic immaturity of American men as a group deserves less sympathy than criticism; for, although pathologically understandable, it serves nonetheless to rationalize patriarchal attitudes that oppress women." Elizabeth Ammons, *Edith Wharton's Argument with America* (Athens: University of Georgia Press, 1980), 178.

The pathologization of fictional and actual bachelors reaches a sharp pitch in David Holbrook's *Edith Wharton and the Unsatisfactory Man*, which maintains that Wharton was neurotically attracted to bisexual men because she was fearful of sexual passion out of devotion to her father—the only male, according to Holbrook, Wharton felt was deserving of her interest. Holbrook characterizes Fullerton as disguising his "fundamental inadequacy" through superior "techniques" of love, such as imbuing his seductions with literary references. According to Holbrook, Wharton's fictional males "fail to commit themselves or develop." In disparaging the bachelor's diminished aesthetic perspective in high modernist art, Holbrook describes Henry James as suffering from "serious schizoid difficulties" because of the novelist's "obsession with subtlety and reticence" in the last years of his life. David Holbrook, *Edith Wharton and the Unsatisfactory Man* (New York: St. Martin's, 1991), 22–36.

27. Edward Carpenter, *Love's Coming of Age* (1896; reprint, New York: Boni and Liveright, Inc., 1911), 130, 140.

The theme of masculine erotic uncertainty is entwined with homosexuality in Wharton's friend André Gide's *Corydon,* a Socratic dialogue on homoerotic eros. "Is not the explanation, the raison d'être of this almost constant superabundance of the male element to be found then in a certain indecision of the sexual instinct (if we dare couple the words 'indecision' and 'instinct')?" Gide asks in discussing same-sex desire. "Must we not admit, sooner or later, that the imperative quality of this instinct remains somewhat ambiguous? And will not nature be comparable to a marksman who, knowing his lack of skill and fearing to miss the target, compensates for the inaccuracy of his aim by the quantity of shots he fires?" André Gide, *Corydon,* trans. Richard Howard (1911; reprint, New York: Farrar, Straus and Giroux, 1983), 49–50. Such formulations foster affinities with Freud's conception of the "polymorphously perverse" infant psyche, simultaneously resisting, through an accent on a superfine, inexplicable erotic "nature," the era's scientific discourse concerning "inversion."

28. Wharton, *The Age of Innocence,* 71, 104.

29. Wharton, *The House of Mirth,* 73.

30. Ibid., 5.

31. Walter Benn Michaels, *The Gold Standard and the Logic of Capitalism: American Literature at the Turn of the Century* (Berkeley: University of California Press, 1987), 226. Michaels argues that *The House of Mirth* is not a critique of market capitalism but a book in which "the love of risk" is "not confined to speculating in stock, playing bridge, or even flirting with Selden" but "appears also—most bizarrely—as the cornerstone of reality."

32. Wharton, *The House of Mirth,* 31.

33. For a history of marriage addressing this issue, see Stone, *Family, Sex and Marriage in England, 1500–1800.*

34. Wharton, *The House of Mirth,* 8–9

35. Ibid., 11.

36. Ibid., 63, 72–73.

37. Georg Lukács, *The Theory of the Novel,* trans. Anna Bostock (Cambridge: MIT Press, 1982), 89. Lukács contrasts the estranged hero of the novel's "adventure of interiority" with the hero of the classical epic, who must always "pass the test, both inwardly and outwardly," and is "only the luminous centre" on which the "unfolded totality of the world" revolves.

38. No aspect of *The House of Mirth* has generated as much critical debate as the novel's ending, not only because of the ambiguity surrounding Lily's intentions when she takes an overdose but because the novel's conclusion resonates with the question of Selden's character. Indeed, the ending of the novel would seem retrospectively to render Selden's offer of a "special kingdom" ironically pointless. Wai-Chee Dimock has argued that Selden is simply another male spectator among numerous others in *The House of Mirth,* "cynically amused by Lily," albeit one without the financial backing to "purchase" the object of his attentions. "For Selden," writes Dimock, "love is a form of exchange, and he will hear nothing but profits." Choosing to disregard the crucial scenes of brief but exalted affection between Lily and Selden, Dimock characterizes Lily's relationship with Lily as wholly economic and *The House of Mirth* itself as overwhelmingly "naturalistic" in its tone and meaning: "Like the others, [Selden] too exudes a cold stinginess, a desire for acquisition without risk and without expenditure." Selden's "republic of the spirit" is, according to Dimock, "less a republic than a refined replica of the social marketplace, of which Selden is a full, participating member." Wharton's book, Dimock concludes, "is fueled by an almost exclusively critical energy directed at the marketplace Wharton disdains. She can only confusedly gesture towards a redeeming alternative: for her, the House of Mirth has no exit." Wai-Chee Dimock, "Debasing Exchange: Edith Wharton's *The House of Mirth,* in *Edith Wharton: Modern Critical Views,* ed. Harold Bloom (New York: Chelsea House, 1986), 129, 131, 137.

39. Wharton, *The House of Mirth,* 184.

40. See Richard A. Kaye, "Textual Hermeneutics and Belated Male Heroism: Edith Wharton's Revisions of *The House of Mirth,*" *Arizona Quarterly* (fall 1995).

41. Wharton, *The House of Mirth,* 73.

42. Bakhtin, *Problems of Dostoevsky's Poetics,* 59. For a fuller discussion of Bakhtin's idea of "unfinalizability," considered as a process of deferral in which "identity is always postponed, and about to be postponed," see Caryl Emerson and Gary Saul Morson, "Penultimate Words," in *The Current in Criticism: Essays on the Present and Future of Literary Theory,* ed. Clayton Koelb and Virgil Locke (West Lafayette, Ind.: Purdue University Press, 1986), 43 – 64. Drawing on Bakhtin's notion of heteroglossia to demonstrate how the interaction of numerous voices—or the failure of such an interaction to take place—affects a social community, Dale M. Bauer has argued for a "feminist dialogical" reading of *The House of Mirth* that views Lily Bart as ruinously misinterpreting available "social texts" and, with Selden, unable to bridge the "gap between speeches and discourses." Dale M. Bauer, *Feminist Dialogics: A Theory of Failed Community* (Stoneybrook, N.Y.: State University of New York Press, 1988), 127.

43. Edith Wharton, "The Great American Novel," *Yale Review,* n.s. 16 (1927), 652.

44. I have several times invoked D. H. Lawrence in characterizing a number of encounters in *The House of Mirth,* and while Lawrence is explicitly evoked in Selden's first name and although a kind of Lawrentian eros dominates certain scenes of intimacy in Wharton's novel, Wharton resists Lawrentian models. If Wharton had been beholden

to a Lawrentian scheme, she would have rendered Selden's "experimentalism" with some of the excitement of unfolding human relations, of their "dark mysteries," which Lawrence decreed as the basic ethic informing his fiction. Neither Lily nor Selden is a figure of the proportions of Lawrence's protagonists; rather, both ultimately falter like the figures of Hardy's fiction, whom Lawrence in highly conflicted terms evaluated in his *Study of Thomas Hardy*—characters such as Jude Fawley and Sue Bridehead who, according to Lawrence, confuse the life-denying strictures of society with some greater cosmic design.

45. Wharton, *The Writing of Fiction*, 109–10.
46. Ibid., 106.
47. Gustave Flaubert, *Sentimental Education*, 65.
48. Wharton, *The Age of Innocence*, 309–10.
49. Ibid., 45.
50. Flaubert, *Sentimental Education*, 419.
51. Wharton, *The Age of Innocence*, 351.
52. Ibid., 113.

5. "ACCEPTABLE HINTS OF INFINITY"

1. The details of these encounters between James and Wilde as well as Wilde's comments on *Dorian Gray* are taken from Ellmann, *Oscar Wilde*, and Leon Edel, *Henry James: The Middle Years* (New York: J. B. Lippincott, 1962).

2. Quoted in Ellmann, *Oscar Wilde*, 178.

3. Ellmann, *Oscar Wilde*, 179.

4. Jonathan Freedman, *Professions of Taste: Henry James, British Aestheticism, and Commodity Culture* (Stanford, Calif.: Stanford University Press, 1990). Freedman offers what is to date the best discussion of the relationship—literary and personal—between James and Wilde, with a particular focus on the problem of aestheticism as it became a successful movement in America.

5. Freedman, *Professions of Taste*, 172–73

6. Wilde, *The Picture of Dorian Gray*, 23–24.

7. Details from the Wilde trials are drawn from Ellmann, *Oscar Wilde*, 435–89.

8. James, *The Tragic Muse*, 29.

9. Ibid.

10. Forster, *A Passage to India*, 49.

11. E. M. Forster, "Jane Austen" (1932) in *Abinger Harvest: Essays on Books, People and Places*, (1936; reprint, New York: Meridian Books, 1955), 151.

12. E. M. Forster, *A Room with a View* (1908; reprint, New York: New American Library, 1986), 315.

13. Henry James might be said to exploit the sinister flip side of the mature woman as tutorial guide in amorous matters in his portrait of Madame Merle in *The Portrait of a Lady*.

14. Forster, *A Passage to India*, 72.

15. E. M. Forster, *Where Angels Fear to Tread* (1905; reprint, London: Camelot Press, 1975), 147.

16. E. M. Forster, *Howards End*, 63.

17. Judging Woolf by both her own criteria (as expressed in "Mr. Bennett and Mrs. Brown") and that of the standard of high Victorian fiction, Forster claimed that Woolf's characters "do live, but not continuously," although he saw *Jacob's Room* as the closest to an exception. Forster, "The Early Novels of Virginia Woolf" (1925), in *Abinger Harvest,* 107.

18. Forster's comments on Joyce are contained in E. M. Forster, *Aspects of the Novel* (1927; reprint, New York: Harvest Books, 1954], 121.

19. D. H. Lawrence, *Sons and Lovers,* 374.

20. Woolf made her influential distinction between "Georgians" and "Edwardians" in her 1919 essay "Modern Fiction" and then again in her "Mr. Bennett and Mrs. Brown" (1923).

21. *The Manuscripts of "A Passage to India,"* ed. Oliver Stallybrass (London: Edward Arnold, 1978), 580. Oddly, Stallybrass notes Forster's insertion of the passage from *Women in Love* but offers no explanation for it.

22. Cynthia Ozick, "Morgan and Maurice: A Fairy Tale," in *Art and Ardor: Essays* (New York: Alfred Knopf, 1983).

23. E. M. Forster, "Terminal Note," in *Maurice* (1971; reprint, New York: New American Library, 1973), 246.

24. *Maurice* has generated exceptionally divergent responses among critics, with many of the novel's readers divided as to whether it stands as sentimental, embarrassing self-revelation or, alternately, a breakthrough (in thematic if not in formal terms). Richard Dellamora has argued for *Maurice* as an exemplary text for an alternative history of literary modernism, in which the thematics of same-sex relations takes a primary place. Richard Dellamora, "E. M. Forster at the End," *Apocalyptic Overtures: Sexual Politics and the Sense of an Ending* (New Brunswick, N.J.: Rutgers University Press, 1994), 83–97.

25. In the opening line of his 1932 essay on Austen, Forster wrote: "I am a Jane Austenite and therefore slightly imbecile about Jane Austen." Forster, "Jane Austen," in *Abinger Harvest,* 140.

26. Virginia Woolf, "The Novels of E. M. Forster," in *Collected Essays,* vol. 1 (London: Hogarth Press, 1966), 349.

27. Forster, *A Passage to India,* 19.

28. Cynthia Ozick, "Morgan and Maurice: A Fairy Tale," 72.

29. In a striking series of revisions, Forster deliberately renders the event in the Marabar caves in highly ambiguous terms. At least three different versions of the Marabar caves scene in Forster's drafts of his novel, a work he began in 1913, indicates that Forster hoped to avoid the suggestion that a rape had occurred, preferring to depict the encounter as a hallucination by Miss Quested. In earlier drafts of the novel, Forster moved from an initial manuscript in which Miss Quested is the victim of an actual attempt of rape by a physically violent man, possibly Dr. Aziz but more probably someone else, to a draft in which Adela and Dr. Aziz seem to voluntarily, if rather passively, move toward a display of carnal feeling, to the far more enigmatic version that we tend to consider the "true" text of *A Passage to India.*

30. Forster, *A Passage to India,* 71.

31. Ibid.

32. Ibid., 77.

33. Ibid., 42.

34. The sense that communication is continually frustrated in *A Passage to India* has led to some wrongheaded claims, however, suggesting that language itself is collapsing in Forster's text. Bette London argues, for example, that "In place of the distinctly discernible Forsterian voice of the earlier novels—urbane, ironic, assured—*Passage* projects a narrative gone mad: a shifting, slippery, unplaceable voice that seems to take its timbre from whatever voice it happens to be near. This voice, split by contradictory articulations, figures a crisis in narrative authority and English identity that posits the liberal humanist author as 'mimic man': master impersonator and impersonated human being." This tends to distort the tone (cool, resolved) and method (not radically dialogical but serenely univocal) of the novel. Bette London, "Of Mimicry and English Men: E. M. Forster and the Performance of Masculinity," in *"A Passage to India": Theory in Practice*, ed. Tony Davies and Nigel Wood (Buckingham, England: Open University Press, 1994), 103.

35. Forster, *A Passage to India,* 156.

36. The postcolonial theoretical critique that has attended to Forster in recent years has understood *A Passage to India* as a fantasy of Anglo-Indian relations—a homoerotic daydream masquerading as humanist project. If humanists such as Lionel Trilling once saw Forster as a novelist of conflicted liberalism, recent critics of Forster's writing have chosen to view the writer as naïvely unable to contain in a seamless way the contradictions at the heart of British Imperialism, a conflict exemplified by Cecil Fielding. Noting that Forster once felt compelled to burn what his biographer P. N. Furbank has called his "indecent" short stories, Sara Suleri claims that such an "erotic immolation . . . surely informs the excisions of intimacy" in *A Passage to India.* "To turn to the cross-cultural friendship that subsists between Aziz and Fielding," Suleri concludes, "is in its most overdetermined sense of the term to approach a cultural 'nothing'." Sara Suleri Goodyear, "Forster's Imperial Erotic," from *The Rhetoric of English India* (1992), reprinted in *E. M. Forster: Contemporary Critical Essays,* ed. Jeremy Trambling (New York: Macmillan, 1995), 157.

37. See, for example, Louise Dammer, "What Happened in the Cave?" *Modern Fiction Studies* (autumn 1961), 258–70.

38. Jeremy Trambling, introducing a recent collection of essays on Forster, claims that "Though *A Passage to India* is sometimes discussed as modernist, it is no more so than D. H. Lawrence's novels, which remain largely antagonistic to modernism's experimentation and interest in language at the level of the signifier and the signified." Leaving aside this unusual characterization of Lawrence as anti-modernist, Trambling's remark relies on a single, unified conception of modernism as denoting a single school. Jeremy Trambling, introduction to *E. M. Forster: New Casebooks* (London: Macmillan, 1995), 2.

39. Bloomsbury's reputation as a sort of Brook Farm of bisexual Transcendentalism almost entirely depends on the sexual relations of its members as opposed to their theoretical contributions to the question of same-sex eros. Despite the close attention devoted to homosexual affairs by Bloomsbury and its inspired attacks on middle-class morality, such followers as Lytton Strachey contributed few theoretical or creative insights to questions concerning same-sex eros. Although Forster once called Bloomsbury the "only genuine *movement* in English civilization," he claimed he was not an authentic member of the Bloomsbury set. See S. P. Rosenbaum, ed. *The Bloomsbury Group: A Collection of Memoirs, Commentary and Criticism* (Toronto: University of

Toronto Press, 1975) and Richard A. Kaye, "Bloomsbury," in *The Gay and Lesbian Literary Heritage*, ed. Claude Summers (New York: Henry Holt, 1995).

40. Lawrence, *Women in Love*, 189.

41. Lawrence, "Foreword" to *Women in Love*, 486.

42. Forster, *A Passage to India*, 14.

43. Ibid., 22.

44. Ibid., 30.

45. Ibid., 317.

46. Lawrence, *Women in Love*, 481.

47. Lawrence, letter to Edward Garnett (June 5, 1914) in *The Selected Letters of D. H. Lawrence*, ed. James T. Boulton (Cambridge: Cambridge University Press), 78.

Selected Bibliography

Allen, Grant. *Falling in Love with Other Essays on More Exact Branches of Science*. London: Smith, Elder, and Co., 1889.

———. *Charles Darwin*. New York: D. Appleton and Co., 1893.

Anderson, Beatrice. "The Unmasking of *Lady Susan*." In *Jane Austen's Beginnings: The Juvenilia and Lady Susan*, edited by J. David Grey, 193–203. Ann Arbor, Mich.: UMI Research Press, 1989.

Armstrong, Nancy. *Desire and Domestic Fiction: A Political History of the Novel*. New York: Oxford University Press, 1987.

Auerbach, Nina. *Communities of Women*. Cambridge, Mass.: Harvard University Press, 1978.

———. *Woman and the Demon: The Life of a Victorian Myth*. Cambridge, Mass.: Harvard University Press, 1982.

———. *Romantic Imprisonment: Woman and Other Glorified Outcasts*. New York: Oxford University Press, 1985.

Austen, Jane. *Emma*. 1816. Reprint, New York: Penguin, 1981.

———. *Pride and Prejudice*. 1813. Reprint, vol. 2, The Novels of Jane Austen. Edited by R. W. Chapman. 3d ed. London: Oxford University Press, 1932.

———. *Lady Susan, The Watsons, and Sandition*. Edited by Margaret Drabble. New York: Penguin, 1984.

———. *Northanger Abbey*. 1818. Reprint, New York: Penguin, 1985.

Bakhtin, Mikhail. *The Dialogic Imagination: Four Essays*. Edited by Michael Holquist, translated by Caryl Emerson and Michael Holquist. Austin: University of Texas Press, 1981.

———. *Problems of Dostoevsky's Poetics*. Translated and edited by Caryl Emerson. Minneapolis: University of Minnesota Press, 1984.

Balzac, Honoré de. "La Duchesse de Langeais," in *The History of the Thirteen*. Translated by Herbert J. Hunt. New York: Penguin, 1987.

Barthes, Roland. *Mythologies*. Translated by Annette Lavers. New York: Hill and Wang, 1972.

———. *The Pleasure of the Text*. Translated by Richard Miller. New York: Hill and Wang, 1975.

———. *A Lover's Discourse*. Translated by Richard Howard. New York: Farrar, Straus and Giroux, 1978.

Baudelaire, Charles. "Le Peintre de la vie moderne," 1859, in *Oeuvres Complètes*. Vol. 2. Paris: Pléiade, 1963.

Beardsley, Monroe, and Elizabeth Beardsley. *Philosophical Thinking: An Introduction*. New York: Harcourt Brace Jovanovich, 1965.

Beer, Gillian. *Darwin's Plots: Evolutionary Narrative in Darwin, George Eliot, and Nineteenth-Century Fiction.* London: Routledge, 1983.

Beerbohm, Max. *The Illustrated Zuleika Dobson.* 1911; reprint, New Haven, Conn.: Yale University Press, 1985.

Bender, Bert. *The Descent of Love: Darwin and the Theory of Sexual Selection in American Fiction, 1871–1926.* Philadelphia: University of Pennsylvania Press, 1996.

Benjamin, Walter. "Paris, Capital of the Nineteenth Century." In *Reflections,* edited by Peter Demetz, 146–62. 1955; reprint, New York: Schocken, 1986.

Bersani, Leo. *The Freudian Body: Psychoanalysis and Art.* New York: Columbia University Press, 1986.

———. *A Future for Astyanax: Character and Desire in Literature.* Boston: Little Brown and Co., 1976.

Boone, Joseph Allen. *Tradition Counter Tradition: Love and the Form of Fiction.* Chicago: University of Chicago Press, 1987.

Bourget, Paul. *Physiologie de l'amour moderne.* Paris: Alphonse Lemerre, 1890.

Brantlinger, Patrick. *Rule of Darkness: British Literature and Imperialism, 1830–1914.* Ithaca, N.Y.: Cornell University Press, 1988.

Brontë, Charlotte. *Jane Eyre.* 1857. Reprint, New York: Signet, 1960.

———. *Villette.* New York: Oxford University Press, 1980.

Brooks, Peter. *Reading for the Plot: Design and Intention in Narrative.* New York: Vintage, 1985.

Butler, Judith. *Gender Trouble.* New York: Routledge, 1989.

Butler, Marilyn. *Jane Austen and the War of Ideas.* Oxford: Oxford University Press, 1987.

Carpenter, Edward. *Civilization: Its Cause and Cure and Other Essays.* 5th ed. London: Swan Sonnenschein, 1897.

Casta-Rosaz, Fabienne. *Histoire du flirt: les jeux de l'innocence et de la peversité, 1870–1968.* Paris: Bernard Grasset, 2000.

Castle, Terry. *Masquerade and Civilization: The Carnivalesque in Eighteenth-Century English Culture and Fiction.* Stanford, Calif.: Stanford University Press, 1986.

Congreve, William. "The Way of the World," in *Four Great Restoration Comedies.* Edited by John Russell Brown and Bernard Harris. New York: Capricorn, 1967.

Craft, Christopher. *Another Kind of Love: Homosexual Desire and English Discourse, 1850–1920.* Berkeley: University of California Press, 1994.

Darwin, Charles. *The Origin of Species by Means of Natural Selection; or The Preservation of Favoured Races in the Struggle for Life.* Edited by J. W. Burrow. 1859. Reprint, New York: Penguin, 1985.

———. *The Descent of Man, and Selection in Relation to Sex* Princeton, N.J.: Princeton University Press, 1981.

Dean, Tim. *Beyond Sexuality.* Chicago: University of Chicago Press, 2000.

DeJean, Joan. *Tender Geographies: Women and the Origins of the Novel in France.* New York: Columbia University Press, 1993.

Dellamora, Richard. *Masculine Desire: The Sexual Politics of Victorian Aestheticism.* Chapel Hill: University of North Carolina Press, 1990.

de Rougemeont, Denis. *Love in the Western World.* 1956. Reprint, New York: Pantheon, 1974.

Dijkstra, Bram. *Idols of Perversity: Fantasies of Feminine Evil in Fin de Siècle Culture.* New York: Oxford University Press, 1986.

Dollimore, Jonathan. *Sexual Dissidence: Augustine to Wilde, Freud to Foucault.* Oxford: Clarendon, 1991.

Eliot, George. *The Mill on the Floss.* 1860. Reprint, New York: Oxford University Press, 1981.

———. *Middlemarch.* 1871–72. Reprint, London: Penguin, 1965.

———. *Daniel Deronda.* 1876. Reprint, London: Penguin, 1995.

Ellmann, Richard. *Oscar Wilde.* New York: Knopf, 1988.

Empson, William. *Seven Types of Ambiguity.* 1947. Reprint, New York: W. W. Norton, 1966.

Flaubert, Gustave. *Sentimental Education.* 1869. Reprint, translated by Robert Baldick. New York: Penguin, 1964.

Forster, E. M. *Howards End* and *A Room with a View.* 1910; 1903. Reprint, New York: New American Library, 1986.

———. *A Passage to India.* 1924. Reprint, New York: Penguin, 1974.

Foster, Hannah Webster. *The Coquette.* 1797. Edited by Cathy N. Davidson. Reprint, New York: Oxford University Press, 1987.

Foucault, Michel. *The History of Sexuality: An Introduction.* Translated by Robert Hurley. New York: Pantheon, 1978.

———. *Discipline and Punish: The Birth of the Prison.* Translated by Alan Sheridan. New York: Vintage, 1995.

Gagnier, Regenia. *Idylls of the Marketplace: Oscar Wilde and the Victorian Public.* Stanford, Calif.: Stanford University Press, 1986.

———. *Subjectivities: A History of Self-Representation in Britain, 1832–1920.* New York: Oxford University Press, 1991.

Gamble, Eliza Burt. *The Evolution of Women: An Inquiry into the Dogma of Her Inferiority to Man.* New York: G. P. Putnam's Sons, 1894.

Gilbert, Sandra, and Susan Gubar. *The Madwoman in the Attic: The Woman Writer and the Nineteenth-Century Literary Imagination.* New Haven, Conn.: Yale University Press, 1979.

Gilbert, William Schwenk, and Arthur Sullivan. *The Complete Plays of Gilbert and Sullivan.* New York: W. W. Norton, 1976.

Gilman, Charlotte Perkins. *Women and Economics: A Study of the Economic Relations between Men and Women As a Factor in Social Revolution.* Edited by Carl N. Degler. New York: Harper and Row, 1966.

Girard, René. *Deceit, Desire, and the Novel: Self and Other in Literature.* Baltimore: Johns Hopkins University Press, 1966.

Hardy, Thomas. *Collected Poems.* New York: Macmillan, 1920.

———. *Far from the Madding Crowd.* 1874. Reprint, Oxford: Oxford University Press, 1993.

———. *Tess of the D'Urbervilles: A Pure Woman.* Edited by David Skilton. 1891. Reprint, New York: Penguin, 1978.

———. *Under the Greenwood Tree.* 1872. Reprint, London: Methuen, 1974.

Harth, Erica. *Cartesian Women: Versions and Subversions of Rational Discourse in the Old Regime.* Ithaca, N.Y.: Cornell University Press, 1993.

Homans, Margaret. *Bearing the Word: Language and Female Experience in Nineteenth-Century Women's Writing.* Chicago: University of Chicago Press, 1986.

Jacobus, Mary. *Reading Women: Essays in Feminist Criticism.* New York: Columbia University Press, 1986.

James, Henry. *Daisy Miller.* 1878. Reprint, New York: Oxford University Press, 1985.

——."Gustave Flaubert," in *Literary Criticism.* New York: Library of America, 1984.

——. *The Tragic Muse.* New York: Harper and Brothers, 1960.

Jameson, Frederic. *The Political Unconscious: Narrative as a Socially Symbolic Act.* Ithaca, N.Y.: Cornell University Press, 1981.

Johnson, Claudia. *Jane Austen: Women, Politics, and the Novel.* Chicago: University of Chicago Press, 1988.

Kaye, Richard A. "Edith Wharton and the 'New Gomorrahs' of Paris: Homosexuality, Flirtation, and Incestuous Desire in *The Reef.*" *Modern Fiction Studies* 43.4 (1997):860–97.

Knoepflmacher, U. C. *George Eliot's Early Novels: The Limits of Realism.* Berkeley: University of California Press, 1968.

——. *Laughter and Despair: Readings in Ten Novels of the Victorian Era.* Berkeley: University of California Press, 1971.

Kristeva, Julia. *Desire in Language.* New York: Columbia University Press, 1980.

Kucich, John. *Excess and Restraint in the Novels of Charles Dickens.* Athens: University of Georgia Press, 1981.

——. *Repression in Victorian Fiction: Charlotte Brontë, George Eliot, and Charles Dickens.* Berkeley: University of California Press, 1987.

Kundera, Milan. *Immortality.* Translated by Peter Kussi. New York: Grove Weidenfeld, 1991.

Langbauer, Laurie. *Novels of Everyday Life: The Series in English Fiction, 1850–1930.* Ithaca, N.Y.: Cornell University Press, 1999.

Laqueur, Thomas. *Making Sex: Body and Gender from the Greeks to Freud.* Cambridge, Mass.: Harvard University Press, 1990.

Lawrence, D. H. *Sons and Lovers.* 1913. Reprint, edited by Helen Baron and Carl Baron. Cambridge: Cambridge University Press, 1992.

——. *Women in Love.* 1921. Reprint, edited by David Farmer, Lindeth Vasey, and John Worthen. Cambridge: Cambridge University Press, 1987.

Leckie, Barbara. *Culture and Adultery: The Novel, the Newspaper, and the Law, 1857–1914.* Philadelphia: University of Pennsylvania Press, 1999.

Levine, George. *The Realistic Imagination: English Fiction from Frankenstein to Lady Chatterley's Lover.* Chicago: University of Chicago Press, 1981.

——. *Darwin and the Novelists: Patterns of Science in Victorian Fiction.* Chicago: University of Chicago Press, 1988.

Lewes, George Henry. *Ranthorpe.* 1847. Reprint, edited by Barbara Smalley. Athens: Ohio University Press, 1974.

Litvak, Joseph. *Caught in the Act: Theatricality in the Nineteenth-Century English Novel.* Berkeley: University of California Press, 1992.

Litz, A. Walton. *Jane Austen: A Study of Her Artistic Development.* Oxford: Oxford University Press, 1965.

Mason, Michael. *The Making of Victorian Sexuality.* Oxford: Oxford University Press, 1994.

McKeon, Michael. *The Origins of the English Novel, 1600–1740.* Baltimore: Johns Hopkins University Press, 1987.

Michie, Helena. *The Flesh Made Word: Female Figures and Women's Bodies.* New York: Oxford University Press, 1987.

Miller, D. A. *Narrative and Its Discontents: Problems of Closure in the Traditional Novel.* Princeton, N.J.: Princeton University Press, 1981.

———. *The Novel and the Police.* Berkeley: University of California Press, 1988.

Mudrick, Marvin. *Jane Austen: Irony as Defense and Discovery.* Princeton, N.J.: Princeton University Press, 1952.

Pater, Walter. *The Renaissance.* 1873. Reprint. Oxford: Oxford University Press, 1986.

Paxton, Nancy. *George Eliot and Herbert Spencer: Feminism, Evolutionism, and the Reconstruction of Gender.* Princeton, N.J.: Princeton University Press, 1991.

Pearsall, Ronald. *The Worm in the Bud: The World of Victorian Sexuality.* Toronto: Macmillan, 1969.

Peters, Julie Stone. *Congreve, the Drama, and the Printed Word.* Stanford, Calif.: Stanford University Press, 1990.

Phillips, Adam. *On Flirtation.* Cambridge, Mass.: Harvard University Press, 1994.

Plotz, John. *The Crowd: British Literature and Public Politics.* Berkeley: University of California Press, 2000.

Polhemus, Robert M. *Erotic Faith: Being in Love from Jane Austen to D. H. Lawrence.* Chicago: University of Chicago Press, 1990.

Poovey, Mary. *The Proper Lady and the Woman Writer: Ideology as Style in the Works of Mary Wollstonecraft, Mary Shelley, and Jane Austen.* Chicago: University of Chicago Press, 1984.

———. *Uneven Developments: The Ideological Work of Gender in Mid-Victorian England.* Chicago: University of Chicago Press, 1988.

Roberts, Warren. *Jane Austen and the French Revolution.* New York: Macmillan, 1979.

Russett, Cynthia. *Sexual Science: The Victorian Construction of Womanhood.* Cambridge, Mass.: Harvard University Press, 1989.

Sedgwick, Eve Kosofsky. *Between Men: English Literature and Male Homosocial Desire.* New York: Columbia University Press, 1985.

———. *Epistemology of the Closet.* Berkeley: University of California Press, 1990.

———, ed. *Novel Gazing: Queer Readings in Fiction.* Durham, N.C.: Duke University Press, 1997.

Shaw, Bernard. *Candida: A Pleasant Play.* 1895. Reprint, New York: Penguin, 1985.

Showalter, Elaine. *A Literature of Their Own: British Women Novelists from Brontë to Lessing.* Princeton, N.J.: Princeton University Press, 1977.

———. *Sexual Anarchy: Gender and Culture at the Fin de Siècle.* New York: Viking, 1990.

Shuttleworth, Sally. *George Eliot and Nineteenth-Century Science: The Make-Believe of a Beginning.* Cambridge: Cambridge University Press, 1984.

Simmel, Georg. *On Women, Sexuality and Love.* Translated and edited by Guy Oakes. New Haven, Conn.: Yale University Press, 1984.

———. *On Individuality and Social Forms: Selected Writings.* Edited by Donald N. Levine. Chicago: University of Chicago Press, 1976.

———. *The Sociology of Georg Simmel.* Translated and edited by Kurt H. Wolff. New York: The Free Press, 1950.

Spacks, Patricia Meyer. *Desire and Truth: Functions of Plot in Eighteenth-Century English Novels.* Chicago: University of Chicago Press, 1990.

Stone, Lawrence. *The Family, Sex, and Marriage in England, 1500–1800.* New York: Harper and Row, 1977.

Tanner, Tony. *Jane Austen.* Cambridge, Mass.: Harvard University Press, 1996.

———. *Adultery and the Novel: Contract and Transgression.* Baltimore: John Hopkins University Press, 1966.

Thackeray, William Makepeace. *Pendennis.* 1848–1850. Reprint, Oxford: Oxford University Press, 1994.

———. *Vanity Fair.* Edited by John Sutherland. 1847–48. Reprint, Oxford: Oxford University Press, 1983.

Thompson, James. *Between Self and the World: The Novels of Jane Austen.* University Park: Pennsylvania State University Press, 1988.

Turgenev, Ivan. *Fathers and Sons.* 1862. Translated by Ralph E. Matlaw. New York: W. W. Norton, 1966.

Vidal, Mary. *Watteau's Painted Conversations: Art, Literature, and Talk in Seventeenth- and Eighteenth-Century France.* New Haven, Conn.: Yale University Press, 1992.

Watt, Ian. *The Rise of the Novel: Studies in Defoe, Richardson, and Fielding.* 1957. Reprint, Berkeley: University of California Press, 1964.

Weeks, Jeffrey. *Coming Out: Homosexual Politics in Britain from the Nineteenth Century to the Present.* London: Quartet, 1977.

———. *Sex, Politics, and Society: The Regulation of Sexuality since 1800.* London: Longman, 1981.

Weinstein, Philip M. *The Semantics of Desire: Changing Models of Identity from Dickens to Joyce.* Princeton, N.J.: Princeton University Press, 1984.

Wharton, Edith. *The House of Mirth.* 1905. Reprint, New York: Penguin, 1983.

———. *The Reef.* New York: Collier, 1986.

———. *The Age of Innocence.* 1921. Reprint, New York: Charles Scribner's Sons, 1970.

———. *A Backward Glance.* New York: Charles Scribner's Sons, 1934.

———. *The Writing of Fiction.* New York: Charles Scribner's Sons, 1925.

Wheelwright, Philip. *The Burning Fountain: A Study in the Languages of Symbolism.* Bloomington: Indiana University Press, 1968.

Wilde, Oscar. *The Picture of Dorian Gray.* 1890–91. Reprint, Oxford University Press, 1974.

Wollstonecraft, Mary. *The Vindication of the Rights of Woman.* Edited by Miriam Brody. 1792. Reprint, New York: Penguin, 1983.

Yeazell, Ruth Bernard. *Fictions of Modesty: Women and Courtship in the English Novel.* Chicago: University of Chicago Press, 1992.

Index

Page references to illustrations are in italics